CHANGING WORLD

Leaving Certificate
HUMAN Geography

CHARLES HAYES
UNA NATION

Gill Education
Hume Avenue
Park West
Dublin 12
www.gilleducation.ie

Gill Education is an imprint of M.H. Gill & Co.

Design and print origination in Ireland by Design Image.

The paper used in this book is made from the wood pulp of managed forests.
For every tree felled, at least one tree is planted, thereby renewing natural resources.

For permission to reproduce photographs, the authors and publisher
gratefully acknowledge the following:

© Alamy: 6, 11, 13T, 13B, 14, 23L, 29T, 29B, 32B, 33, 34, 36T, 36C, 36B, 37, 38, 51, 54, 60, 63T, 65, 66, 67, 78, 80L, 84B, 86L, 88, 91, 93B, 95B, 99C, 99L, 99R, 112, 113T, 113B, 122B, 123, 129T, 129B, 134, 145T, 147T, 147C, 148, 156, 159B, 160T, 160CB, 160B, 162, 163T, 163B, 167T, 171T, 171B, 173, 174T, 174B, 175C, 176, 177, 180T, 180C, 180B, 189, 190, 191, 197, 199, 201, 203, 204T, 204B, 206B, 210, 212, 216T, 216B, 221B, 222C, 223T, 225L, 225R, 227T, 238T, 240C, 241C, 241B, 242CL, 242BL, 244T, 244B, 245T, 245B, 246B, 247CR, 247B, 248, 254T, 254C, 254B, 256, 257T, 257B, 258, 260C, 260B, 262T, 262B, 263C, 265C, 265B, 266T, 276T, 276B, 277BR; © Collins Agency: 136, 137T, 240T; © Corbis: 12, 32T, 39, 56, 127, 169, 211, 213L, 221T, 222TL, 226, 269T, 269B, 270, 273B, 276C; © The Irish Examiner: 50, 85, 108T, 108B; © Finbarr O'Connell: 115, 131; © Getty Images: 23B, 27, 30, 31T, 31B, 41T, 41B, 43T, 43B, 53B, 58, 59, 69, 77T, 77B, 80R, 86R, 117T, 138, 141, 144T, 160CT, 164, 166, 167B, 172, 175B, 179, 184, 188L, 188R, 192, 194, 200, 202, 205T, 205B, 206T, 213R, 220, 221C, 222TR, 222CL, 222CR, 222BL, 222BR, 223CL, 223CR, 227B, 228C, 229, 230, 238C, 242CR, 242BR, 243, 246T, 247CL, 249, 250T, 250L, 251, 252, 262C, 263B, 267, 268B, 273T, 275, 277L, 277TR; © Imagefile: 63B, 64, 95C, 109, 122T, 137B, 193, 217, 241T; © Inpho: 219, 236; © Irish Times: 57B, 140, 269C; © Press Association: 21, 57T, 152, 228L, 253, 264, 266B; © Peter Barrow: 81, 93T, 95T, 106, 128, 139, 144B, 145B, 146, 154; © Photocall Ireland: 22, 42, 53T, 117B, 126, 147B, 157; © Photolibrary: 175T; © RTÉ Stills Library: 159T; © Topfoto: 268T; Courtesy of McGoldrick Art & Photography, Will McGoldrick: 84T, Courtesy of NASA: 1; Courtesy of TG4: 240B; Courtesy of Youghal County Museum: 83.

The author and publisher are grateful to the following for permission to reproduce copyrighted material:

'Dust storms blowing country across the Atlantic', by Nick Middleton reprinted by permission of *The Times*; 'The Case of Mr. Luyindula', courtesy of Trocaire; 'The intense isolation of asylum seekers in Ireland' reprinted by permission of *The Irish Times*; 'Irish politicians become embroiled in the "hijab at school" controversy' by Patricia McDonagh reprinted by permission of the *Irish Independent*.

The authors and publisher have made every effort to trace all copyright holders, but if any has been inadvertently overlooked we would be pleased to make the necessary arrangement at the first opportunity.

Contents

Web Resources

Chapter 1: Population Distribution and Density

Population Distribution: Short interactive quiz based on the concept of population distribution from the Internet Geography website.
www.bit.ly/yX7cuY

Population Density: Short interactive quiz based on the concept of population density from the Internet Geography website.
www.bit.ly/AcpYws

Chapter 2: Population Change Over Time

Population Change: This BBC News video clip explains how world population has changed over time and what is projected to happen in the future.
http://bbc.in/vFArCm

Population Statistics: The Worldometers website provides real time world statistics on population, birth rate, death rate and net population growth.
www.bit.ly/JNqC

Population Growth: This simulator from Annenberg Learner depicts population growth and changing population pyramids for several countries. Choose a country from the drop down menu – you can even change birth and death rates to see how the population is affected by variations in these factors.
www.bit.ly/wDqgpa

Population Pyramids: This animated video clip from the French National Institute of Population Studies explains the structure of population pyramids.
www.bit.ly/A2cJ18

Population Pyramids Ireland: A range of population pyramids for Ireland from 1990 to 2050 from the Nation Master website.
www.bit.ly/q92lYv

Note: All web resource links are case sensitive.

Chapter 3: Causes and Effects of Overpopulation

Overpopulation: This interactive lesson on overpopulation from National Geographic describes the causes and effects of overpopulation. The lesson includes images and videos and there is also a tab on deforestation and desertification, both of which are related to overpopulation.
http://on.natgeo.com/y9gLow

Overpopulation in the Sahel Region: A summary of desertification as a result of rising birth rates and overpopulation in the Sahel region from the Barcelona Field Studies Centre.
www.bit.ly/AlBX3D

Overpopulation in Darfur: This How Stuff Works video discusses the life of internally displaced people in the overpopulated Darfur region of Sudan.
www.bit.ly/zJ5Ps8

The Aral Sea: A history of the Aral Sea including an interactive map showing the drying of the lake over time and its effects, from the Central Asian Online Travel Company.
www.bit.ly/oN1jSB

Chapter 4: Migration

Migration Map and Statistics: This interactive world migration map allows you to access data and graphs on donor and receiver regions from the Migration Policy Institute USA.
www.bit.ly/qVtrJR

Irish Migration Patterns: Statistics on migration patterns in Ireland from the Migration Policy Institute USA including: net migration, immigration, emigration, asylum seekers and citizenship. Access the data by selecting categories from the menu.
www.bit.ly/82GrRZ

Migration: This BBC interactive lesson on migration includes an introduction to migration, reasons for migration, an animation showing global migration patterns since 1900, migration policies and an end-of-lesson quiz.
http://bbc.in/yVWCoU

Racism against Migrants: A short BBC documentary based on racist attacks against migrants in Northern Ireland. It examines the attitudes of people towards migrants and highlights issues that arise due to migration.
http://bbc.in/wGUTPg

Racism against Migrants – the Turban Issue: A short BBC documentary on the wearing of Muslim headscarfs by migrants. It examines the attitudes of people towards migrants and highlights issues that arise due to migration.
http://bbc.in/xz4anD

Rural-to-urban Migration in Kolkata: Case study 2 from the S-cool revision website is a summary of rural-to-urban migration in Kolkata. It includes the causes and effects of rural-to-urban migration.
www.bit.ly/yCELjB

Chapter 5: Human settlement – Location, Historic Settlement and Settlement Patterns

Settlement Site: This interactive lesson from the BBC on identifying and describing settlement sites includes diagrams, activities and an end-of-lesson quiz.
http://bbc.in/zLHUcO

Settlement Types and Patterns: This Magic Studio interactive drag and drop activity is based on settlement types and patterns.
www.bit.ly/zn9s58

Historic Settlement in Youghal: The Youghal Heritage website explains the historic settlement of Youghal from pre-historic times to the 18th century.
www.bit.ly/yJNAJO

Chapter 6: Rural Planning Strategies

Ireland's National Development Plan 2007–2013:
www.bit.ly/y85GWl

Waterford County Development Plan 2011–2017:
www.bit.ly/wlAQnR

South Dublin County Development Plan 2010–2016:
www.bit.ly/aVpkPv

Cork County Development Plan 2009:
www.bit.ly/xUf2Me

Galway County Development Plan 2009–2015:
www.bit.ly/zGUpzX

Donegal County Council Plan 2012–2018:
www.bit.ly/yyfLOR

Chapter 7: Urban Hierarchy and the Central Place Theory

Central Place Theory: This animation from Wikimedia.org illustrates Christaller's Central Place Theory. It shows the location of large cities, towns, villages and hamlets in relation to one another as part of the Central Place Theory.
www.bit.ly/A8sry2

Chapter 8: Urban Functions

Urban Functions: This BBC interactive lesson based on identifying functions of settlements includes activities, diagrams, an OS map and an end-of-lesson quiz.
http://bbc.in/yEvzHE

Changing Functions of Cork City: This history of Cork City from Cork County Council describes how the city and the functions of the city have changed over time.
www.bit.ly/zceUh5

Chapter 9: Land Use Zones in Urban Areas

Land Use Models: The S-cool revision website features a summary of three urban land use models. It describes, with diagrams, land uses in urban areas and includes a section on urban zoning.
www.bit.ly/gOorN7

Map of Dublin: This Google map shows Dublin's city centre.
www.bit.ly/y9tezm

Chapter 10: Urban Problems

Urban Sprawl in Dublin: This RTÉ News report on urban sprawl in Dublin discusses the causes and effects of urban sprawl, as well as measures to be taken to reduce these effects.
www.bit.ly/wZOkEI

Traffic Congestion in Dublin: A traffic map and traffic images provided by the National Roads Authority allow you to check traffic around Ireland in real time.
www.bit.ly/ybYvRY

Dublin Bike Scheme: The Dublin Bike Scheme website includes information about the scheme, images and maps of the bike stations and cycling routes in the city.
www.bit.ly/hG8g6D

Urban Decay in Detroit: This video clip from the *Guardian* discusses urban decay in the city of Detroit and the methods being used to renew the city.
www.bit.ly/97VUiS

Chapter 11: Air, Water and Waste – Environmental Issues in Urban Areas

Environmental Issues in the Bronx: Short video from How Stuff Works about environmental problems in the Bronx area of New York City including air pollution, water pollution and waste disposal, and a project that has been undertaken to reduce these problems.
www.bit.ly/vZdU5o

Air Pollution in China: This short video, 'Longing for Blue Skies', from the Asia Society discusses the causes and effects of air pollution in China and the rest of the world. A collection of images called 'Room with a view' can also be accessed which shows air quality in Beijing on a day-to-day basis.
www.bit.ly/6JVz2J

Chapter 12: Heritage Issues in Urban Areas

Protection of Georgian Buildings: The Irish Georgian Society website contains a list of buildings that are at risk around Ireland and that need protection as heritage sites.
www.bit.ly/wN31Tf

The Development of Wood Quay: An account by RTÉ of the protests against the building of civic offices at Wood Quay in the 1970s.
www.bit.ly/A6r2Ao

Chapter 13: Urbanisation and Urban Problems in the Developing World

Urban Problems in Sao Paulo: This short Discovery Channel video clip on Sao Paulo, Brazil looks at Sao Paulo's urbanisation and the problems this has caused. It focuses primarily on traffic congestion.
www.bit.ly/A2R3Ms

Shanty Towns: A short documentary video clip from Metacafe based on shanty towns in Africa.
www.bit.ly/xT4lj8

Shanty Town Development: This animated interactive lesson on shanty town development from Staffordshire Learning Net discusses the stages of development and highlights the need for infrastructure and services.
www.bit.ly/pPrHVp

Urban Problems: A summary of urban problems in developing regions and possible solutions to these problems is provided by the S-cool website.
www.bit.ly/xOtkmL

Chapter 14: Future Urban Issues

The Green City of Masdar: A Planet Green video clip about the development of Abu Dhabi's green city Masdar. This development demonstrates the ideal future for our cities with increased public transport, 100% renewable energy and improved waste management.
www.bit.ly/wk1yXS

Solar Energy: A short Discovery Channel video clip about solar energy as a key to a sustainable future.
www.bit.ly/hZFcKO

Wind Energy: A short How Stuff Works video clip about wind energy as a key to a sustainable future.
www.bit.ly/x9oqK2

Ghettoization in Urban Areas: The BBC website reports how children are being educated in socially, ethnically and racially divided ghettos in London.
http://bbc.in/q9fgqh

Chapter 15: Soils

Soil Types: Interactive lesson from the Smithsonian Institute on soil types called 'The Earth's Skin Types'. Select a soil type for information and a map on that soil.
www.bit.ly/ye6tVf

Soil Formation: This summary of soil formation from Annenberg Learner focuses on soil forming factors.
www.bit.ly/ww4y4f

Soil Structure: This summary of soil horizons from Annenberg Learner includes images and diagrams.
www.bit.ly/yZSQWh

Chapter 16: Human Interference with Soils

Deforestation in the Amazon: This video clip from the *Guardian* on deforestation by cattle ranchers in the Amazonian Rainforest.
www.bit.ly/LUaXM

Desertification and the Sahel: Fact file on desertification from desertification.com including causes, effects and a case study of the Sahel region.
www.bit.ly/AdvLiT

Soil and Water Conservation: This video clip from the Water Channel on soil and water conservation in Africa focuses on three methods of conservation: land terracing, sand dams and planting trees.
www.bit.ly/x1aljR

Chapter 17: Biomes

Biomes: Short Discovery Channel video introducing biomes as regions with similar climates, soils, flora and fauna.
www.bit.ly/xd4i4Y

Types of Biomes: Interactive lesson on biomes from the Teachers Domain: click on a biome to find out about climate, soil type and location of that biome.
www.bit.ly/vj1Yxh

Hot Desert Biome: A short Discovery Channel video clip on the desert biome: it introduces the characteristics of the biome including climate conditions, flora and fauna.
www.bit.ly/zoj8G7

Chapter 18: How Human Activities Alter Biomes

Deforestation in the Tropical Rainforest Biome: BBC News video report on deforestation in the tropical rainforest biome of the Amazon basin. An audio report also discusses native forest people dying due to human interference in the Amazon.
http://bbc.in/zFHg5s

See also resources for Chapter 16: Human Interference with Soils.

Chapter 19: Racial Patterns and Impacting Factors

Racial Grouping: This How Stuff Works video on racial classification focuses on the birth of distinct racial categories.
www.bit.ly/zGnDgG

Ireland's Multicultural Society: This BBC news report on 'Ireland's new multicultural mix' looks at how the rise of immigration in Ireland has changed Irish society. The article focuses on Gort, Co. Galway which has become home to a large Brazilian community.
http://bbc.in/xDd8Cs

Chapter 20: Language and Religion as Cultural Indicators

World Languages: The Nations Online website includes information on the number of languages spoken in each continent as well as the most commonly spoken languages in the world.
www.bit.ly/dGT7iN

Changing English Language: An interactive account from the BBC of how the English language has changed over time.
http://bbc.in/8vwUx4

The Irish Language: This article from Gaeilge.org on the history of the Irish language discusses measures taken to promote the language throughout the 20th century and the questionable future of the language.
www.bit.ly/yQTVBH

Chapter 21: State Boundaries, Nationality and Related Problems

The Muslim Religion in Europe: A country guide from the BBC to the Muslim religion in Europe – use the interactive map to select a country, examine its Muslim population and their background.
http://bbc.in/zbTwCR

Conflict in Northern Ireland: A brief guide by the BBC to the conflict in Northern Ireland which was caused by cultural, religious and political divisions.
http://bbc.in/6a9btl

The Northern Ireland Archives – Living with the Troubles: An archive of video clips from the BBC TV show Panorama. The archive contains a range of video clips based on different aspects of the Troubles in Northern Ireland.
http://bbc.in/yUWYsf

Chapter 22: Yugoslavia – the Life and Death of a Culturally Diverse European State

The Break-up of Yugoslavia: A timeline from the BBC of the break-up of Yugoslavia from 1990–2006.
http://bbc.in/Av7WJS

Population distribution

The term **population distribution** refers to *the way in which people are dispersed* (spread out) across the world, a country, a region or any other *geographical area.*

You will see from Figure 1 that the world's human population is very *unevenly distributed.* Some areas are crowded and are described as being *densely populated.* Other areas have very few people and are described as being *sparsely populated.* Densely populated areas enjoy several *positive factors* that encourage human settlement. Sparsely populated areas usually have a combination of *negative factors* that discourage human settlement. Some of those positive and negative features are listed on the next page.

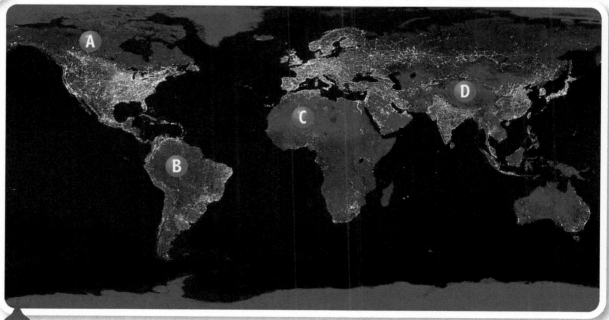

1 The world at night. This satellite image shows well-lit highly populated regions, as well as dark or almost dark regions that are very lightly populated regions.

(a) Name four principal highly populated regions.

(b) Why do you think the regions labelled **A** to **D** are very lightly populated? You can use the information on pages 2 and 3 to check some of your answers.

Some positive factors that attract human settlement

- Favourable *climate* with no extremes of temperature or precipitation levels.
- Flat or gently sloping *land* that is fertile and easy to build on.
- Enough wealth and levels of *development* to stimulate industry and jobs.
- *Accessibility* to coasts and to other highly populated areas.
- Good transport and other *infrastructure*.

Negative factors that discourage human settlement

- *Climatic* extremes (too hot, too cold, too dry or too wet).
- Steep and infertile *land* that is difficult to farm or build on. Very high mountains where oxygen levels and low atmospheric pressure make human survival difficult.
- Insufficient wealth or *development* to stimulate industry or jobs.
- *Inaccessibility*.
- Poor transport and other *infrastructure*.

Northern Canada – very sparsely populated

- Long, dark and bitterly *cold* winters discourage human settlement and agriculture.
- *Remoteness* and few roads make the region inaccessible.
- Human communities are small and scattered. Population *growth is low*.

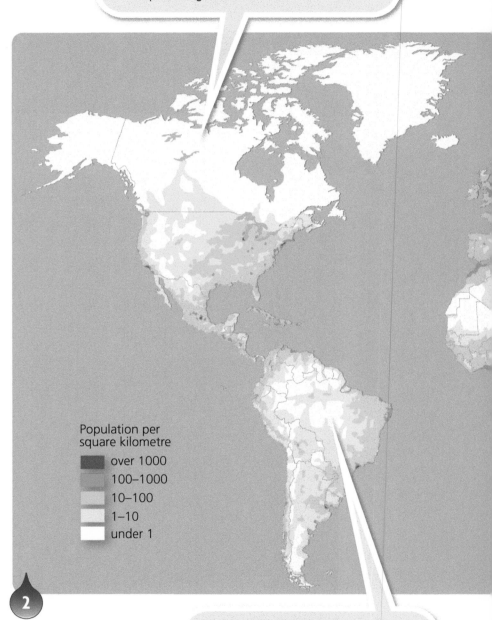

Population per square kilometre

- over 1000
- 100–1000
- 10–100
- 1–10
- under 1

2

Some densely and sparsely populated regions of the world

Amazon Basin – sparsely populated

- *Hot, wet* rainforest conditions discourage human settlement.
- *Infertile soils* discourage agriculture.
- Despite some in-migration, most of this region is quite *inaccessible* and contains very few roads or towns.

Western and Central Europe – very densely populated

- A generally moderate climate and vast areas of low-lying fertile land have allowed Western Europe to support profitable *agriculture* and large *rural populations*.
- The presence of coal led to the early growth of *industry* and large industrial *cities* in countries such as Germany and Britain.
- Former imperial powers such as Britain and France also derived much wealth from their *colonies*. This wealth stimulated economic development.
- *Low birth rates* have led to very low or 'negative' population growth. *In-migration* maintains population levels in some areas.

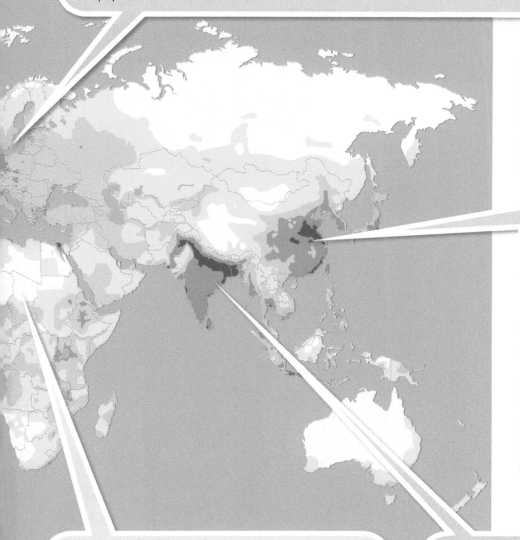

East Asia – very densely populated

- Fertile rice-growing regions such as in Vietnam, the Philippines and eastern China support large *rural* populations. Fertile soils vary from alluvium in the floodplains of China's Yellow River to volcanic soils on the Indonesian island of Java.
- Countries such as China and Japan are highly *industrialised* and contain many huge *cities* such as Beijing and Tokyo. China is the world's leading manufacturing nation.
- Population continues to grow at an annual rate of nearly 2 per cent in countries such as Vietnam. China's population is declining because of its government's 'one-child' policy.

The Sahara Desert – very sparsely populated

- Extreme *drought* makes agriculture and human survival very difficult.
- Much of the *land* is rocky or stony and is *inaccessible*.
- The *Nile valley* is one of the few densely populated areas. Alluvial soil and river water for irrigation allows agriculture to thrive.

The Indian sub-continent – very densely populated

- Fertile rice-growing regions in the Ganges and Indus river basins support huge *rural populations*.
- The region includes huge and rapidly growing *cities* such as Mumbai and Kolkata. There has been rapid *industrial growth* in such cities.
- *High birth rates* result in rapid population growth.

Calculating population density

Example

The Republic of Ireland is $70.283km^2$ in size and its total human population is 4,581,269. Calculate the population density of the Republic of Ireland.

$$\frac{\text{Total population}}{\text{Size of area}} \quad \frac{4,581,269}{70,238} = 65.2$$

Ireland has a population density of *65 people per km^2*.

Now calculate the population densities of each of the countries listed below.

Country	Total population	Total land area (km²)
France	62,227,432	545,630
Haiti	9,203,083	27,560
Japan	127,704,000	374,744

Population density

Population density is used to help measure the distribution of people throughout the world. It is calculated by *dividing the total population of an area by the size of that area*. It is usually represented as the *average number of people per square kilometre*.

It is important to remember that the calculation of population density *averages* may hide big population *variations within areas*. Canada, for example, has a very low population density of 3 people per square kilometre. But population densities within Canada vary greatly. Southern regions around Montreal and Toronto are densely populated while vast tracts of northern Canada are virtually uninhabited.

Skills activity

The table shows the population densities of selected countries in the world.

Using graph paper, draw a suitable graph to illustrate the data shown in the table.

Country	Population per km²
Brazil	22
Ireland	65
Mali	10
USA	32
South Africa	36

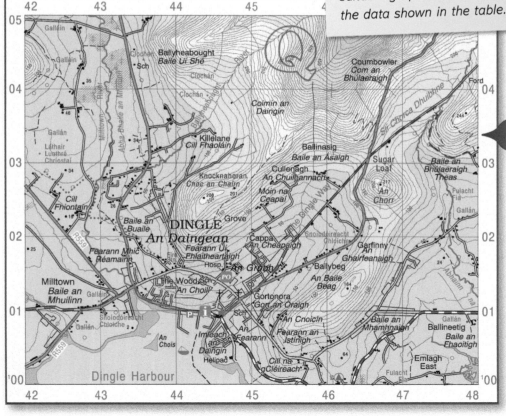

3 Examine this map extract of the Dingle area.

(a) *Explain, using evidence from the map, why the area to the east of easting 44 and north of northing 03 has such a low population density.* (LC Higher Level – 30 marks)

(b) *Account for the low population density in the vicinity of the Milltown River north of northing 03.*

(c) *Explain* three *reasons for the development of the urban area of Dingle/An Daingean at this site.*

Case Study:
Population distribution in the Italian Mezzogiorno

Revise
pages 306–307
of your
Changing World
core textbook.

The Mezzogiorno region of southern Italy is home to almost 21 million people and has an average population density of 140 per square kilometre. Its population is, however, very unevenly distributed (see Figure 4 on page 6). Some coastal areas are densely populated and experience population increase, while much of the interior is sparsely populated and experiences population decline. The basic reason for this is that coastal areas are generally more economically developed than interior areas.

Coastal areas

- The Mezzogiorno's best **agricultural land** is in coastal areas. Such areas include places of rich volcanic soil close to Mount Vesuvius and small but fertile alluvial coastal plains in places such as the Metapontino area in the 'instep' of Italy. The Cassa per il Mezzogiorno and the EU's Common Agricultural Policy (CAP) set up irrigation schemes and other initiatives that allowed small but intensive farms to prosper in such coastal areas.

- The Mezzogiorno's largest **cities** are all on or near the coast. They include Naples, Palermo, Bari, Brindisi and Taranto. The Cassa per il Mezzogiorno chose such urban areas as 'growth-poles' of manufacturing industry and helped to develop in them *heavy industries* such as steel mills, oil refineries and petro-chemical plants. *Light, footloose industries* such as computer manufacturing were also attracted to coastal cities because of the large and relatively low-wage labour force that was available there.

- **Tertiary activities** such as tourism have provided valuable employment in coastal resorts such as Sorrento and in historic sites such as Pompeii.

- Job opportunities in coastal cities have attracted **in-migration** from economically depressed interior areas. Such migration has further boosted the populations of coastal areas.

Interior areas

- The interior of the Mezzogiorno is dominated by the rugged and steep-sided Apennine Mountains. **Agriculture** in such areas is confined mainly to sheep farming – an activity that can maintain only sparse human population densities.

- Hilly terrain, poor roads and an absence of vibrant urban areas prevent the development of large-scale **industry** throughout most of the interior.

- **Tertiary economic activities** are also poorly developed. Tourism, for example, is severely hampered by poor access to many upland areas and by a general shortage of hotels and other amenities.

- With few employment opportunities outside farming, many young people are forced to leave remote interior villages in search of work. The mountain village of Aliano in Basilicata provides a typical example of this. Since the 1960s the population of Aliano has fallen by more than 25 per cent as a result of **out-migration**. Most migrants are young adults and this has contributed to steadily falling birth rates and to an ongoing spiral of population decline.

Terms to know

Types of industry
Heavy industries process large amounts of bulky raw materials. They include steel making, chemical manufacturing, etc. *Light industries* concentrate mainly on the manufacture of smaller consumer goods such as computers, clothing etc. *Footloose industries* are those that can thrive in a wide range of locations.

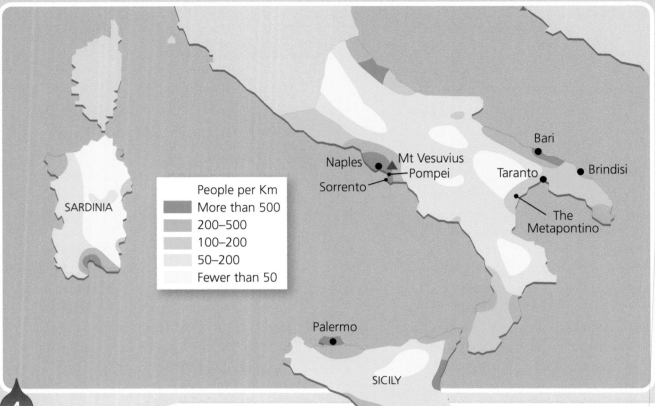

People per Km
More than 500
200–500
100–200
50–200
Fewer than 50

SARDINIA

Naples
Sorrento
Mt Vesuvius
Pompei
Bari
Brindisi
Taranto
The Metapontino

Palermo

SICILY

4

Contrasting population densities in the Mezzogiorno.

(a) *Use the map to contrast general population densities of interior areas with those of coastal areas.*

(b) *Account for some of those contrasts.*

A village in the interior of the Italian Mezzogiorno.

(a) *Why do areas such as this experience declining population densities?*

(b) *How do such declining densities affect population distribution in southern Italy?*

Sum Up

- **Population distribution** refers to the spread of people throughout an area.
- People are **unevenly distributed** throughout the world.
- Regions such as East Asia possess **positive factors** that encourage dense population.
- Regions such as the Sahara Desert endure **negative factors** that result in very sparse populations.
- **Population density** is the average number of people per square kilometre.
- The population of Italy's **Mezzogiorno** is unevenly distributed. Richer coastal areas are more densely populated than poorer interior areas.

Activities

1. The table in Figure 5 refers to the populations of the counties of Connacht in 2006. Using graph paper, draw a graph that shows the data in the table. (LC Ordinary Level – 30 marks)

2. The information in Figure 6 relates to the size of counties in Connacht. Use Figure 5 and Figure 6 together to calculate the population densities of Counties Mayo and Sligo.

3. Examine the world map in Figure 7, which shows density of population by country.
   (a) Identify examples of each of the following:
   - Two areas of high population density.
   - Two areas of low population density.
   (b) Account for the population densities of one densely populated area and of one sparsely populated area that you identified in question (a) above.
   (LC Higher Level sample paper – 30 marks)

4. Describe and explain, using examples that you have studied, the difference between the terms *population density* and *population distribution*. (LC Higher Level – 30 marks)

County	Population
Galway	231,670
Leitrim	28,950
Mayo	123,839
Roscommon	58,768
Sligo	60,894

5 Total populations of Connacht counties

County	Size
Galway	6,148
Leitrim	1,588
Mayo	5,527
Roscommon	2,547
Sligo	1,837

6 Sizes of Connacht counties (in sq. km)

7

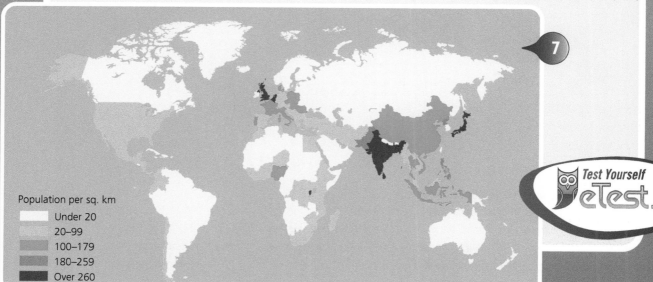

Population per sq. km
- Under 20
- 20–99
- 100–179
- 180–259
- Over 260

Test Yourself eTest.ie

2 Population Change over Time

World population growth

Figure 2 illustrates the growth over time of the world's human population. The population of our planet has grown from less than half a billion in the Middle Ages to nearly seven billion in the year 2010.

- Up to the eighteenth century, population growth was very slow and often fluctuated as a result of frequent **famines**, **wars** and **plagues**.
- After 1750, **agricultural**, **industrial** and **medical revolutions** in Europe resulted in improved food production, hygiene and medicine. This stimulated steady population growth, especially in Europe.
- Since 1950, the world's population growth has been so rapid that it is referred to as a **population explosion**. This dramatic growth is especially pronounced in developing (Third World) countries.

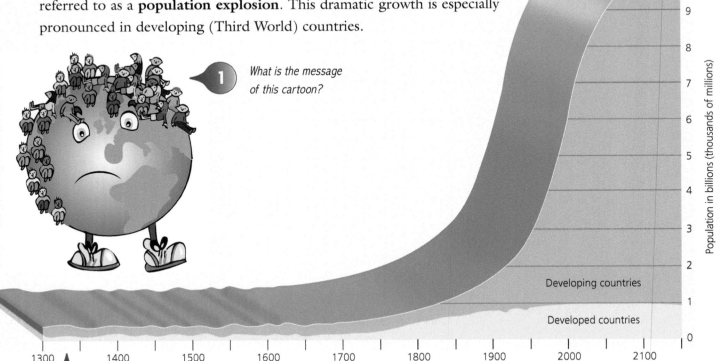

1 What is the message of this cartoon?

2 World population growth over time.
(a) What was the total world population in the year 2000?
(b) Approximately what will the world's total population be in the year 2050?
(c) Describe briefly the differing trends shown for the more developed and the less developed countries:
(i) up to the present time; and (ii) in the future. (LC Higher Level questions)

8

The components of population change

Three key components determine population change. These variable components are **fertility** (births), **mortality** (death) and **migration** (movement). Each of the terms below relates to how we calculate population change. *Learn these terms.*

Terms to know

- **Birth rate:** the number of live births per thousand of population per year.
- **Death/mortality rate:** the number of deaths per thousand of population per year.
- ***Natural increase:** when birth rate exceeds death rate the difference between the two is called natural increase. Natural increase figures are given per thousand of population.
- ***Natural decrease:** when death rate exceeds birth rate the difference between the two is called natural decrease. Natural decrease figures are given per thousand of population.
- **Total fertility rate (TFR):** the average number of births per woman.
- **Population replacement level:** the total fertility rate at which a population precisely replaces itself from one generation to the next. Ireland's population replacement level is currently calculated as a TFR of 2.1.

*Natural change is a term that is sometimes used to describe natural increase or natural decrease.

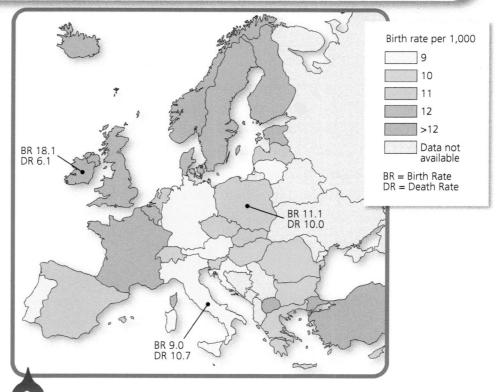

3 Some European birth rates and death rates in 2007.

(a) What was the birth rate of the Netherlands in 2007?

(b) What was Switzerland's birth rate?

(c) Define the term 'mortality rate'.

(d) Rank the following countries according to their birth rates: Portugal, Ireland, Sweden, Greece, Belgium.
(Place the country with the highest birth rate at the top of your ranking.)

(e) Calculate the natural increase or the natural decrease for Ireland, Poland and Italy.

(LC Higher Level questions)

Some factors that affect birth rates and death rates

Natural change in population depends on a combination of birth rates and death rates. Some factors that affect these rates are listed in the box below.

Some factors affecting:	
Birth rates	*Death rates*
Attitudes towards children	Food supplies
The status and education of women	Hygiene and medicine

Birth rates

Attitudes towards children

Attitudes towards children generally tend to be different in economically developed and developing parts of the world. These attitudes depend on **economic security** and people's **standard of living**.

Children in developed countries are usually expensive to raise because they must be educated and maintained with a comfortable standard of living for many years. In Ireland, the average annual cost of raising a child is reckoned to exceed €8,000 a year. The prospect of such an **economic burden** reduces birth rates because it encourages many adults to limit the size of their family.

In developing countries, children are often regarded as **economic assets**. Most children of the Third World poor receive little formal education and may work from an early age to help in the home or on the land or to contribute to meagre family incomes. In Third World countries such as India, large families are also seen by many as the best means of offering parents support and security in old age (see Figure 4). These factors increase birth rates because they encourage many poor people to have large families.

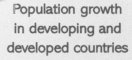

Population growth in developing and developed countries

The populations of most developing countries in the *South* are growing much more rapidly than those of developed countries in the *North*. Birth rates in the South continue to be much higher than those in the North. But the difference in death rates between North and South has decreased significantly. This means that natural increase in the South exceeds that in the North.

Some factors that affect birth rates and death rates in the North and South are examined on these pages.

Terms to know

- The *South*: a term used to describe the economically developing 'Third World' or 'majority world'.
- The *North*: a term used to describe the economically developed 'First World'.

We have no old age pension. So we will need our children to support us when we are old.

But some of our children may die.

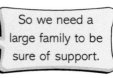

So we need a large family to be sure of support.

4

The status and education of women

The status and education of women can greatly affect birth rates throughout the world.

Gender equality and high levels of **female education** have contributed in the following ways to declining fertility rates in developed countries such as Ireland.

- Educated women are likely to be well informed about *family planning* issues.
- They may choose to pursue *professional careers* rather than to have large families.
- They may decide to *postpone child-rearing* for many years and so have few fertile years available to them in which to have children.

In Ireland, where most university graduates are women, the average fertility rate is 1.98. This is below the natural replacement level of 2.1.

Female students at Trinity College Dublin.
Comment on some general relationships between gender equality, prolonged formal education and family size.

In Third World countries, **poor and uneducated women** may not be fully *informed* on family planning issues and may not always have the *confidence* to decide the size of their family with their partner. In strictly Islamic countries such as Afghanistan, women are traditionally expected to *obey* their husband's wishes and to pursue the role of mother. This contributes to Afghanistan's high birth rate of 47 and its total fertility rate of 5.6. *Traditions* of young motherhood also contribute to large families and to high birth rates. In sub-Saharan African countries such as Zambia, more than one-third of teenage girls give birth before reaching the age of 18. Zambia has a high natural increase of 38.

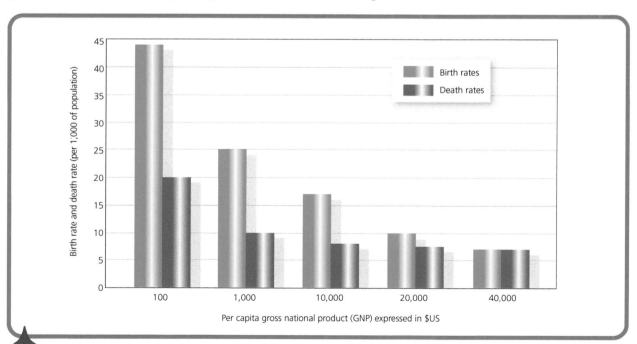

5 This graph shows a general worldwide relationship between birth rates, death rates and wealth.

(a) What general effect does increasing wealth have on birth rates? Refer in your answer to information given in the graph.

(b) Attempt to account for the general relationship between birth rates and increased wealth.

(c) 'Death rates tend not to fall below a base rate of 5–10, irrespective of increases in wealth.' Why do you think this is so?

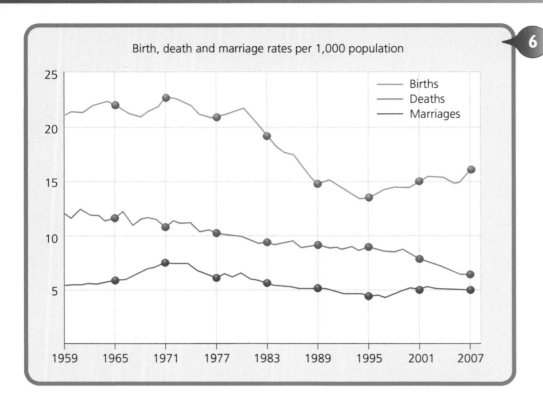

Birth, death and marriage rates per 1,000 population

— Births
— Deaths
— Marriages

1959 1965 1971 1977 1983 1989 1995 2001 2007

6 Birth, death and marriage rates over time. Examine the graph and answer the following questions:

(a) What was the marriage rate per thousand in 1989?

(b) When did the death rate first drop below 10 per thousand?

(c) What was the general trend in the birth rate between 1983 and 1995?

(d) Briefly explain the term 'natural increase'.

(LC Higher Level questions)

Death (mortality) rates

Food supplies

The supply and distribution of food plays a major role in mortality rates. **Improved and more balanced diets** have been partly responsible for a gradual rise in life expectancy levels and for a fall in death rates throughout the developed world. Mortality rates in Britain, for example, fell from approximately 42 in the year 1810 to approximately 15 in 2010. This was partly due to improved food supplies associated with the Agricultural Revolution.

Food shortages and the **uneven distribution** of food wealth leave more than one billion people hungry or malnourished in the South. Famines have killed millions of people and have inflated death rates in countries such as Ethiopia in 2002. But improved food yields in Third World countries such as India, together with more efficient global emergency food aid, have reduced such death rates. Bangladesh, which lost 1.5 million people to a devastating famine in 1974, now has a relatively low death rate of 7.6.

Emergency food aid distributed to victims of an earthquake in Haiti in 2010. Aid such as this helps to reduce death rates in Third World countries.

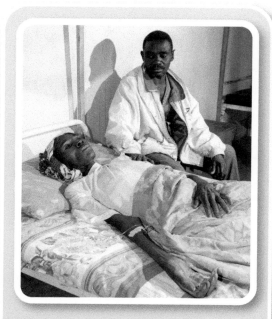

AIDS

AIDS stands for *Acquired Immune Deficiency Syndrome*. It is caused by a virus called **HIV** that is normally passed from person to person by sexual or by blood-to-blood contact. HIV gradually weakens the immune system so much that the human body is unable to fight disease without the help of expensive medicines. With the destruction of their immune systems, most AIDS victims die of chest infections and other normally curable ailments.

Sub-Saharan Africa is the region most heavily affected by HIV. In 2008, the region contained more than two-thirds of the world's HIV-infected people. The epidemic has a devastating impact, not only on death rates, but also on households, businesses, public services and national economies.

Hygiene and medicine

Hygiene and medical care have improved greatly over time in most parts of the world. Piped water, sewerage schemes and preventive medicines are now commonplace in almost all developed countries. In the South, contaminated water supplies still lead to outbreaks of illnesses such as hepatitis and typhoid. Such **water-borne diseases** contribute to high death rates in places such as the **bustees** or shantytowns of the Indian cities of Mumbai and Kolkata. But **improved water schemes** and the benefits of **new medicines** have now helped to reduce death rates throughout many parts of the South. Developing countries such as Cuba have made medical care an important cornerstone of their development agendas. By 2010, Cuba's death rate of 7.6 was lower than that of the United States.

AIDS has reversed the reduction of death rates in many parts of sub-Saharan Africa – a region that now endures 72 per cent of all the world's AIDS-related deaths. The southern African state of Swaziland lost so many people to AIDS that life expectancy there was halved to 37 years between 1990 and 2007.

A scene in Kolkata, India.

(a) 'Water taps are more important than hospital beds to the health of a country.' Explain why you agree or disagree with this statement.

(b) How do water taps such as the one shown here affect mortality rates in the countries of the South?

Development and population change – the demographic transition model

People who study population are called **demographers**. Demographers have discovered that, as any country or region develops economically, its birth rates and death rates (and therefore its natural population growth) change predictably. Demographers have drawn up a simplified idea called a *geographical model* to show how these changes take place. This model is called the **demographic transition model** or the population transition model. The model shows that population change takes place in **five different stages**. As a country or region develops economically it moves from one stage to the next.

Study **Figure 7**, which explains the demographic transition model.

A **geographical model** is anything that shows a simplified or idealised version of a complicated geographical truth. Many models use diagrams to illustrate their ideas. They assist our understanding of geography, though they provide only simplified general views of reality.

Some uses of the Demographic Transition Model

1   The model shows that when a country first begins to develop economically, its population expands rapidly. This helps to explain the present world **population explosion,** as most people live in countries that are at Stage 2 or 3 of the model.

2   The model also shows that, as a country continues to develop, its population growth begins to moderate and eventually goes into negative growth. This is heartening information. It suggests that, if living standards can be improved significantly in developing countries, the **world population will eventually stabilise.** It is interesting to note that annual global population growth – though still high – has already moderated from 2 per cent in the late 1960s to 1.3 per cent at the present time.

3   The model helps to explain **changes over time in Ireland's population.** Ireland had a large natural increase up to the early twentieth century when most of the country passed through Stage 2 of demographic transition. Only massive emigration kept our population in check during that period. Ireland is now economically developed and is at Stage 4 of the model. Over the next 20 years, our population will 'age' as a greater proportion of people move into older age groups. Our population will then enter Stage 5 of the model and will begin to experience natural decrease.

A mother with her children in Ethiopia.

(a) *Judging by this photograph, at which stage of the demographic transition model is Ethiopia likely to be?*

(b) *Suggest some reasons for high birth rates in Ethiopia.*

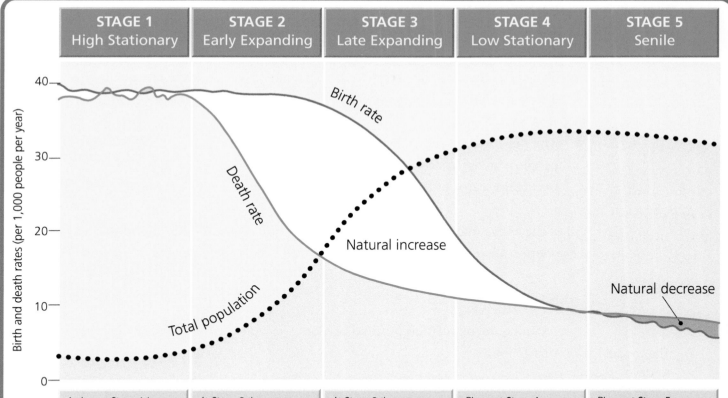

STAGE 1 High Stationary	STAGE 2 Early Expanding	STAGE 3 Late Expanding	STAGE 4 Low Stationary	STAGE 5 Senile
A place at **Stage 1** is economically very poor. Birth rates are high because children are economically useful and are a means of security for elderly parents. But death rates are also high and fluctuate because of frequent wars and periodic plagues and famines. Total population is low and may fluctuate or **grow very slowly**. Europe was at this stage during the Middle Ages. Only a *few remote areas* in the Third World are now at this stage.	At **Stage 2** the economy starts to develop. Birth rates remain high because of tradition and the low status of women. Death rates fall dramatically because of better hygiene, food and medicines. A big gap opens between birth rates and death rates, and this results in a **population explosion**. Europe was at this stage during the Industrial Revolution of the 18th and 19th centuries. Many Third World countries, such as *Mali* and *India*, are now at this stage.	At **Stage 3** the economy continues to improve. Parents begin to plan the size of their family when they realise that almost all their children are likely to survive to adulthood. Birth rates therefore begin to fall rapidly. Death rates fall less rapidly than birth rates, so **the rate of population growth slows down**. Europe passed through this stage in the late 19th and early 20th centuries. Third World countries such as *Brazil* are now at this stage.	Places at **Stage 4** are economically developed. Birth rates are low because many women work outside the home and because children are considered costly to raise. Most people live long lives, so death rates are also low. Population therefore **increases only very slowly**. Europe reached this stage in the second half of the 20th century. *Ireland* is now at this stage.	Places at **Stage 5** are economically affluent. People are so concerned with material comforts that they have very few children. A **natural decrease** occurs as birth rates fluctuate and usually fall below death rates. Only inward migration prevents a more rapid decline in total population numbers. Some European countries, such as *Germany* and *Italy*, have now reached Stage 5 of the population transition model.

7 The demographic transition model.

(a) Name one stage of this model where the birth rate and the death rate are nearly equal.

(b) At what stage of the model is the natural increase highest?

(c) At what stage of the model is the total population lowest?

(d) At what stage is the total population growing most rapidly? Why?

(e) At what stage is the total population declining? Why?

(f) Define each of the following terms: birth rate; death rate; natural increase; natural decrease.

Population structure

When we study the population **structure** or **make-up** of a country or area, we can examine the following:

- The **age structure**: the proportions of people who are in different age groups.
- The **sex structure**: the proportion of males to females in each age group.
- The **dependency ratio**: the proportion of young and old people who are dependent on the economically active (working) sector of the population.

Revise pages 188–189 of your Changing World core textbook.

All of the above information is contained in a single diagram called a **population pyramid**. (*Population pyramids are examined on pages 188–189 of the* Changing World *core textbook.*)

Skills practice

1   Examine the population pyramid of Cork City in Figure 8. Then answer the questions that follow.

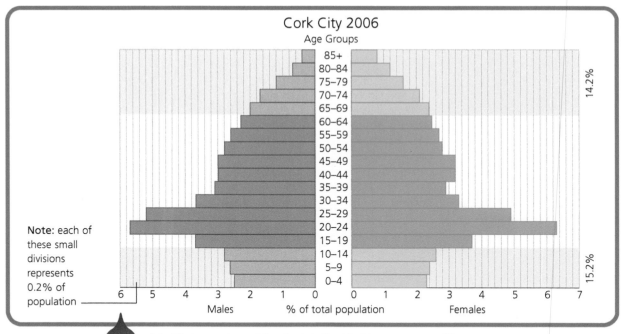

Cork City 2006

Note: each of these small divisions represents 0.2% of population

8   (a) *What percentage of females is in the 10–14 year age group?**
(b) *Which age group is the largest?**
(c) *Are there more males or more females in the 80–84 age group?**
(d) *Calculate the percentage of children (male and female) in the 0–4 age group.**
(e) *Are there more males in the 40–44 age group than there are females in the 50–54 age group?*
(f) *Approximately what percentage of females are aged 80 years or more?*
(g) *What total percentage of people are in the 0–14 age groups?*
(h) *Calculate the total percentage of people in the 15–64 age groups.**
(i) *Offer one possible explanation for the large proportion of people in the 20–29 age groups.*
(j) *Suggest one way in which the population structure of Cork City might differ from that of a city in the developing world.**

(**LC exam question*)

2 The table of percentages in Figure 9 shows the population of Ireland in 2010 classified according to age and sex. Using graph paper, draw a suitable graph to illustrate this data.

(LC Higher Level question)

Ireland's population by age and sex 2010 **9**

Age group	Males (%)	Females (%)
0–14	21	20
15–24	15	15
25–44	32	31
45–64	21	21
65 +	11	13
Total	100	100

Types of population pyramid

There are **three** basic types of population pyramid. They are called **progressive**, **stationary** and **regressive** pyramids. These pyramid types represent countries or regions at different stages of demographic transition. As a country develops economically, its pyramid shape changes gradually from progressive to stationary to regressive.

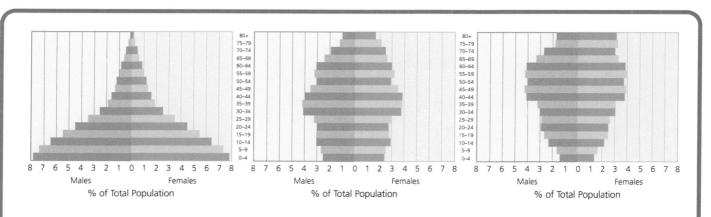

- **Progressive:** Progressive pyramids are the most 'pyramid shaped'. They have wide bases and they narrow progressively towards pointed tops. These pyramids are typical of countries such as *Mexico* that have *high birth rates and high death rates* and that are at Stages 1 to 3 of demographic transition.

- **Stationary:** Stationary pyramids are rather square in shape because all age groups are well represented in them. These pyramids represent countries such as *Ireland* in which *birth rates are moderate and life expectancy is quite high*. Such countries are at Stage 4 of demographic transition.

- **Regressive:** Regressive pyramids have rather wide tops, bulging middle sections and narrow bases. They represent countries such as *Italy*. Italy contains *more old people than young children* and has reached Stage 5 of demographic transition.

10 Progressive, stationary and regressive pyramid types

How to describe contrasts between population pyramids

You may be required to describe and explain the differences between two contrasting population pyramids. The sample descriptions provided here refer to the population pyramids in Figure 11. Read these examples carefully. Then answer the questions relating to Figures 12 and 13 on the next page.

Tanzania

A

Male   Female

80+
75–79
70–74
65–69
60–64
55–59
50–54
45–49
40–44
35–39
30–34
25–29
20–24
15–19
10–14
5–9
0–4

3.5 3.0 2.5 2.0 1.5 1.0 0.5 0.0   0.0 0.5 1.0 1.5 2.0 2.5 3.0 3.5

Population (in millions)

Germany

B

80+
75–79
70–74
65–69
60–64
55–59
50–54
45–49
40–44
35–39
30–34
25–29
20–24
15–19
10–14
5–9
0–4

Male   Female

4.0 3.5 3.0 2.5 2.0 1.5 1.0 0.5 0.0   0.0 0.5 1.0 1.5 2.0 2.5 3.0 3.5 4.0

Population (in millions)

11 Population pyramids of Tanzania and Germany

Sample descriptions

Examine three major differences between the population structures of Tanzania and Germany as shown in Figure 11.

The **base** of pyramid A is much broader than the base of pyramid B. This shows that Tanzania's population has a much greater proportion of children than Germany's. Tanzania is shown to have almost 3 million females and just in excess of 3 million males in the 0–4 age bracket alone. Germany, on the other hand, has a total of only 4 million children in the same age category.

These contrasts reflect the fact that birth rates in Tanzania are much higher than they are in Germany. This is because children in Third World countries such as Tanzania are regarded as economic assets and a means of economic security for elderly parents. Children in developed countries such as Germany are costly to rear and educate. This causes many German parents to have small families – usually of one or two children only.

Tanzania's 'progressive-type' pyramid **narrows very rapidly** from its base upward. This is typical of pyramids that represent countries at Stage 2 of demographic transition. Such countries have high death rates among children and young people and this is shown by the fact that there are fewer than 3 million people in the 25–29 age bracket in Tanzania.

Germany's 'regressive' pyramid, on the other hand, **bulges in the middle** sections. It shows that 3.5 million females and more than 3.5 million males are aged between 35 and 39 years. Such 'middle age' bulges are typical of developed countries in which death rates are low and where family planning has increased over the past 40 years.

The **top of pyramid A** is very narrow or pointed, which is typical of progressive-type pyramids. The top of pyramid B, on the other hand, is broad in the fashion of regressive pyramids. This reflects the fact that few people survive to old age in Tanzania, while many people survive to beyond the age of 80 years in Germany. Fewer than 0.2 million (200,000) people are shown to reach 80 years in Tanzania, while in Germany this age is exceeded by more than 2 million females alone.

Uncertain food supplies and poor medical care reduce life expectancy rates in Third World countries such as Tanzania. Most people in Germany enjoy food security, high living standards and excellent medical care. This results in high average life expectancy rates there.

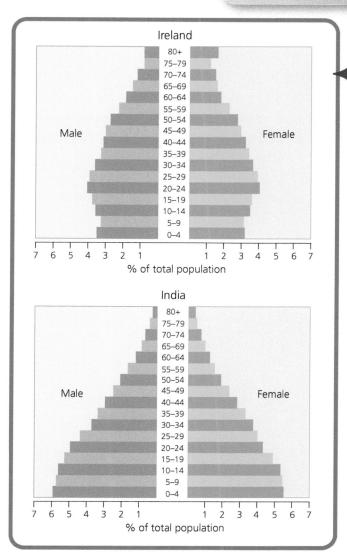

12 Population pyramids of Ireland and India. *Describe and account for two major differences between the population structures of Ireland and India.*

Figure 13 contains two superimposed population pyramids that show the population of Japan in 1950 and the predicted population of Japan in 2050. The pyramid outlined here in **black** refers to the **1950** population, while the pyramid outlined in **red** refers to the projected **2050** population. *Describe two principal contrasts between the population of Japan in 1950 and the projected population of Japan in 2050.*

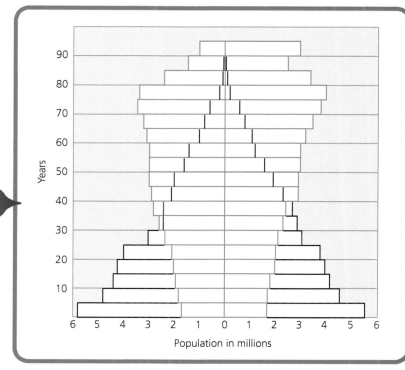

Dependency ratio

The dependency ratio is the ratio between the non-working and the working populations of a country or region. For the purpose of calculating dependency ratio,* people under the age of 15 years are considered to be young dependants, while people at or over the age of 65 are all considered to be elderly dependants. People between the ages of 15 and 64 are considered to be economically active.

*Either real numbers or percentages of people may be used when calculating the dependency ratio. Percentage figures are usually easier to use.

Calculating the dependency ratio

The following **formula** is used to calculate the dependency ratio:

$$\frac{\text{Population under 15 + Population at or over 65}}{\text{Population between 15 and 64}} \times 100$$

Sample question and solution

Question

The grid in Figure 14 shows census statistics for the population structure of Ireland in 2002. Use these statistics to calculate Ireland's dependency ratio.

14

Age (years)	Numbers	Percentage
65 and over	436,001	11
15–64	2,653,774	68
0–14	827,428	21
Totals	3,917,203	100

Solution

$$\frac{\text{\% young dependants + \% elderly dependants}}{\text{\% working population}} \times 100$$

$$\frac{11 + 21}{68} \times 100 = \frac{32}{68} \times 100 = \frac{3,200}{68} = 47 \text{ (to nearest whole number)}$$

This means that there are 47 dependants for every hundred workers. This dependency ratio is written as 47:100.

The answer is *47:100*.

The importance of dependency ratios

The dependency ratio can indicate a great deal about the economic problems or wellbeing of a country. A high dependency ratio is usually bad news. It indicates that the economically active population might need to be taxed heavily in order to maintain pensions, education, health care and other services for large proportions of dependants.

Activities

1. *Use Figure 8 on page 16 to calculate the dependency ratio for Cork City in 2006.*
2. *Do activity 7 on page 25.*

Case Study:
Challenges of Ireland's ageing population

Ireland has a 'greying' or ageing population. This means that our proportion of elderly dependants is growing and is likely to grow steadily over time. Our ageing population will increase Ireland's current dependency ratio of 47. This case study examines two challenges associated with Ireland's ageing population.

1 Increasing pension costs

An increasing ratio of elderly people creates a **growing demand for pensions**. Some pensions are 'contributory pensions' that employees help to pay for throughout their working lives. Many other people receive smaller 'non-contributory' old age pensions from the age of 66. Increasing demands for pensions will prove costly for the state. This presents Ireland with a serious problem, especially in times of economic recession and severe national debt. There are no easy solutions to this problem.

- Ireland could **cut pension rates**. But this would be unfair to people who contributed to their pensions throughout their working lives. It would also create severe hardship for many elderly old age pensioners, some of whom already live on the brink of poverty.

- Another solution might be to raise the **pension eligibility age**. This would reduce pension costs: but it would force people to remain longer in the workforce and would therefore reduce the number of jobs available to young people. It might also result in lower labour productivity and in more illness-related absenteeism from work on the part of older workers.

- Ireland could increase **income tax** levels to meet its rising pension costs. But our rising dependency ratio means that a smaller and smaller proportion of working people will be available to pay such taxes. Other forms of **taxation** – such as taxes on betting and on high-value luxury items – might provide a limited but more sociably acceptable means of helping to meet Ireland's rising pensions costs.

Grey power – angry older people protest outside Dáil Éireann.
Greater numbers of older people may have a growing influence on Irish politics. How is this likely to affect any moves to reduce old age pensions or to raise the pension eligibility age?

2 Medical and social needs

The **medical and social needs** of elderly people create other economic and moral challenges.

*The **government medicines scheme** places a monthly limit on the cost of prescription medicines to non-medical card holders.

- The occurrence of serious medical conditions such as heart disease, stroke and cancer generally increases with age. These conditions also require expensive, long-term treatments in the forms of diagnostic tests, hospital care and pharmaceutical medicines. The provision of such **medical care** is a big challenge to Ireland's already struggling and cash-strapped Health Service Executive (HSE) and to the country's tax-funded government medicines scheme.* The announcement that our government medicines scheme is to make greater use of effective but less costly generic medicines should help to reduce costs somewhat.

- Ireland's ageing population creates the need for a greater number of suitable, purpose-built and well-run **retirement homes**. Tax breaks for building such homes, along with rigorous inspections of their operations, might help to meet this growing need.

- Our ageing population creates the prospect of more elderly people being alone, lonely and in dire need of **social contacts**. The dangers of this might be alleviated by public awareness drives, by government support for localised 'active retirement' groups and by increased financial allowances for home care assistants.

This active retirement group is helping to meet the social needs of older people

- The world's **population grew** slowly up to 1750. Since 1950, population growth has been so rapid that it is referred to as a **population explosion**.
- Population change is affected by **birth rates**, **death rates** and **migration**.
- **Birth rates** are lower in developed countries of the North than they are in developing countries of the South.
  - Child rearing is expensive in developed countries. But *children* can be *economic assets* and sources of economic security for many Third World parents.
  - *Gender equality* and high levels of *female education* have reduced birth rates more in developed countries than in developing countries.
- **Death rates** in the North are low because of high levels of *food supplies*, *hygiene* and *medical care*. Factors such as improved water schemes have lowered death rates in the South, although *AIDS* has increased death tolls in sub-Saharan Africa.
- The **demographic transition model** states that as countries develop economically their birth rates and death rates change predictably. Countries pass through five development stages. As they do so, big population increases at Stages 2 and 3 give way to natural decrease at Stage 5.
- The demographic transition model helps to explain the present world population explosion. It also predicts that population growth will moderate as more countries develop economically.
- **Population pyramids** are used to illustrate *age structure, sex structure* and *dependency ratio*.
  - **Progressive** population pyramids represent Third World countries that have high birth rates, high death rates and rapid population growth. **Stationary** pyramids represent countries such as Ireland that have little natural increase. **Regressive** pyramids represent countries that have relatively 'old' populations and that experience natural decrease.
  - Population pyramids of **developing countries** with high birth and death rates tend to have **broad bases** and **narrow peaks**. Population pyramids of developed countries with low birth and death rates have narrow bases and wide peaks (see Figure 15).

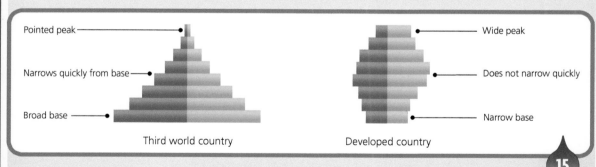

Pointed peak · Narrows quickly from base · Broad base

Wide peak · Does not narrow quickly · Narrow base

Third world country   Developed country

15

- The **dependency ratio** provides an approximate ratio between the non-working population and the working population. It is calculated as follows:

$$\frac{\text{People under 15 + People 65 and over}}{\text{People between 15 and 64}} \times 100$$

- Ireland's ageing population gives rise to **economic challenges** that relate to growing demands for pensions, medical care and retirement home care.

Test Yourself
eTest.ie

Activities

1. The table in Figure 16 provides census information on changes in the population of the Republic of Ireland between 1901 and 2006. Using graph paper, draw a suitable graph or chart to illustrate the information given in Figure 16.

2. Read the newspaper extract in Figure 17 and answer the questions below.

Year	Total in millions
1901	3.2
1926	2.9
1946	2.2
1961	2.8
1991	3.5
2002	3.9
2006	4.2

16 Population of Ireland 1901–2006

Ireland's population is set to increase to 6.7 million by 2050, according to official forecasts compiled by the European Union. The 52 per cent increase – up from a current population of around 4.4 million – would make Ireland one of the fastest growing countries in Europe. Ireland's population is expected to be significantly older, with a quarter aged 65 or over, and one in ten aged 80 or older.

Irish Times, 27 August 2008   **17**

   (a) What was the population of Ireland when the news extract was written?
   (b) What is the predicted population in 2050?
   (c) Explain two difficulties that a rise in population can cause for a country.

   (LC Ordinary Level – 30 marks)

3. Explain each of the following terms:
   ● mortality rate   ● total fertility rate
   ● natural change   ● population replacement level.

4. Explain two reasons why the population in poorer developing countries grows faster than the population in wealthier developed countries.

   (LC Ordinary Level – 40 marks)

5. Examine Figure 18 below. The three sketches labelled **A**, **B** and **C** represent different types of population pyramids, each representing the population of a different country. Identify which of these sketches represents:
   (a) A country with a 'stationary' population.
   (b) A country that is at Stage 2 of demographic transition.
   (c) A country at the 'senile' stage of demographic transition.
   (d) A Third World country such as Sudan.
   (e) A 'regressive' population pyramid.
   (f) A country with a need for many primary schools.

18

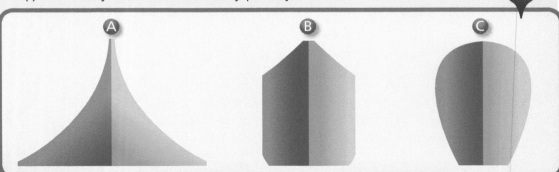

6. Figure 19 contrasts the population (age and sex) profiles of Irish Travellers with those of the total population of Ireland.
   (a) Approximately what percentage of Travellers are under 5 years of age?
   (b) Approximately what percentage of Travellers survive to be 80 years or more? Attempt to account briefly for this percentage.
   (c) Which is greater, the percentage of male Travellers in the 30–34 age category or the percentage of female Travellers in the 40–44 age category?
   (d) Referring to Figure 19, describe *two differences* between the profiles of the two groups shown.

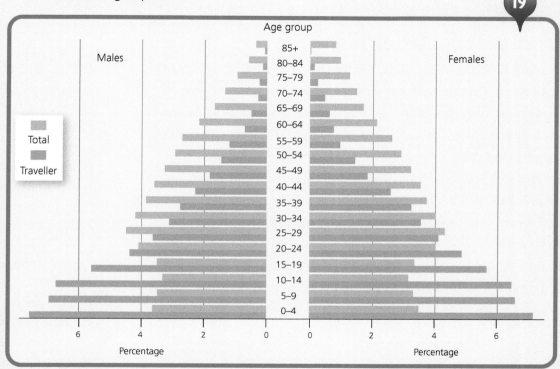

7. (a) Calculate the *dependency ratio* for the European region referred to by the statistics in Figure 20.
   (b) Why might statistics such as those provided in Figure 20 prove useful to national or local governments?

Selected population statistics of a European region by age in 2011

Age group	Males	Females	Persons
0–14	253,534	231,988	485,522
15–19	89,001	87,845	176,846
20–24	91,665	91,321	182,986
25–44	295,009	294,652	589,661
45–64	90,856	96,709	187,565
65 and over	66,321	94,776	161,097

8. Name and explain two difficulties that an ageing population can cause for a country.
                            (LC Higher and Ordinary Level – 30 marks)

Causes and Effects of Overpopulation

What is overpopulation?

Overpopulation occurs when there are **too many people in an area for the resources of that area to provide adequate living standards**.

You will see from this definition that the term overpopulation does not merely refer to size and density of population. It refers rather to the **population in relation to resources**. For example:

- The Netherlands has a huge population density of 420 people per square kilometre. But the Netherlands is *not* overpopulated because it has the **carrying capacity** (resources) to maintain its people comfortably.
- Ethiopia has an average population density of only 60 per square kilometre. Yet Ethiopia *is* overpopulated because it does not have the resources to provide an adequate standard of living for all its people.

Other important terms

Underpopulation occurs when there are *not enough people in an area to fully exploit the area's resources*. In such cases, an increase of population usually leads to increased living standards. In-migration is therefore sometimes encouraged in underpopulated areas.

Optimum population: A point can be reached when there are *just enough people in an area to make the best possible use of its resources*. When this happens, the area is said to enjoy ideal or optimum population. This precise, knife-edged balance between underpopulation and overpopulation is *almost impossible to achieve* in practice. This is because the economically 'ideal' population for any area will change with each slight variation in an area's economic fortunes.

Photograph A shows a scene from the Sahel region of Africa. Photograph B shows part of Manhattan in New York.
Which one of these photographs shows the more overpopulated area? Explain your choice.

Some causes of overpopulation: an introduction

- The **unwise use of resources** such as farmland or mineral deposits can result in the depletion of those resources.
- **Cultural influences** such as gender inequality or some religious traditions can lead to high birth rates and rapid population growth.
- **Low income levels** cause some poor people to regard children as possible sources of economic security. This can contribute to high birth rates and population growth.
- Improved agricultural and medical **technology** has increased food supplies and reduced death rates. This, in turn, has contributed to rapid population growth. **Mechanisation** can also lead to widespread **unemployment**, which is a symptom of overpopulation.

The strange story of the Aral Sea

The Aral Sea in Central Asia was once one of the world's largest lakes. It was fed by waters from the Syr and Amu rivers (see Figure 1). In the 1960s, it supported up to 30 million people along or close to its shores.

In the 1960s, the government of the former Soviet Union began to divert irrigation water away from the Syr and Amu rivers. This turned out to be an unwise use of water resources. The Aral Sea began to shrink so much that its former ports were left abandoned up to 50 kilometres from the new, reduced lakeshore. As lakeshore agriculture, fishing and lake trading all collapsed, the area around the Aral became an overpopulated economic wasteland. People responded to the new situation by migrating away from the area.

The map in Figure 1 shows how the Aral Sea shrank over time. The photograph shows fishing boats stranded on the now exposed seabed.

Some results or symptoms of severe overpopulation

- Inadequate **food supplies**, which can sometimes result in malnutrition or even famine.
- Crowded **housing** and inadequate **sanitation**.
- Widespread **disease** resulting from inadequate food, sanitation or housing.
- Environmental pressure that can result in air, water, noise and visual **pollution**.
- **Economic stagnation**, widespread unemployment and poverty.
- **Out-migration** from overpopulated areas.

27

Case Study 1:
Overpopulation in Kolkata

Kolkata is the capital city of the state of West Bengal in Northern India. It is a heavily overpopulated city that cannot provide adequate living standards for its astonishingly high population density of **33,000 per square kilometre**. One third of Kolkata's 16 million people are crammed into in poor shantytowns called **bustees**. Many of these bustees are among the world's most overpopulated places.

Overpopulation in Kolkata is associated with:

- **High** (although declining) **birth rates** that are typical of the region's position in Stage 3 (the 'late expanding stage') of demographic transition.

- **Massive in-migration** from rural areas of West Bengal and from the neighbouring country of Bangladesh

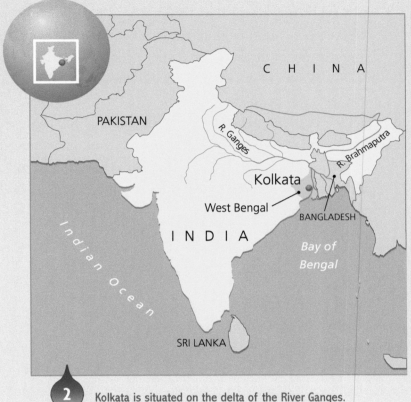

2   Kolkata is situated on the delta of the River Ganges. It has developed along the River Hooghly, which is a distributary of the Ganges.
What is a delta and what is a distributary?

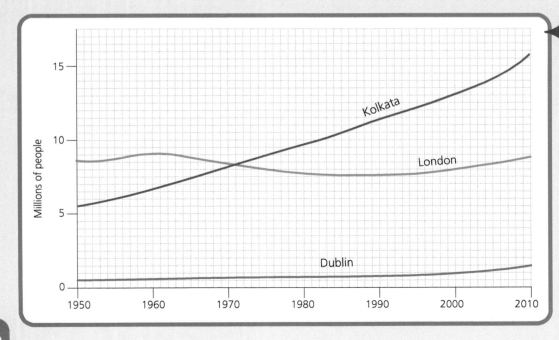

3

Populations of the urban areas of Kolkata, London and Dublin between 1950 and 2010.

(a) State the approximate population of Kolkata in 1950 and in 2010.

(b) In which year did the population of Kolkata overtake that of London?

(c) In which year did the population of Kolkata reach 10 million?

(d) By approximately how many million did the population of Kolkata exceed that of Dublin in the year 2010?

(e) Suggest two possible reasons for the 'population explosion' in Kolkata's population.

Causes of overpopulation

A combination of causes affects in-migration and high birth rates in Kolkata. In this case study we will examine two of those causes: the **influence of society and culture** and the **impact of technology**.

1 The influence of society and culture

- The **status of women** in India has traditionally been inferior to that of men. More than 60 per cent of Indian women are illiterate because girls are still generally given fewer educational opportunities than boys. Many poorer and more conservative parents consider the formal education of females to be something of a 'waste' of scarce financial resources. They expect their daughters to marry young and to pursue the roles of wife, homemaker and mother. Many girls still enter into arranged marriages in their mid- to late teens. With little formal education or life experience, these girls tend to have little say on the subject of family planning or the size of their family. They usually have relatively large families and this contributes to high birth rates, to population growth and to overpopulation.

- A **desire for male children** is very strong in Indian culture. Male children are often valued because they carry the family name down to future generations. Sons are also valued economically. They are more likely than daughters to contribute earning power to the family household. On marriage, they are also likely to add their bride's dowry to the family wealth.

  Poor parents in India realise that hard work, limited diet and inadequate medical care will cause them to age quickly. They also realise that, in a country with very few state benefits for the aged, they may eventually rely for survival on their economically active sons. But infant mortality rates – especially among boys – has been high among India's poor. Many parents therefore have many children in the hope that they will have enough surviving sons to provide for them in their old age.

An elderly beggar in Kolkata.
Why is fear of destitution in old age a contributory cause of overpopulation in Kolkata?

A Hindu bride in Kolkata.
Many Indian brides marry in their teens. They therefore have many years of fertility available to them throughout their married lives. This contributes to high fertility rates.

29

2   The impact of technology and science

The **Green Revolution** has had a profound impact on agriculture and on population in countries such as India. The Green Revolution began in the 1960s, when scientists developed new 'miracle' strains of rice, wheat and other cereals. These strains were high-yielding, drought-resistant and needed only a short growing season. At that time India was faced with a growing threat of food shortages, so the Indian government imported 18,000 tonnes of the new seeds.

The 'miracle seeds' of the Green Revolution came with a hidden price. They required the use of expensive pesticides, artificial fertilisers and modern farm machinery. Richer farmers, who could afford to invest in these requirements, enjoyed large yields and profits and therefore benefited greatly. But many poorer farmers – whose yields were now hopelessly uncompetitive – went out of business and sold their tiny farms. Other small farmers incurred such heavy debts in trying to purchase seeds and fertilisers that they too were driven off the land. Many of these landless *peasants migrated* to the streets or the shantytowns of Kolkata in search of work. They were joined there by unemployed farm labourers who had lost their jobs because of more mechanised agriculture. Kolkata thus experienced a wave of immigration that served to increase its levels of overpopulation.

Kolkata has benefited greatly from technological improvements in **preventive medicine**. It has benefited particularly from the invention of disposable-syringe vaccinations that are effective, cheap and easy to administer even in the poorest conditions. Many children throughout Kolkata are now vaccinated against preventable but potentially fatal infections such as measles and whooping cough. Such advances have greatly *reduced infant mortality* rates throughout India. Partly because of this, life expectancy has increased from an average of **20** years a century ago to an average of **60** years today. Increased life expectancy contributed – at least in the short term* – to rising population levels and therefore to overpopulation in Kolkata.

*It is expected that in the *longer term*, increased life expectancy will reduce overpopulation by encouraging people to have smaller families. This appears to be happening already in India, where the total fertility rate (TFR) had moderated to 2.76 in 2010. This was less than half of India's TFR figure for 1950.

How did the Green Revolution and increased mechanisation in agriculture contribute to overpopulation in Kolkata?

Some effects of overpopulation in Kolkata

1 Unplanned, overcrowded bustees

One effect of overpopulation in Indian cities such as Kolkata has been the rapid growth of shantytowns called **bustees**. These hastily built slums have grown up mainly around the expanding fringes of the city, where millions of rural migrants attempt to settle. Because Kolkata grew so rapidly, its bustees developed in an unplanned way. Their narrow alleyways wind chaotically around the homes of Kolkata's poor.

About one-third of Kolkata's population – more than 5 million people – are crammed into bustees. One shantytown, a place called Barabazar, contains an incredible 100,000 people per square kilometre! Most bustee families live in tiny, overcrowded houses that are sometimes no bigger than average-sized Irish garden sheds. Many people – especially newer migrants – live in makeshift one-roomed huts that they make from wood, straw, plastic sheeting or flattened metal barrels.

Most bustees began as 'squatter camps', where people did not own the land on which their huts were built. In time, however, most bustee dwellers gained legal title to their homes.

Other people – the poorest of all – have no homes. They are called 'pavement people' because they live on Calcutta's streets, under its bridges or even in unused sewerage pipes.

Overcrowded bustees in Kolkata.
What human problems might arise from overcrowding such as that shown in these photographs?

2   Inadequate services

Even the most basic public services are inadequate in the poorer areas of Kolkata.

- While most people have some access to **clean water**, it is usual for up to 40 families to depend on a single street tap for their water supply. Some drinking water has been poisoned by lead from old lead piping. Many homeless 'pavement people' have no access at all to clean water. They are forced to rely on unfiltered water supplies that were originally intended only for street cleaning or fire fighting.

- Proper **sanitation** facilities such as flush toilets are very rare in Calcutta's bustees. Human effluent runs through open sewers in narrow laneways. Heavy monsoon rains flood these drains and often wash sewage into water supplies and into people's houses. This endangers lives by leading to occasional outbreaks of deadly diseases such as cholera and of gastroenteritis, which is particularly dangerous to infants.

- Most bustee **schools** are poorly built, badly equipped and extremely short of money. Many classrooms do not even have seats, tables or desks and few children have textbooks of their own. It is very difficult, therefore, for pupils to make progress at school. Some children – especially girls – do not attend school at all. Their parents are so poor that they need their children to work from an early age.

- Despite the fact that Kolkata has an underground rail system, its **public transport** is generally very inadequate. Most buses are old and are so overcrowded that some passengers hang on from the outside.

How do the photographs on this page illustrate inadequate services in poor areas of Kolkata?

Solutions to overpopulation in the Third World

Third World countries such as India have relied on massive **birth control** schemes to reduce birth rates and thus to resolve or ease their overpopulation problems. Government agencies in India have given widespread publicity to the benefits of family planning. Free family planning advice and free or cheap contraceptives have been made available. Over 100,000 people have been employed at a single time in birth control projects, some of which included very controversial offers of transistor radios and even pay rises to young men who agreed to be sterilised.

But high birth rates in Third World countries have been related closely to underdevelopment and poverty. Birth control succeeds best, therefore, when it is combined with **social and economic development**. Ways must be found to develop Third World regions so that people there will no longer feel dependent on large families for economic security. When this happens, attitudes to family size tend to change gradually. Very large families come to be regarded as economically burdensome rather than economic necessities. Parents then begin to plan smaller families. This change has already happened in economically developed countries such as Germany and is already beginning to happen in rapidly developing countries such as India, which has now entered Stage 3 – the late expanding stage – of demographic transition.

Third World development will not be easy to achieve. It will demand justice, generosity and prolonged effort on the part of developed as well as developing nations. Yet it appears to offer the only workable and humane means of overcoming the world's present overpopulation problems.

A family planning poster in India. Intense government campaigns have contributed to a significant increase in family planning in India, where 48 per cent of married women now use some form of contraception. This is an almost four-fold increase from 13 per cent in 1970. India's birth rate has fallen steadily over time, though it is still high enough to result in continued long-term population growth.

Case Study 2:
Overpopulation in the Sahel

The Sahel is a long, narrow region that stretches for more than 5,000 kilometres across Africa. It lies between the Sahara Desert to the North and Africa's **savanna*** grasslands to the south (see Figure 4). The Sahel has traditionally been covered by grasslands and scattered trees that supported millions of farmers and **nomadic herders***. But this situation has changed dramatically in recent decades. The Sahel has now become an overpopulated region that can no longer adequately support its human population.

You can read more about the Sahel on pages 189–194 of this book.

Legend:
- The Sahel
- Direction of desertification

0   km   600

N

4

The Sahel.

(a) Use the information on this map to describe the extent and location of the Sahel. Refer to the approximate length, width and area of the region. Refer to its latitude, its orientation (the direction in which its long axis points) and the countries which it partly occupies.

(b) 'Sahel' is the Arabic word for 'shore' or 'boundary area'. Why do you think the Sahel is so called?

Population and resources in the Sahel. The concept of overpopulation takes into account the **population** and the **resources** of a country or a region. The average population density of the Sahel is a mere 30 people or so per square kilometre. But this modest population density exceeds the **carrying capacity** of the region's resources. The area is therefore overpopulated.

Causes of overpopulation

Rapid population growth and the **overuse of resources** are two major causes of overpopulation in the Sahel.

1 Rapid population growth

The human population of the Sahel has grown from approximately 19 million in 1961 to more than 50 million in 2011. This is because most countries of the Sahel are at Stage 2 (the early expanding stage) of demographic transition and have high birth rates, falling death rates and therefore high rates of natural population increase. Niger, for example, has an annual birth rate of 52 (per thousand), which is one of the highest in the world. Its death rate, on the other hand, declined rapidly from 22 to 14 between 2003 and 2011. This means that by 2011 Niger had a big natural increase of 38 per thousand.

- **High birth rates** throughout the Sahel have been influenced by **economic poverty** and by **traditional customs and female status**.
  - Most people in the Sahel live in deep **economic poverty**. For example, Niger's **GDP per capita*** is a mere US$163 – less than one per cent of Ireland's figure. Poor people in Third World countries often live in fear of destitution in old age. They know that when they can no longer work they must usually rely on their adult children to support them. They may also rely on young children to assist with household or other duties and sometimes to contribute by their work to meagre family incomes. Poor people therefore feel an economic need for children. But many people fear that some of their children might die young. They therefore tend to have large families to ensure that they have enough children to meet their needs.
  - **Traditional customs and the status of women** contribute to high population growth. In rural parts of Nigeria, for example, very few girls remain at school beyond their teens. It is customary for many women there to marry in their late teens. Once married, a woman is expected to obey her husband's wishes regarding family size. Many men and women regard large families as a blessing from God and a sign of maternal virtue. Such traditions contribute to Nigeria's total fertility rate of 5.0 – one of the highest in Africa.
- **Falling death rates** throughout the Sahel have been linked to improvements in **preventive medicine**. Vaccinations against 'childhood' diseases such as measles and whooping cough have, for example, helped to reduce **infant mortality rates.*** Niger's infant mortality rate now stands at 77 – just over half its 1965 figure.

Terms to know

- **Savanna:** large areas of tropical grasslands that typically contain scattered trees and shrubs.
- **Nomadic herders:** people who move with their cattle along set routes in search of fresh pastures.
- **GDP per capita:** gross domestic product per capita is the total value of all goods and services produced in a country in a year, divided by the population of that country. GDP is usually expressed in terms of US dollars.
- **Infant mortality rate:** the number of infants who die under the age of one year, expressed as the number of deaths per 1,000 live births.

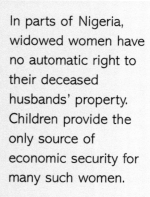

Fact

In parts of Nigeria, widowed women have no automatic right to their deceased husbands' property. Children provide the only source of economic security for many such women.

2 Overuse and depletion of natural resources

The principal natural resources of the Sahel are *soil*, *water* and *natural vegetation* in the form of grass and trees. As the population of the region has increased, these resources have been overused and depleted. The Sahel became overpopulated when its resources could no longer adequately meet the needs of its population.

The resources of the Sahel are overused by the processes of **overgrazing**, **overcultivation** and **cutting trees**.

- **Overgrazing:** Cattle herding has for centuries been the Sahel's principal economic activity. As the human population has increased, so has the number of cattle and goats. The animals overgraze the land by grazing it beyond its **carrying capacity**. They remove grass cover and even eat the bark of young trees and shrubs. This leaves the soil bare and vulnerable to wind erosion. Many **wells** have been dug to provide watering places for animals. Too many cattle congregate around these wells, causing the land there to become overgrazed and trampled. The overuse of wells has also used up precious ground water that has taken hundreds of years to build up.

- **Overcultivation:** Rapid population growth has forced many people to cultivate the land excessively in order to provide enough food for themselves and their families. In such cases the land is not allowed to rest or is not fertilised sufficiently between crops. The soil then becomes progressively more bare and barren.

- **Cutting trees:** Most people in the Sahel rely on firewood for **heating and cooking**. As the population has increased, more and more trees have been cut to provide for these needs. Huge areas – especially those close to large urban areas – have now been almost completely denuded of trees. This leaves the soil bare and exposed to wind erosion. It also damages soil by depriving it of much-needed organic matter that leaves and other plant litter provide. Another problem is that when firewood becomes scarce many people are forced to use dried **animal dung as fuel**. This dung would normally fertilise the soil, so its use as fuel contributes further to soil infertility and degradation.

Overgrazing, overcultivation and gathering firewood – three ways in which the resources of the Sahel are depleted

Some effects of overpopulation in the Sahel

1 Desertification

The resources of the Sahel have been damaged and degraded through overuse. *Water tables** have fallen seriously in the vicinity of overused wells. Natural vegetation has been stripped from the land by overgrazing, overcultivation and tree cutting. Bare, dry soil has then been exposed to the elements and has been massively eroded and blown away by frequent dust storms (see news article below). When the topsoil of a Sahel area is removed, that area becomes barren and bare like the neighbouring Sahara Desert. This spread of desert conditions is called **desertification**. The Sahel is experiencing desertification on a scale exceeding that of anywhere else in the world. It is estimated that desert conditions in parts of the Sahel are expanding southwards at a rate of up to 10 kilometres a year. These expansions have devastating consequences for millions of inhabitants of the Sahel. Desertification in the Sahel has contributed to increased poverty, food shortages and even **famines** in areas such as central Sudan (2010) and Chad (2010). It has also resulted in large-scale human **migrations** away from desertified areas. Such migrations and their effects are examined on the next page.

Dust storms blowing country across the Atlantic

Adapted from an article by Nick Middleton in The Times

The West African State of Mauritania is blowing away. Every year, 100 million tonnes of topsoil – much of it from the fragile Sahel zone – is sucked up by the burning desert winds and carried out over the North Atlantic.

The reasons for this ecological disaster are drought and desertification Drought has plagued this area since the late 1960s. Overgrazing, overstocking and the cutting of woody shrubs for fuel, coupled with a population explosion, all spelt disaster when the drought came. The resulting desertification of Mauritania has been like an advancing tide of sand.

Since the 1960s, dust storms in the Sahel of Mauritania have increased considerably.

The storms often advance as a wall of dust, hundreds of metres high, engulfing all in their path and reducing visibility to near zero. The dust gets in your eyes, up your nose, through doors and windows, coating everything in a thick layer of red dust. Cars and airports are brought to a standstill, radio communications are affected. But worst of all, the soil is lost, piling up on the bed of the Atlantic Ocean.

Find Mauritania and the city of Nouakchott on the map in Figure 4.

A dust storm approaches a village in the Sahel.

(a) According to the news extract, what are the **effects** of dust storms in Mauritania?

(b) What **reasons** does the extract give for the 'ecological disaster' associated with dust storms?

Terms to know

● **Water table:** the level below which the ground is saturated with water.

2 Migration

A lack of resources, hunger and other hardships associated with overpopulation forced millions of people out of the rural Sahel from the late 1960s onwards. **Out-migrants** from the region numbered 5 million in 1995 alone.

● Many migrants moved to **urban areas** both within and outside the Sahel region. This resulted in the rapid growth of cities in the Sahel. The population of Senegal's capital of Dakar, for example, grew from under 1 million in 1965 to 2.5 million in 2010. Since most in-migrants to these cities are poverty-stricken *ecological refugees,** their mass arrival in cities has resulted in the rapid growth of unplanned, overcrowded shantytowns at the edges of cities such as Nouakchott. Very poor housing, inadequate services and dire poverty are all commonplace in these shantytowns.

● Mass migrations within and from the Sahel have resulted in **tensions** and even **violence** between migrants and the original inhabitants of the areas to which migrants moved. Such migrations have even contributed to all-out civil wars in countries such as Sudan (see opposite).

● Migrations have seriously affected the rural areas that migrants left. Many of these **source areas** have lost a high proportion of young, energetic adults. This has increased their economic dependency ratios. Most migrants tend to be males, so the sex ratios of source areas have also been altered. Such areas have been left with a greater proportion of unmarried or unpartnered females.

Migrants from rural areas of the Sahel in a 'bidonville' or shantytown in Dakar, Senegal. *What challenges might such people encounter in their new homes? Try to be specific.*

Terms to know

● **Ecological refugees:** people who are forced from their homes because of adverse environmental situations such as severe drought.

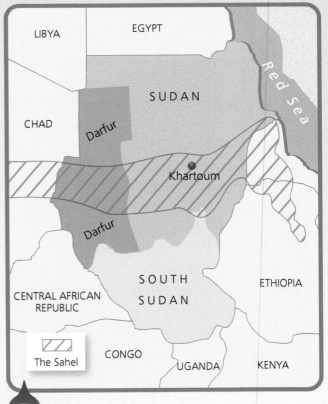

5 Sudan, the Sudanese province of Darfur and the newly independent state of South Sudan

Overpopulation and Civil War in Sudan

Most Sudanese people are of Muslim Arabic stock and the country has a mainly Muslim Arabic government. But Sudan also contains many black people who live in the western region of Darfur and in the south of the country where most people are Christian (see Figure 5). Old tensions exist between those cultural groups.

The Sahel region runs east–west through the middle of Sudan. Migrations caused by drought and overpopulation in the Sahel inflamed cultural tensions and contributed to armed conflict in Sudan.

Severe drought and overpopulation forced many Arabic cattle herders to migrate southwards. In doing so, they entered the traditional territories of black Christian farmers. Competition for land and water inflamed tensions between the two groups and became a contributory cause of two disastrous civil wars.

- One war broke out in 1983 between Arabic government forces and black southern rebels. It lasted for 20 years and resulted in two million deaths. In 2011, South Sudan became an independent state.
- No sooner had the first civil war ended than another broke out in the Darfur region. This caused 2.25 million deaths in an area nearly six times the size of Ireland. It also led to the destruction of hundreds of villages and to millions of people being driven from their homes.

Civil war in Darfur.
This village was burned by pro-Government forces. The war in Darfur caused so much suffering that in 2007 the United Nations sent Irish and other troops on a peacekeeping mission to the region.
How did overpopulation contribute to war in Darfur?

Some possible long-term solutions to overpopulation in the Sahel

Population

Reduced birth rates might be achieved through long-term economic development, combined with culturally sensitive birth control programmes. (This solution was examined in relation to India on page 33.)

Resources

1   Firewood might in some instances be replaced by **solar power** as a source of energy. Prolonged sunny conditions make the Sahel an ideal location for solar power. But the introduction of solar panels would be initially very expensive and would require massive aid from economically developed countries.

2   Many cattle herders measure their wealth and importance by the number of **cattle** that they possess. This leads to the existence of very large herds of poor-quality cattle. It would be helpful if people could be persuaded to reduce the number of cattle they own and to settle for fewer, more productive animals.

3   **Drought-resistant grasses and trees** might be planted and used to stabilise soil and so reduce wind erosion.

The impact of population growth rates on development

In general

There is a **complex relationship** between population growth rates and economic development.

- A **growing population** will provide an expanding, youthful *labour force* for manufacturing and other economic activities. It will also provide a growing *market* for goods and services. These factors tend to stimulate economic development. But an expanding population will also place increased *demands on resources* such as land, fuel and food, as well as on education, health and social services. If the resources of a country cannot meet these increased demands, that country will become overpopulated and may suffer from economic decline.

- A country that has a stable population or that experiences **negative population growth** (population decline) is less likely to experience excessive demands on its resources. On the other hand, it is likely to have an *ageing population* with increasing proportions of its people in older age groups. Such a country may have to rely on *immigrants* to supplement its ageing and shrinking workforce. Its economy will also be required to provide for an increasing proportion of elderly dependants.

Skills activities

1. Examine the graphs in Figure 6.
   (a) Which of the three age groups shown is expected to increase between 1950 and 2050?
   (b) What is the projected increase for that age group between 1950 and 2050?
   (c) Identify some likely economic effects of that increase.
   (d) What is meant by the term 'dependency ratio'?
   (e) Will the dependency ratio of Germany be greater or less in 2050 than it was in 1950?
   (f) Explain briefly how this trend is likely to affect the German economy.

2. Examine the statistics in Figure 7. Using graph paper, illustrate these statistics by means of three appropriately labelled percentage bars.

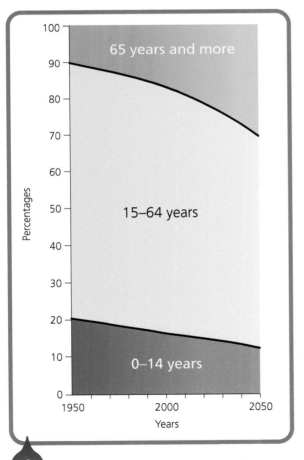

6 The changing age profile of Germany between 1950 and 2050 (projected)

	1846	**1976**	**2006**
65 years and over	9	17	19
15–64 years	53	63	67
0–14 years	38	20	14

7 The percentage age profile of an Irish parish in 1846, 1976 and 2006

In developed countries

- In the *eighteenth and nineteenth centuries*, countries such as Britain and present-day Germany passed through the early expanding stage of the demographic transition. Their **populations expanded rapidly** at that time and this helped to stimulate enormous economic growth. Their growing and youthful *workforces* were used (and often abused) to run coal mines, iron foundries and factories that were the chief motors of the **Industrial Revolution**. Expanding populations also provided the *increasing markets* for textile and iron products that fuelled continued industrial growth. Growing numbers of young men manned the *armies and navies* that allowed Britain and Germany to conquer colonies such as India and German East Africa (mainly present-day Tanzania). These colonies were exploited as sources of cheap raw materials and as captive markets for manufactured products. Their exploitation was vital to the continued economic growth of Imperial Britain and Germany. Rapid population increase therefore played a vital role in the **economic expansion** of those countries.

- Countries such as Germany have *now* reached the fifth ('senile') stage of demographic transition. Their populations are experiencing **natural decreases** as death rates exceed birth rates. Germany's natural decrease is now 0.2 per cent per annum. This situation helps to ease demand and stress on *resources* such as water supplies and land. But it means that Germany's native **population is ageing** and that the country must sometimes rely on immigrants to supplement its *declining native workforce*. It also means that Germany now has increasing proportions of *elderly dependants* who require old age pensions, medical care, retirement home care and other expensive assistance. These requirements create costly obligations that must be met by the German economy.

Then: workers in an old British cotton mill.
How did a relatively young age profile once help to stimulate economic growth in Britain?

Now: older people enjoying an outing.
How might a 'greying population' affect the economies of countries such as Britain or Germany?

In developing countries

Most countries of the developing world are now at stages two and three of demographic transition. Their birth rates exceed their death rates and this is resulting in **rapid population growth**. This growth has enormous implication for economic development. The countries involved have high and **growing dependency ratios** because of their growing proportions of young people. Young dependants require food, clothing, housing, education and employment, none of which is easily provided by weak Third World economies. In many Third World countries, therefore, rapidly growing populations tend to **hinder economic development** and contribute to high levels of **unemployment** and **underemployment**. Unemployment and underemployment lead in turn to **population migrations** that cause further economic problems (see the box, right).

Some rapidly developing countries have, however, managed to use large youthful populations as motors of economic growth. These **newly industrialised countries** (NICs) include China and India. China has used its vast, disciplined and sometimes poorly paid workforce to make it one of the world's leading manufacturing nations. Thirty-eight per cent of India's population is under the age of 15. But India has invested heavily in educating a skilled and inexpensive workforce that attracts numerous foreign investors and stimulates massive industrial growth. It is now estimated that India produces twice as many university science graduates for its workforce as the USA and Canada put together.

Unemployment, migrations and economic problems

High levels of unemployment have caused some skilled Third World people to emigrate to richer countries in search of well-paid jobs. This is type of emigration is referred to as the **'international brain drain'**. The economies of many Third World countries are damaged by this brain drain because they cannot afford to lose skilled and educated people.

High levels of rural unemployment have been a leading cause of massive **rural to urban migration** in Third World countries. This migratory trend has serious socio-economic implications for both rural and urban areas:

- Many **rural areas** lose their cleverest and most energetic young adults to out-migration. This contributes to **economic stagnation** in rural areas, which become dominated by older, less energetic and less innovative people.
- In-migration results in the rapid growth of **unplanned slums** or shantytowns in Third World cities such as Kolkata (India) and Mexico City. It also results in the **unsustainably rapid growth** of these cities. The population of Mexico City, for example, has grown from 1 million to more than 20 million in the past 50 years.

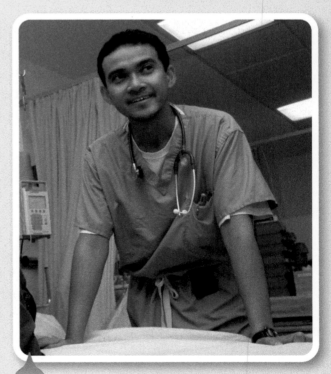

Irish hospitals benefit greatly from the expertise of doctors and nurses who come from Third World countries such as Pakistan and the Philippines. *How might the 'brain drain' of such skilled people to Ireland affect the economy of their home country?*

Population pyramid of India for 2010.

(a) Use this population pyramid to calculate approximately the number of young dependants (people aged 0–15 years) in India in 2010.

(b) India's population pyramid does not widen much between its 20–24 age category and its base. Try to explain why this is so.

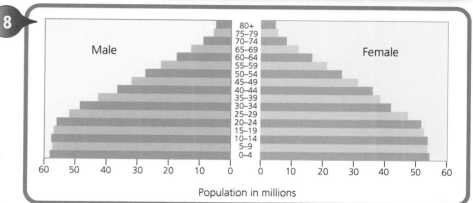

Population in millions

Economic liabilities and assets of India's young population.

The population pyramid in Figure 8 shows that India contains hundreds of millions of young dependants. So many young people place heavy economic demands on educational and other services (circular photograph). But a well-trained and educated young workforce has made India a favoured and growing destination for multinational high-tech industry (main photograph).

Sum Up

- **Overpopulation** happens when there are too many people in an area for the resources of that area to provide adequate living standards.
  - Factors such as the unwise use of resources, cultural influences, low income levels and new technology can all **cause** overpopulation.
  - The **effects** of overpopulation can include inadequate supplies of food, housing and sanitation; as well as disease, pollution, economic stagnation and out-migration.
- **Kolkata** is heavily overpopulated.
- **Causes** of overpopulation in Kolkata include:
  - **Cultural influences:** *women* have traditionally been expected to marry young and to devote themselves to motherhood. Many poor people consider *children* (especially male children) to be economic assets.
  - **Impacts of technology:** the *Green Revolution* caused many poorer farmers and farm labourers to abandon the land and to migrate to Kolkata. Improved *preventive medicines* caused death rates to fall and this also contributed to population increase, leading to overpopulation.
- Some **effects** of overpopulation in Kolkata include:
  - The growth of **overcrowded bustees**, where people live in tiny, overcrowded houses, in makeshift one-roomed huts or even on the streets.
  - **Inadequate services** such as water supplies, sanitation, schools and public transport.
- The best long-term **solution** to overpopulation is social and economic development. This would lead to more family planning and to reduced population growth.
- The **Sahel** is an overpopulated region.
- **Causes** of overpopulation in the Sahel include:
  - **Rapid population growth:** *high birth rates* and *falling death rates* have resulted in rapid population growth. Economic poverty, traditional customs and poor female status have contributed to high birth rates. Improved preventive medicines have contributed to falling death rates.
  - **The overuse and depletion of natural resources:** *overgrazing, overcultivation* and the *cutting of trees* have damaged soil fertility and depleted ground water resources. These resources are now insufficient to meet the needs of the Sahel's growing population.
- Some **effects** of overpopulation in the Sahel include:
  - **Desertification** – the spread of desert conditions. This happens when bare, overused soil is exposed to the elements and blown away in dust storms. Desertification has led to poverty, food shortages and famine in countries such as Sudan.
  - **Massive out-migration** from rural areas. Such migration has led to the rapid growth of cities and shantytowns. It has led to tension and contributed to civil wars in regions such as Darfur. It has also resulted in higher dependency ratios and altered sex ratios in source areas from which migrants moved.
- **Solutions** to overpopulation in the Sahel might include economic development combined with birth control programmes. Precious resources might be conserved by the use of solar power, the planting of drought-resistant grasses and reductions in the size of cattle herds.

- Population growth rates can have complex **impacts on economic development**.
  - A *growing population* might provide plenty of workers and a growing market for goods and services. But it might also make heavy demands on finite resources.
  - A *declining population* might put less pressure on resources. But it will usually result in a shrinking workforce and an ageing population with special requirements.
- **Developed countries** such as Germany had expanding, young populations during the *Industrial Revolution*. These populations created large labour forces and markets for industry. They also manned the armies that helped to make Germany an imperial power. Germany's population now shows a *natural decrease*. Its workforce is declining and its population is ageing.
- Most **developing countries** experience *rapid population growth*. The presence of many young dependants *hinders economic development*. It leads to unemployment, which in turn leads to 'brain drain' emigration and to uncontrolled rural to urban migration. But countries such as China and India use their vast, trained workforces as *motors of rapid industrial growth*.

Activities

1. (a) Explain the term 'overpopulation'.
   (b) Explain two causes of overpopulation in one area that you have studied.

   (LC Higher Level – 30 marks)

2. Examine one cause and one effect of overpopulation, referring to examples that you have studied.

   (LC Higher Level – 30 marks)

3. Explain how the unwise development of a natural resource has created overpopulation in a region that you have studied.

   (LC Higher Level sample paper – 30 marks)

4. (a) Explain in detail one cause of overpopulation in a region that you have studied.
   (b) Describe in detail one problem caused by overpopulation.
   (c) Suggest one solution to the problem of overpopulation.

   (LC Ordinary Level – 40 marks)

5. The table of statistics in Figure 9 shows total fertility rates in Belgium, Ireland and Bangladesh in 1970 and 2003. Using graph paper, suitably illustrate this data in graphical form.

The marking scheme and a sample answer to this question appear on pages 46–47.

Note

Frequently Leaving Cert questions require the following information:
- the meaning of overpopulation
- one or two *causes* of overpopulation with reference to one or two case studies
- one or two *effects* of overpopulation with reference to one or two case studies.

	Belgium	Ireland	Bangladesh
1970	2.2	3.9	7.0
2003	1.6	1.9	2.2

9 Total fertility rates in three countries in different years

45

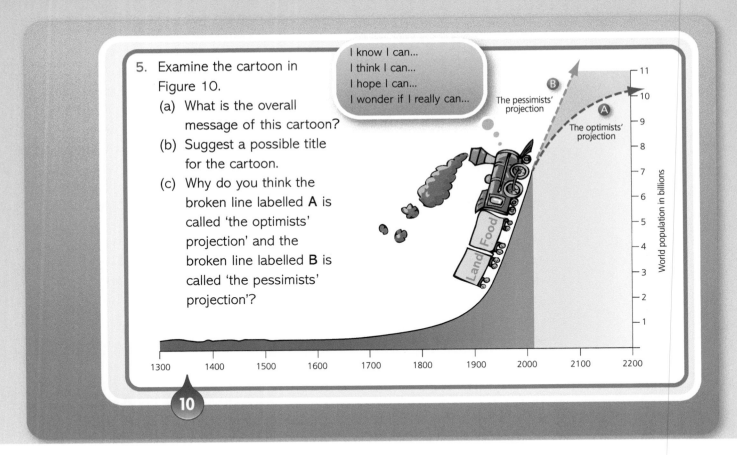

5. Examine the cartoon in Figure 10.
   (a) What is the overall message of this cartoon?
   (b) Suggest a possible title for the cartoon.
   (c) Why do you think the broken line labelled **A** is called 'the optimists' projection' and the broken line labelled **B** is called 'the pessimists' projection'?

I know I can…
I think I can…
I hope I can…
I wonder if I really can…

The pessimists' projection

The optimists' projection

World population in billions

10

Exam training
Leaving Certificate Higher Level question, official marking scheme and sample answer.

The question
(a) Explain the term 'overpopulation'.
(b) Explain two causes of overpopulation in one area that you have studied.

(30 marks)

The marking scheme

Explanation of term	= 4 marks (graded 4-2-0)
Named area	= 2 marks
Two named causes at 2 marks each	= 4 marks
Examination: 10 SRPs* at 2 marks each	
(5 SRPs for each cause)	= 20 marks
Total	= **30 marks**

* Note:
- An SRP (significant relevant point) is a clear piece of geographical information that is relevant to the question asked.
- Try to exceed somewhat the number of SRPs required in the marking scheme. This helps to ensure full or high marks in the event of some of your SRPs failing to score marks.

Sample answer

(a) Overpopulation occurs when there are too many people in an area for the resources of that area to provide adequate living standards. ✓ The term 'overpopulation' does not refer merely to population size or density. ✓ It refers to the population in relation to the resources available. ✓

4/4

(b) <u>Kolkata</u> ✓ in India is an example of an overpopulated area.

2

One cause of overpopulation in Kolkata is the <u>influence of society</u> and culture. ✓

2

The status of women in India and in Kolkata has traditionally been inferior to or at least different from that of men. ✓ Daughters of poorer families are often given little formal education, so 60% of Indian women are illiterate. ✓ Girls are traditionally expected to marry young (often in their late teens) and to then take on the roles of wife and mother. ✓ Most of these women do not have the confidence, the education or the maturity to question this tradition. They therefore tend to have large families. ✓ Other reasons for large families are the traditional wish to have sons who will carry on the family name ✓ and the fear among parents that they themselves may become destitute in old age if they do not have grown-up children to support them. ✓ Large families in Kolkata contribute to rapid population growth and to overpopulation.

10/10

Another cause of overpopulation in Kolkata has been the <u>impact of technology and science.</u> ✓

2

The 'Green Revolution' allowed richer farmers In India to greatly increase their crop yields by growing high-yielding strains of rice and other cereals. ✓ But many farmers could not afford the expensive seeds, fertilisers and technology required to grow these new strains. ✓ They were forced off the land and many migrated to urban areas. ✓ This caused such a 'population explosion' in Kolkata that the city's resources could not cope with the population growth and overpopulation that resulted. ✓ Technological improvements in preventive medicine have resulted in falling death rates and therefore have also contributed to population growth and to overpopulation. ✓ Vaccines against infections such as measles and whooping cough have been particularly effective in reducing infant mortality rates. ✓

10/10

30/30

4 Migration

The term **migration** is normally used to describe *the movement of people to another area or country for more than one year.* On the next page you will find some important terms that relate to migration.

Why people migrate

A combination of **push and pull factors** usually cause people to migrate.

Push factors

Push factors or **repellent factors** are things that force or persuade people to leave their original places of residence. Some principal push factors are:

- **Unemployment or underemployment:** for example in Ireland following the economic recession that began in 2008.
- **Overpopulation** and its resultant difficulties: for example in the Sahel region of Africa.
- **Unrest, war or invasion,** such as that which forced Palestinians from their homes following the foundation and expansion of the state of the Israel. (See photograph opposite.)
- **Religious or racial persecution,** such as the persecution of Jews in Nazi Germany or the eviction of black people from their homes by the former apartheid regime in South Africa.
- **Natural or human disasters,** such as the Great Famine in Ireland or the 2010 flood disaster in Pakistan.

Pull factors

Pull factors or **attractive factors** are things that entice people to migrate to other areas.

- **Economic opportunity,** such as the prospects of employment or higher incomes, is the most common pull factor of in-migration.
- **Better services,** such as health services, educational services and recreational services.
- **Family ties** such as the desire to join spouses or other family members who have already migrated.
- **The promise of freedom** for people who feel persecuted in their original home areas.
- **A desirable climate** attracts some retired migrants to destinations such as the south coast of Spain.

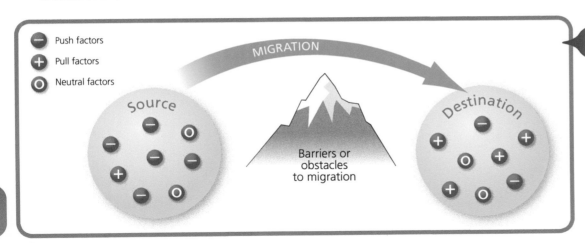

- Push factors
- Pull factors
- Neutral factors

MIGRATION

Source

Destination

Barriers or obstacles to migration

1 Human migration.
(a) Describe the information given by this diagram.
(b) List as many barriers to migration as you can.

Terms relating to migration

- **Internal migration:** migration within a country.
- **International migration:** migration between countries.
- **Immigration:** migration into a country.
- **Emigration:** migration out of a country.
- **Net migration:** the difference or 'balance' between the number of immigrants and the number of emigrants in a country.
- **Source (donor) area:** the area that migrants leave.
- **Destination (host or receiver) area:** the area to which people migrate.
- **Refugee:** a person who, because of real or believed danger or oppression, leaves his or her country and is unwilling or unable to return.
- **Asylum seeker:** a person who has fled his or her own country and applies to the government of another country for protection as a refugee.
- **Barrier to migration:** anything that makes migration difficult or impossible Barriers might range from the cost of travel to government restrictions on immigration.
- **Voluntary migration:** migration in which the migrant moves by choice. Most migrations are voluntary.
- **Forced migration:** migration in which the migrant has no choice but to move.

Why do people leave their native country?

Example 1: Economic migrants Agata and Borys Krol

Agata Krol and her husband Borys once worked in a state-owned textile factory near Warsaw in their native Poland. When the factory closed following the collapse of Communist rule, Borys found permanent *work so hard to find* that he was pushed eventually into contemplating emigration. When Poland joined the European Union in 2004, it became possible for Polish people to migrate easily to Ireland, which was then welcoming Central European immigrant workers to fuel its 'Celtic Tiger' economic boom. Attracted by this *economic opportunity*, Borys migrated to Ireland in 2005. He quickly obtained work in Dublin's then thriving construction industry. Agata later migrated to Ireland, mainly to be with her husband.

Example 2: Political migrant Guy Bertrand Nimpa

Guy Bertrand Nimpa, who now resides in Ireland, is a refugee from Cameroon in West Africa. When Guy campaigned for civil rights in his native land he was detained without trial. *Fear for his safety* persuaded Guy to leave Cameroon. He fled to Ireland and successfully sought asylum here. A *promise of freedom* was the principal pull factor that attracted Guy to Ireland. But he also enjoys teaching in Cork, where he has qualified as a teacher of mathematics and physics and has taken a higher multi-media degree at University College Cork.

Forced migrants.

These Palestinian refugees were forced from their homes as a result of the founding of the state of Israel in 1948. Approximately 0.75 million Palestinians were driven from their homes at that that time.

Changing migration patterns in Ireland 1950–2010

Throughout the **1950s**, Ireland experienced its highest **emigration** rates since the 1880s. More than 400,000 people left Ireland in the 1950s, mostly for Britain or the United States. A combination of **push and pull factors** was responsible for this high emigration.

Period	Economic situation	Net migration
1950s	Stagnation	Emigration
1960s–1970s	Expansion	Slight immigration
1980s – early 1990s	Recession	Emigration
1996–2008	Boom	Immigration
From 2008	Recession	Emigration

2 Summary of migration patterns

- Ireland was suffering from **economic stagnation**. Manufacturing industry was very limited outside large urban areas such as Dublin, while mechanisation in agriculture was beginning to reduce the demand for farm labourers. Tens of thousands of people were unemployed and many more were underemployed or very poorly paid. This situation helped to **push** Irish people towards emigration.

- Britain, on the other hand, was experiencing a post-World War II **economic boom**. The rebuilding of war-damaged buildings was still going on in the early 1950s and this created a huge demand for overseas construction workers. Industry too was booming and huge industrial plants such as the Ford car factory at Dagenham near London provided well-paid, steady work for many thousands of Irish immigrants. These economic opportunities were the principal **pull factor** for Irish migrants. But many young people also wished to experience a real or imagined 'bright lights' **social life** in cities such as London. Ties with and support from **family members** who had already emigrated also encouraged many people to leave Ireland.

Rural to urban migration was a form of internal migration that increased in Ireland in the 1950–2010 period. Aspects of rural to urban migration in Ireland will be examined on pages 62–67.

An Irish family leaving Cobh, Co. Cork for the USA in 1953.

(a) Why were emigration rates from Ireland high during the 1950s?

(b) Was emigration good or bad for Ireland at the time? Explain your point of view.

The **1960s and 1970s** saw a reversal in migration patterns. Emigration from Ireland decreased steadily, while more than 104,000 Irish emigrants returned to live in Ireland throughout the 1970s. This caused Ireland to enjoy slight **net immigration,** when immigration figures exceeded those of emigration. This reversal was the result of more job opportunities in Ireland, which in turn was due to the following factors or events:

- A **worldwide economic boom** helped to stimulate the economies of countries such as Ireland.
- The Irish government, under Taoiseach Séan Lemass launched the **First Programme for Economic Expansion**. This programme attracted foreign investment by offering government grants and tax breaks for industry.
- In 1973, Ireland joined the **European Economic Community** or EEC (now the European Union/EU). The EEC also began to pump huge amounts of capital into Ireland in the form of agricultural subsidies, assistance for road improvements and other forms of economic aid.

Heavy government debts and **economic recession** plunged Ireland back into mass **unemployment and emigration** throughout the **1980s and early 1990s**. Emigration reached a peak in 1989 when 70,000 people left our shores. Most Irish emigrants of the 1980s and 1990s were well educated and skilled and a significant number of them took up well-paid jobs in EU countries such as Germany. The departure of so many well-educated and well-trained emigrants is referred to as a **brain drain**.

Number of migrants from five countries who took up work in the Republic of Ireland in 2005	
Poland	63,528
Lithuania	22,812
Latvia	10,332
Slovakia	9,024
Czech Republic	6,210

3 Using graph paper, draw a suitable graph or graphs to illustrate the information given in the table in Figure 3.

Irish emigrants in the early 1990s.
Did emigration at this period differ in any ways from that of the 1950s? Explain.

The period **from 1996 to 2008** saw a huge drop in emigration and a dramatic influx of immigrants into Ireland. By the late 1990s, Ireland's net immigration rate was ranked second only to that of Luxembourg within the 15-member European Union (EU). By 2005 more than 10 per cent of people living in Ireland had been born outside the country. Reasons for this **dramatic wave of immigration** include the following.

- This was a period of explosive growth in the **Celtic Tiger economy**. An economic boom focused largely on construction and on exports by multinational companies created a huge demand for labour, especially in the building industry. This demand could not be met in Ireland alone and so created an urgent need for immigrant workers. Many immigrants came from Central European countries, such as Poland, Lithuania and Latvia, that joined the European Union in 2004. When Ireland announced that it would allow unrestricted immigration from these **new EU countries**, tens of thousands of immigrants came in search of employment. Some brought their families with them, further increasing immigrant numbers.

- A much smaller number of immigrants were **asylum seekers**. They numbered just over a thousand in 2002 but their numbers swelled to a peak of more than 11,000 in 2006. Asylum seekers typically came from non-EU countries, such as Nigeria, and applied to the Irish authorities for protection as refugees. Asylum seekers are not allowed to work while their applications are being considered – a process that can sometimes take years to complete.

You will learn more about **asylum seekers** on page 57.

Overspending, personal debt and uncontrolled profits and greed brought the Celtic Tiger boom to an abrupt end in **2008**. Boom was followed by bust as the Irish economy collapsed into deep and sudden **recession**. By 2010, more than 455,000 unemployed people had joined the Irish dole queues. A severe job shortage in Ireland caused a rise in emigration and a corresponding fall in immigration. Ireland had once again become a country of **net emigration**.

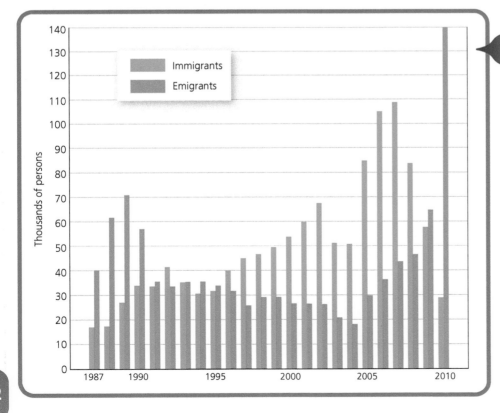

4 Numbers of immigrants to and emigrants from Ireland between 1987 and 2010.

(a) In which year did the greatest number of people emigrate?

(b) In which year did the number of immigrants first exceed the number of emigrants?

(c) In which year did immigration peak?

(d) In what year did immigration most exceed emigration?

(e) Calculate net immigration in 1999.

(f) Account for the large number of emigrants from Ireland in 2010.

Some effects of migration

Migration has many positive and negative impacts on both donor and host countries and regions. Some of these impacts are examined below.

Positive impact on donor countries
The economic dividend

- Many migrants come from overpopulated countries that suffer from high levels of **unemployment** or underemployment. Migration provides a '**safety valve**' that allows some unemployed people to go elsewhere in search of work. This reduces unemployment in host countries. It also reduces demands for dole or other unemployment assistance. Such a 'safety valve' helped Ireland through periods of high unemployment in the 1950s and the 1980s, when more than half a million Irish people emigrated to Britain, the USA and other countries in search of work.

- Most working migrants send some of their earnings home to support their families. These sums are called '**remittances**' and they often play an important role in the economic welfare of migrants' families and home countries. Remittances from Polish workers in Ireland, for example, have been used to educate children, to help aged parents and even to renovate family homes in Poland. They have also helped to stimulate the Polish economy by injecting money into it. It was estimated in 2004 that remittances amounted to the equivalent of US$250 billion globally, or twice the amount of all foreign aid to developing countries.

- Many migrants return eventually to work in their native country. When they do, they often bring with them valuable professional **skills** that they acquired abroad. This may be the case, for example, for Pakistani or Philippine doctors and nurses who currently work in Irish hospitals.

A Polish construction worker in Ireland in 2005 (above) and a Pakistani surgeon working in an Irish hospital (below).
What benefits and what disadvantages might the emigration of these migrants have for their native countries?

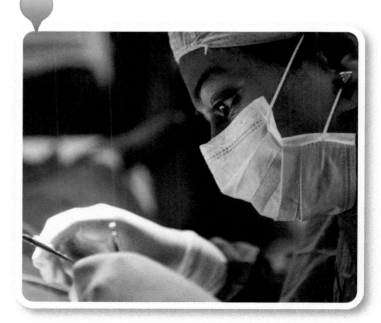

Negative impact on donor countries
The loss of young and trained people

A large proportion of migrants tend to be young, energetic and highly trained people whose departure can be a great loss to their donor areas and countries.

- A 'brain drain' occurs when highly educated and trained people emigrate in search of well-paid employment. Donor countries will have invested heavily in the education and training of those migrants and their departure means that other countries will benefit from their much-needed skills. The loss of too many highly skilled people hinders economic recovery or development in donor countries. This was the case in Ireland in the 1980s, when thousands of our business, computing and engineering graduates were lost to emigration.

- The loss of energetic young adults can lead to **depopulation and decay** in rural areas. The out-migration of young adults resulted in the decline of some rural parishes in the West of Ireland throughout the 1950s and the 1980s. Schools, shops and entertainment centres closed down for want of local initiative and support, while some local GAA teams struggled to survive for want of suitable players. The out-migration of young adults also reduced birth rates and this contributed further to a **spiral** of depopulation and ultimate decay.

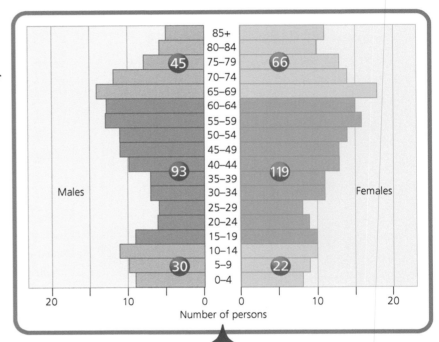

5 The population structure of a small rural community in Calabria, Southern Italy.

(a) How does this population pyramid suggest that the community referred to may be experiencing depopulation?

(b) Calculate the population ratio for the community shown.

Signs of rural out-migration in Co. Clare.

Discuss in detail one cause and one effect of out-migration from rural areas in Ireland.

Positive impact on host countries
Enriching the economy

- Many host countries suffer from **labour shortages** that are met by incoming migrants. This was the case in Ireland during the Celtic Tiger economic boom of 1996–2008. At that time, rapid economic growth was made possible only by the arrival of hundreds of thousands of workers from Poland, Lithuania and other countries. Such migrants supplemented the Irish workforce and became the backbone of industries such as construction, on which the Celtic Tiger boom was largely based. Ireland's need for migrant labour was then so strong that foreign workers filled two-thirds of all our job vacancies in 2006.

- Host economies also benefit from the high-level and useful **skills** of some migrants. In Ireland's case, these skills range from the medical expertise of Indian doctors to the culinary skills of Italian pizza chefs.

- Migrant workers **contribute indirectly** to the economies of host countries by paying taxes and by increasing the home market for goods and services.

Negative impact on host countries
The danger of poorer wage and employment conditions

Many immigrants are poor people who may be in desperate need of employment. Some – especially those with poor knowledge of the language of the host country or with lower-level skills – may be willing to work for **poorer pay and employment conditions** than normally pertain in the host country. The exploitation of such workers might lead to wider economic injustice by depressing pay and working conditions for all workers. The Irish Congress of Trade Unions (ICTU) recognised this danger in 2007, when it revealed that non-English-speaking migrants earned 31 per cent less than Irish employees who did similar work. Only the existence of a legal minimum wage then seemed to prevent the danger of a 'race to the bottom' in Irish pay and working conditions.

There is a further danger that poorly paid or exploited immigrants might be blamed wrongly for any future fall in wage or working conditions. They might then become targets of **racist or xenophobic abuse.** (Racism and xenophobia are examined further on page 56.)

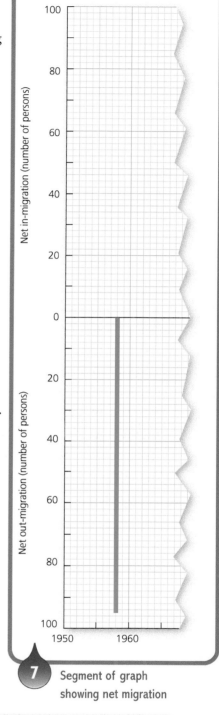

7 Segment of graph showing net migration

Skills activity

The table in Figure 6 below gives simulated in-migration and out-migration figures for an Irish town during selected years from 1958 to 2010. Calculate the **net migration** figures for each of the years given. Then use graph paper to illustrate these net migration figures in graphical form. You can use the segment of graph in Figure 7 to help you design your graph.

Year	1958	1973	1989	2006	2010
Number of in-migrants	7	36	18	140	26
Number of out-migrants	102	34	76	41	80

6 Simulated in-migration and out-migration figures for an Irish town

Ethnic, racial and religious issues that arise from migration

A wave of immigration accompanied Ireland's economic boom in the Celtic Tiger years of 1996 to 2008. Immigrants from many parts of the world contributed new languages, music, food and fashion that have enriched Ireland with its first real experience of **multiculturalism**. Many immigrants, for their part, have absorbed aspects of Irish culture and have became what has been called 'the new Irish'.

'New Irish' people participate in a St Patrick's Day parade in Dublin. Immigration has provided Ireland with many benefits of multiculturalism. But it has also given rise to some difficult ethnic, cultural and religious issues.

But the road to ethnic and racial harmony and integration is not always easy. It sometimes has to surmount barriers of **ethnic disadvantage**, **xenophobic** or **racist attitudes** and feelings of **isolation** among immigrants.

- Many new immigrants find themselves seriously **disadvantaged** in host countries such as Ireland. This is particularly true of immigrants who do not speak English well. Language barriers can create social and academic difficulties for immigrant schoolchildren and have led to the exploitation of some immigrant workers. In 2007, non-English-speaking workers in Ireland earned only 69 per cent of the wages earned by Irish employees who did similar work.

- **Xenophobic and racist attitudes** have sometimes resulted in verbal harassment and physical attacks on immigrants. The Economic and Social Research Institute (ESRI) reported in 2006 that 35 per cent of immigrants to Ireland had experienced some form of harassment in public places. In Northern Ireland, there have been several instances of life-threatening arson attacks on the homes of Chinese immigrants.

Terms to know

- **Race:** the division of humankind into subgroups based on physical features.
- **Ethnic group:** a large group of people who have distinct cultural features such as language, customs, etc.
- **Xenophobia:** an irrational fear or distrust of foreigners.
- **Racism:** an irrational belief that some racial or ethnic groups are inferior to others. Most racists discriminate on the basis of skin colour and are of the impression that the group to which they belong is superior to others.

A result of racial hate.
One result of arson attacks that drove Chinese and other immigrants from their homes in Belfast, Larne and other locations in Northern Ireland in 2010. Extreme loyalist elements have been suspected of carrying out some of the attacks.

● Ethnic disadvantage and xenophobia can all intensify the **isolation** and vulnerability that immigrants feel in a new land. These feeling encourage migrants from the same source country to live close to each other for mutual support. This custom has led to the growth of economically poor immigrant **ghettos** in countries such as the USA, Britain and France. The development of large ghettos such as East Harlem in New York and Southall in London serve only to increase feelings of social isolation and alienation among migrants and their descendants. These feelings have sometimes spilt over into anger and rioting, such as happened in some mainly Arabic ghettos in France in 2005.

The intense isolation of asylum seekers in Ireland

A 'living hell' is how Faycal Daoud describes his life in a centre for asylum-seekers in the West of Ireland.

'The food is bad, the rooms are dirty, the beds are ripped and there is nothing to do – we can't work or study. People just sit around every day getting depressed.'

Faycal lives under the **direct provision** system that was set up by the government for asylum seekers in Ireland. Under this system, the government pays private firms to provide beds and three meals a day for the asylum seekers. More than 6,000 people now live in privately run centres – one-third of them have lived there for more than three years. Asylum seekers have no right to work or to study. To survive, they get a basic weekly allowance of €19.10 per adult and €9 per child.

In Faycal's centre, I saw ripped beds and sheets, peeling paint, exposed electrical wiring and communal bathrooms out of order and nailed shut. One man had to attend hospital following an infestation of bed bugs in his room. In another bedroom a man lay on his bed sleeping at 4 p.m. 'He doesn't go out any more. He is depressed,' explained my guide.

Mental illness is a big challenge facing residents who have to live in close quarters and with no privacy for several years. Such people are extremely isolated. They live permanently under stress and have very limited means. Suicidal feelings are common among them.

(Adapted from an article in the Irish Times, *28 August 2010.)*

Faycal Daoud in an Irish centre for asylum seekers.

How does the Irish state's direct provision system contribute to feelings of isolation among asylum seekers in Ireland?

Measures the Irish government could take to assist refugees and asylum seekers

1   **Shorten the waiting time for asylum applicants.** On arrival in Ireland, each asylum seeker must apply formally for asylum either at a Refugee Applications Centre or at a Garda station. The applicant might then spend several years awaiting a final decision on his/her application. During that period, asylum seekers are forced to live in what can be isolating and depressing conditions under the direct provision system. The long periods that applicants spend in this system raise the cost of the system for the Irish state. Any means of speeding up the decision-making process would be helpful. It would allow successful applicants to move more quickly into mainstream society and might also save money for Irish taxpayers.

2   **Increase support services.** The Refugee Information Service has proved invaluable to asylum seekers and refugees. It is confidential and independent and it offers free information, advice and referral services. But it is available only in parts of Dublin and Galway. If the Refugee Information Service were extended throughout Ireland, it would help to reduce social isolation and anxiety among people who await a state decision on their refugee status.

Religious issues and migration

The **religious beliefs and traditions** of some immigrants may differ visibly from those of most people in host countries. Such displays of 'difference' among immigrants can lead to unease among some local people, who may feel that immigrants should 'blend' into local religious (or non-religious) culture.

The issue of 'religious visibility' among immigrants has emerged in Ireland and other European countries in relation to the wearing of female Muslim religious dress. In 2008, a debate developed in Ireland as to whether girls should be permitted to wear the **hijab**

The hijab is rather like a scarf that leaves the face exposed and is fastened under the chin. Some Muslim women wear the hijab as a garment of modest dress in keeping with their religious beliefs.

(Islamic headscarf) in schools. The governments of France (2004) and Belgium (2008) had already banned hijabs in schools on the grounds that wearing the hijab promotes segregation and gender inequality among young people. Muslims were angered by the rulings. They stated that the hijab represents modest dress for many Muslim women. They believed that banning the hijab in schools was a denial of reasonable religious rights and was the result of anti-Islamic prejudice. Ireland's Department of Education and Skills has made no recommendations regarding the hijab in schools and many Irish schools see the wearing of Islamic headscarves as a private matter of religious expression. Nevertheless, the debate on the issue may have increased a sense of cultural isolation among Ireland's growing Muslim community. It also shows that migration can sometimes lead to religious issues of a divisive nature.

Irish politicians become embroiled in the 'hijab at school' controversy

In September 2007 a Muslim couple in Ireland asked that their daughter be allowed to wear the hijab in class. The principal of the post-primary school involved referred the request to the Department of Education and Science and the matter soon became an issue of debate among politicians.

Ruairi Quinn of the Labour Party was of the opinion that immigrants who come to Ireland should conform to the culture of this country. 'Nobody is formally asking them to come here,' he stated. 'In the interests of integration and assimilation, they should embrace our culture.' 'Irish girls don't wear headscarves,' he added, 'I believe that in a public school situation they should not wear a headscarf.'

Brian Hayes of Fine Gael thought that Ireland should not be going down the route of multiculturalism. He agreed with Deputy Quinn that the headscarf should not be permitted in school. 'It makes absolute sense,' he said, 'that there should be one uniform for everyone.'

A spokeswoman for the Islamic Society of Ireland said she was 'shocked' at the two deputies' positions. Meanwhile, the director of the National Consultative Committee on Racism and Interculturalism described their interventions as 'ill-thought' and 'disappointing'.

Meanwhile a spokesman for Fianna Fáil's Conor Lenihan [who was then Minister for Integration] said that he had no problem with students wearing hijabs. 'It's not so long since Irish women wore headscarves to church,' he pointed out. 'For those who wear the hijab, it's an issue of modesty, so we must respect that.'

(From the Irish Independent, *Monday 2 June 2008.)*

Ireland's immigration policy

Ireland's immigration policy is based broadly on a work permit system that was reformed in 2007. It features different levels of permission to work in Ireland:

- **Workers from within the European Economic Area (EEA)** may migrate freely to Ireland. The EEA consists of EU countries along with Norway, Iceland and Liechtenstein. (Liechtenstein is a small principality that borders Switzerland and Austria.)

- **Green cards** are given readily to 'elite' workers from outside the EEA who are judged to have much-needed skills that would earn in excess of €60,000 per annum. Green cards are issued initially for two years, after which their holders may be granted permanent residency. Holders of green cards are allowed immediately to bring their spouses and families with them to Ireland.

- **Work permits** are given to lower-skilled non-EEA workers. These permits are limited in number and difficult to obtain. They are valid for two years only, though they might – depending on Ireland's needs – be extended for a further period of up to three years.

- **Intra-company transfer permits** allow multinational companies to move staff temporarily between factories in different countries. These permits usually facilitate the movement of senior management, people with special skills and trainees.

Facts

Prior to 2007, work permits were given to the employers of immigrant workers rather than to the migrants themselves. This system led to the scandalous abuse of some migrant workers who had no option but to remain with their initial employer or face deportation.

Some other rules on immigrants

- Migrant workers enjoy the same employment rights as Irish workers.
- Migrant workers must be resident in Ireland to be eligible for social welfare benefits.
- Green card or work permit holders may be given permanent residency after two years and may apply for Irish citizenship after five years of permanent residency.
- Asylum seekers may not engage in work or normal study programmes until they have the same rights as other Irish nationals. Persons refused refugee status may be deported.

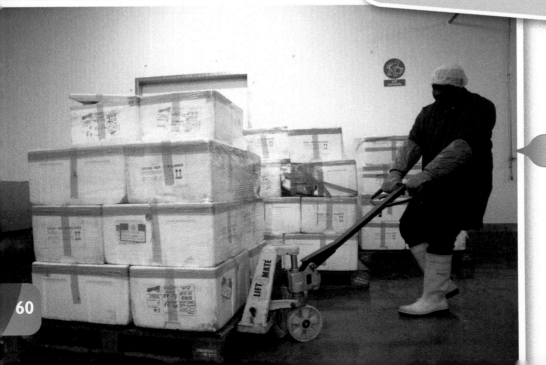

A non-EEA migrant worker in Ireland.
(a) What type of card or permit is this worker likely to possess?
(b) What rights and limitations are attached to the type of card or permit that you identified in your answer to question (a)?

Moves towards a common European immigration policy

Since the 1970s, individual EU states have developed their own individual immigration policies. But different EU countries have different rules, some stricter than others.

Increased immigration into the EU – an annual average of 1.8 million in recent years – has led to demands for the creation of a common European immigration policy that would regulate immigration more evenly throughout the EU. It would also help to prevent **illegal immigration**, which has grown rapidly since the early 1990s (see box). It could also combat the illegal **human trafficking** of poor people into Europe for the purpose of virtual slave labour or prostitution.

Since 1999, EU leaders have **moved gradually towards** the creation of a common European immigration policy. In 2005, they set up an EU border guard called *Frontex*. In the following year they set up a European *Border Patrol Network* on the EU's southern borders. They have also set up a *fingerprint database of asylum seekers*. The purpose of this is to stop people seeking asylum in an EU state if they have already been refused asylum in any other EU country.

Some people fear that a future common policy might adopt a 'fortress Europe' approach that would simply clamp down on all 'unnecessary' immigration. It is important that any future common policy blends caution with a humane approach towards prospective immigrants.

Why illegal immigration into the EU has grown

- The **collapse of the Soviet Union** in 1992 led to fewer border controls on the EU's eastern borders.
- As the **EU expanded** to 27 member states, its outer borders became ever larger and more difficult to patrol.
- The EU **Schengen Agreement** of 1995 removed all border controls between many EU states. Illegal immigrants, once inside the EU, could then move more freely from country to country.

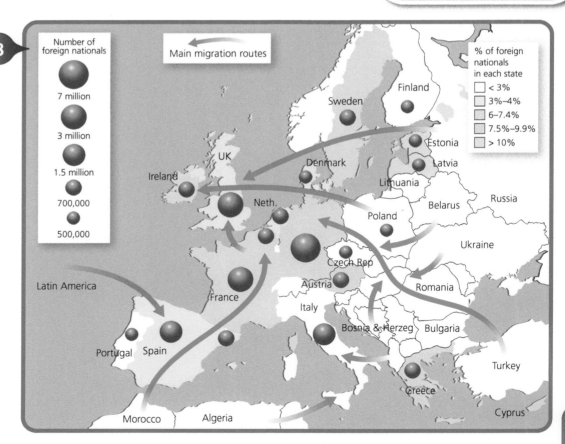

Migration patterns in and around Europe. **8**

(a) Which country contains the greatest number of foreign nationals? What are the main source countries of these foreign nationals?

(b) Approximately how many and what percentage of foreign nationals are shown to be in the Republic of Ireland?

(c) This map relates to statistics gathered prior to 2006. How and why might the number of foreign nationals in Ireland have altered since that time?

Rural to urban migration in Ireland

Ireland, like most countries, is becoming more and more urbanised. This is largely because of the movement of people from rural to urban areas. Rural to urban migration is particularly marked **from the West of Ireland to Dublin** and to the *Greater Dublin Area (GDA)*, where 40 per cent of our population now live.

Urban and rural populations (numbers and percentages) in the Republic of Ireland between 1925 and 2011.

(a) How many people lived in rural areas in 1925?

(b) By how much did the rural population decline (i) in real terms and (ii) as a percentage of the total population between 1925 and 2011?

(c) In what year did the urban population equal the rural population in number?

(d) In what year was the rural population at its lowest?

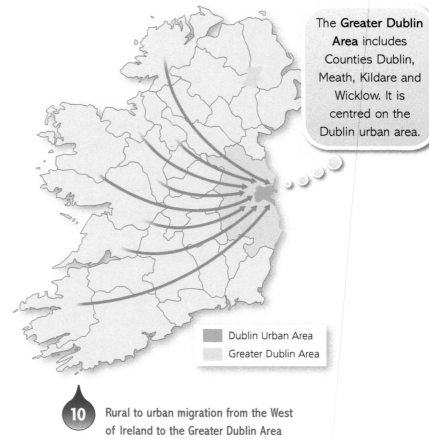

The **Greater Dublin Area** includes Counties Dublin, Meath, Kildare and Wicklow. It is centred on the Dublin urban area.

Dublin Urban Area
Greater Dublin Area

10 Rural to urban migration from the West of Ireland to the Greater Dublin Area

9

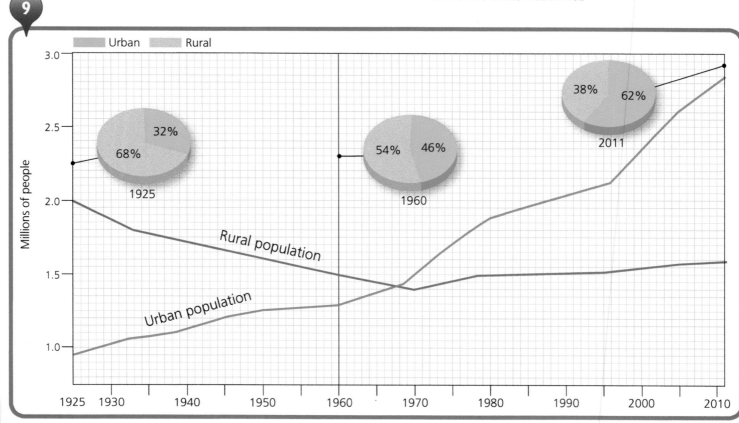

Why people migrate from the West of Ireland to Dublin

Employment opportunities

Employment is limited in many rural areas of the West. Farming, for example, offers a viable living to fewer and fewer people, especially in areas of poor, challenging land such as in parts of Connemara and South Kerry.

Dublin, on the other hand, offers a wide variety of employment opportunities, especially for trained and educated internal migrants. The GDA is an economic **core area** that attracts more industrial and commercial enterprises than any other part of Ireland. Dublin has numerous industrial estates and **business parks** such as those at Park West and Sandyford. It is also the hub of Ireland's **financial services**. Centres such as the International Financial Services Centre (IFSC) at Custom House Quay offer thousands of well-paid jobs in banking, finance and computing. Dublin also contains the headquarters of the **Civil Service**, which has traditionally attracted large numbers of recruits from rural areas.

These **push and pull factors** cause many young people from counties such as Mayo, Donegal and Kerry to migrate to Dublin in search of improved wages and a wider choice of jobs.

Dublin's International Financial Services Centre (IFSC) was built to contain up to 400 banks, insurance companies and other businesses. This business hub employs skilled workers from all parts of Ireland.

Social life and services

Limited entertainment and other amenities in some rural areas make the 'bright lights' of Dublin seem exciting to many young migrants. Some are attracted by the endless variety of bars, restaurants, nightclubs and other such places of **entertainment** available in the capital. There is also a wide choice of theatres (e.g. the Abbey), art galleries (the National Gallery), museums (the Natural History Museum) and concert centres (the Point). Sports fans can attend GAA matches at Croke Park or soccer and rugby games at the Aviva Stadium.

Dublin's third-level **educational institutions** attract thousands of students from the West. These institutions include universities such as University College Dublin, Trinity College and Dublin City University, which between them cater for more than 50,000 students. Some students from the West of Ireland settle permanently in Dublin when they complete their college course.

A nightclub scene at Temple Bar, Dublin. The prospect of a lively social life attracts some young adult migrants from the West of Ireland to Dublin.

Impacts on Dublin of rural to urban migration
Urban sprawl

Unlike most European cities, Dublin has developed relatively few high-rise, high-density housing and office blocks. Instead, it has spread outwards into the countryside to the extent that it is one of the worst cities in Western Europe for **urban sprawl**. The migration of people from rural areas to Dublin has contributed greatly to the city's urban sprawl.

The following **problems** are associated with Dublin's urban sprawl:

- Valuable *farmlands*, such as in north Co. Dublin, have been taken over for building purposes. *Wildlife habitats* in these farmlands have been destroyed or disrupted, forcing animals such as foxes to survive in urban environments.

- Unique *villages* such as Dundrum have been swallowed up by large monotonous *suburbs*. Many of these suburbs suffered from inadequate recreational and other services in the early years of their existence.

- The spread of urban areas into counties Meath, Kildare and Wicklow has increased the number of people *commuting* to and from Dublin City. Inadequate public transport services in some commuter areas have led to the overuse of private cars and to consequent traffic congestion.

Revise page 266 of your *Changing World* core textbook, in which urban sprawl in the GDA is examined in detail. *Urban sprawl* is also examined on pages 138–142 of this book.

Urban sprawl in Dublin

11 What environmental issues relating to urban sprawl in Dublin does this cartoon raise?

Traffic congestion

Migration from rural areas to Dublin has inevitably added to traffic volumes in the GDA. Dublin's transport routes have had to cope with ever-growing volumes of traffic and traffic congestion, especially during morning and evening 'peak times' when most people commute to and from work.

Traffic increased three-fold in the Dublin area in the 15 years up to 2010. Commuting in that area increased by 74 per cent between 2003 and 2008. The traffic congestion associated with these increases has impacted on road haulage costs, delivery schedules and staff punctuality and has reduced productivity. The Dublin Transportation Office (DTO) estimated in 2002 that the annual cost of road congestion amounted to €2 billion.

Dublin's traffic congestion also gives rise to social and health costs that are difficult to quantify. In 2008 it was estimated that many GDA road commuters spent an annual equivalent of nine working weeks in traffic gridlock. Commuters are harmed by the frustration, alienation and sedentary lifestyles to which this situation gives rise.

Traffic congestion is examined further on pages 143–148 of this book.

Congestion in older streets.
Increased numbers of cars have created special problems for older streets that pre-date the popularity of private motor vehicles. This Dublin street is too narrow to accommodate its residents' parked cars.
How might this situation affect residents' quality of life?

Some solutions to urban sprawl in Dublin

- The **National Spatial Strategy (NSS):** a 20-year plan that was launched in 2002. Its purpose is to slow down the rapid outward growth of Dublin by stimulating the development of other urban centres outside Dublin. It has identified nine large centres called 'hubs' and several smaller centres called 'gateways' for special development. Improved transport and communication networks will be provided to assist the development of these hubs and gateways.

- **New towns:** several new towns (e.g. Tallaght and Adamstown) have been built on the western fringes of Dublin. These towns were intended to house some of Dublin's overspill population and so help to prevent or reduce Dublin's continued urban sprawl. Some new towns have themselves become large urban areas – Tallaght has a population of more than 65,000 people. They have, however, so far failed to stop urban sprawl in Dublin.

Revise the National Spatial Strategy and new towns: see page 267 of your Changing World *core textbook.*

Impacts on rural areas of rural to urban migration

Demographic (population) decline

Rural to urban migration has contributed to **population decline** in many Western counties. Between 1926 and 2002, counties Donegal, Leitrim and Mayo lost up to 40 per cent of their populations, largely though out-migration.

The **age structures** of rural areas are also affected by out-migration. It is usually young adults who migrate, leaving source areas with larger proportions of elderly people. This results in declining marriage rates and birth rates in source areas, causing further long-term population decline.

The **sex structures** of some rural areas are also altered. There has been a tendency in many farming areas for the out-migration of young women to exceed that of men. A large proportion of rural young women, on completing post-primary education, migrate to Dublin or other urban areas to attend third-level colleges or later to work as nurses, teachers or civil servants. Men, on the other hand, are more likely to inherit family farms or businesses and therefore to remain in their rural homes. These tendencies create a **sex ratio imbalance** in which the number of men significantly exceeds that of women in many rural areas of the West. This sex ratio imbalance contributes to lower marriage rates, to smaller birth rates and ultimately to population decline.

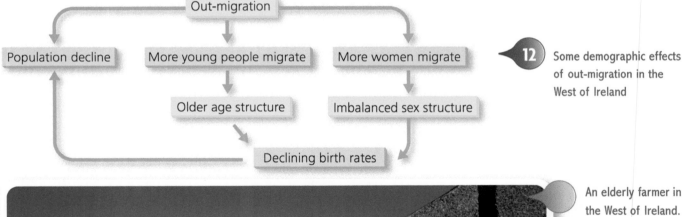

12 Some demographic effects of out-migration in the West of Ireland

An elderly farmer in the West of Ireland. *How has out-migration affected farming and social life in the West of Ireland? Refer in your answer to age ratio, sex ratio and agricultural productivity.*

Social decline

An area needs a certain minimum population density in order to maintain social **amenities** such as cinemas, youth clubs and sports teams. Severe out-migration, especially among young people, has resulted in the decline or collapse of such amenities in parts of the West of Ireland.

More **basic rural services** have also been affected:

● Between 1992 and 2010, nine western counties lost more than 30 per cent of their *post offices*, with a loss of 41 per cent being recorded in Co. Leitrim. Most closures happened in small villages and other rural communities where post offices provide social outlets for people to meet, chat and exchange local news.

● In 2009 *An Bord Snip Nua* proposed the closure of nearly 300 *rural Garda stations*. This has raised security concerns in rural communities, especially among elderly people who live in isolated areas.

Out-migration

Less demand for services

Life more difficult for people remaining

Decline in services

13 A spiral of out-migration and social decline

The collapse or decline of such amenities makes life increasingly difficult for those who remain in source areas and so triggers off a continuous **spiral of migration** and decline (see Figure 13). Such a spiral has seriously damaged the fabric of social life in many rural areas in the West of Ireland.

A rural Garda station in Terryglass, Co. Tipperary. *How might out-migration affect Garda services in rural areas and what effects might this have on people in rural areas of the West?*

Rural to urban migration in the developing world

Case Study:
The effects of in-migration on Kolkata

We saw on page 28 that **Kolkata** is a huge and rapidly expanding city in West Bengal, India. The population of Kolkata now stands at 16 million and is growing steadily.

One **reason for the rapid growth of Kolkata** is massive in-migration from rural areas in West Bengal and from the neighbouring country of Bangladesh. Most of these source rural areas are at Stage 3 (the late expanding stage) of demographic transition. They experience high (although declining) population growth because their birth rates exceed their death rates by up to 3 per cent in some areas. Many rural families survive on tiny, overcrowded farms of less than one hectare. Other people are landless labourers who cannot adequately support themselves or their families. Such people are **pushed** by economic circumstances to migrate to cities such as Kolkata. Some Bangladeshis are forced to migrate because of frequent flooding of the Ganges delta in the south of the country. In 2010, for example, floods drove 100,000 Bangladeshis from their homes. Migrants are attracted to Kolkata by the possibility of some form of employment. Other **pull factors** of the city include access to more healthcare and educational facilities than normally exist in rural areas.

Problems associated with the rapid expansion of Kolkata

1 **Unplanned, overcrowded shantytowns** ———

> **Revise** 'Unplanned, overcrowded bustees' on page 31.

2 **Inadequate services** ————————

> **Revise** 'Inadequate services' on page 32.

Solving the problems associated with Kolkata's rapid growth

Overpopulation, caused by natural increase and in-migration, is a major underlying cause of the expansion of shantytowns and of poor services in Kolkata.

Reduced birth rates would reduce the current natural population increase in Kolkata and help to stem migration into the city from overpopulated rural areas.

Birth control programmes, coupled with **social and economic development**, would appear to be the most effective long-term route to reduce birth rates in Third World areas.

> *Revise 'Solutions to overpopulation in the Third World' on page 33.*

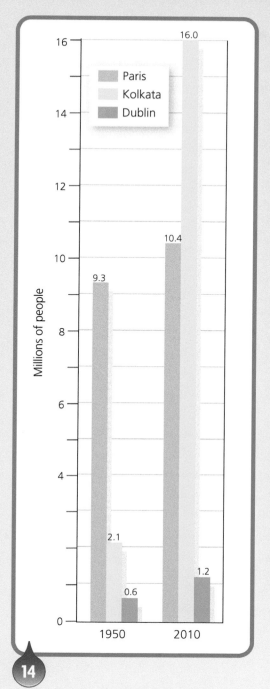

Describe this scene in one of Kolkata's shantytowns

14

Estimated populations of Paris, Kolkata and Dublin Metropolitan Areas in 1950 and in 2010.

(a) *Which of the three cities experienced the least population growth between 1950 and 2010?*

(b) *By how many million people did Kolkata grow between 1950 and 2010?*

(c) *By how much did the population growth of Kolkata exceed that of Paris?*

(d) *Account for the rapid growth in Kolkata's population.*

More about Kolkata's shantytowns

The slums and shantytowns of Kolkata can be divided into three broad groups.

1 The *oldest bustees* are situated in the heart of the city. They originated more than a century ago and are associated with early urbanisation.

2 Other bustees date back to the *1940s or 1950s* and are located near industrial sites or major roads or railways.

3 All bustees are 'registered slums'. Legal ownership of dwellings within them is officially recognised by Kolkata's city council.

4 Towards the fringes of Kolkata there are many *unregistered slums*. Many of these are relatively new and they are occupied by people who migrate in from the country and erect dwellings on land on which they squat (occupy without legal right).

69

Sum Up

- **Migration** is the movement of people to another area or country for at least one year. Repellent factors, such as unemployment, **push** people from source areas. Attractive or **pull** factors, such as economic opportunity, attract people to destination areas.
- **Irish migration patterns have changed over time:**
  - Economic stagnation at home and opportunities abroad caused mass *emigration* from Ireland in the *1950s*.
  - The *1960s and 1970s* brought economic improvement and periods of net *immigration*.
  - Ireland experienced heavy *emigration* and a *brain drain* during the economically depressed *1980s and early 1990s*.
  - The Celtic Tiger economic boom brought a flood of economic *immigrants* (and a much smaller number of asylum seekers) to Ireland from *1996 to 2008*.
  - *Emigration* once again replaced immigration *following the economic collapse of 2008.*
- Migration has **positive and negative impacts** on donor and host countries.
  For **donor** countries:
  - **Positive** impacts: it provides an *economic 'safety valve'* for people seeking employment, leads to *remittances* from emigrants and allows emigrants to learn *new skills* before returning home.
  - **Negative** impacts: a *brain drain* and associated spirals of *social decay and depopulation*.
  For **host** countries:
  - **Positive** impact: immigration can provide a pool of *skilled workers* who contribute to the economy.
  - **Negative** impact: it can be used to *depress wage and employment conditions* for all workers.
- Migration may give rise to the following **ethnic issues:**
  - Some immigrants may be exploited or otherwise *disadvantaged*.
  - Immigrants may face *xenophobia* or *racism*.
  - Emigrants who feel isolated may tend to live in *ghettos*, which breeds further isolation and frustration.
  - *Asylum seekers* under the 'direct provision' system may feel particularly isolated. It would be helpful if the government shortened waiting times and increased support services for asylum applicants.
- Issues may arise regarding the **religious traditions** of some immigrants. Public debate over the wearing of the **hijab** is a case in point.
- **Ireland's immigration policy** allows people from the European Economic Area (EEA) to migrate freely into Ireland. It provides **green cards** to certain elite workers and **work permits** to some lower-skilled workers. It also provides **intra-company transfer permits** to some employees of multinational companies.
- There have been moves towards a **common European immigration policy**. Increased immigration, illegal immigration and human trafficking have created some demands for such a policy.
- There has been considerable **rural to urban migration** from the **West of Ireland to the Greater Dublin Area** (GDA).
- People migrate from the West of Ireland to Dublin in search of:
  - *employment* in sectors such as industry, business and the civil service
  - entertainment, educational and other *amenities*.

Sum Up

- Rural to urban migration has had the following **impacts on Dublin**:
  - *Urban sprawl*, which increases commuting and swallows up farmland and villages.
  - *Traffic congestion*, which increases haulage costs, reduces productivity and undermines commuters' health.
- **Attempted solutions** to urban sprawl in Dublin include the **National Spatial Strategy** and the building of **new towns**.
- Rural to urban migration has had the following **impacts on rural areas** of the West:
  - *Population* decline and alterations in age and sex ratios.
  - A decline in *social amenities*, which contributes in turn to more out-migration.
- People migrate to **Kolkata** from rural areas of West Bengal and Bangladesh. This results in **inadequate services** and the growth of **unplanned shantytowns** in Kolkata.
- Rural and urban **overpopulation** is a major underlying cause of Kolkata's problems. **Birth control programmes** coupled with **social and economic development** would appear to be the best solution to overpopulation.

Activities

1. The graph in Figure 15 shows in-migration, out-migration and net migration in an Irish parish between 1999 and 2011.
   (a) In what year was out-migration at its greatest?
   (b) In which year did in-migration peak and what was the in-migration figure for that year?
   (c) In which year did the number of in-migrants first equal the number of out-migrants?
   (d) Between which two years did net migration show no change?
   (e) In which year did out-migration exceed in-migration by 10 persons?
   (f) Calculate the difference between in-migration and out-migration in 2011.
   (g) State one factor, not mentioned in Figure 15, that would also cause a change in the total population of the parish.
       (Based on LC Higher and Ordinary Level questions)

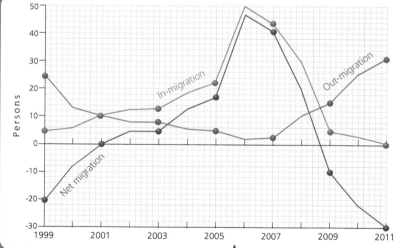

15

In-migration, out-migration and net migration in an Irish parish between 1999 and 2011

2. Explain any two reasons why migrants might leave their native countries.
   (LC Ordinary Level – 40 marks)

3. Examine two major changes in the patterns of Irish migration over the last one hundred years.
   (LC Higher Level – 30 marks)

Activities

4. Read the report from 2005 given in Figure 16. Then answer the questions that follow.
   (a) What is Ireland's population forecast to be in 2020?
   (b) In 2020, how many people are expected to be migrants?
   (c) In which year is it expected that the population of the Irish Republic will reach 6 million?
                                    (LC Ordinary Level – 30 marks)

5. Use the figures in the table in Figure 17 to answer the following questions.
   (a) In which year was immigration greater than emigration for the first time?*
   (b) Calculate the difference between immigration and emigration in 2005.*
   (c) In what year was emigration greatest?*
   (d) Between which years did the greatest increase in natural change occur?
   (e) Calculate Ireland's total population increase in 2005.
                            (*LC Ordinary Level – 30 marks)

6. Explain two reasons why immigration into Ireland increased between 1996 and 2008.
                            (Based on LC Ordinary Level)

7. Examine one positive and one negative potential consequence of human migration.
                                    (LC Higher Level – 30 marks)

8. *'Ethnic and religious issues can arise as a result of migration.'*
   Examine this statement with reference to example(s) that you have studied.
                                    (LC Higher Level – 30 marks)

9. (a) Describe two problems faced by refugees when they seek asylum in a new country such as Ireland.
   (b) Explain two measures that governments could take to help refugees solve these problems.
                                    (LC Ordinary Level – 40 marks)

10. Comment on the need to develop a common immigration policy for countries of the European Union.
                            (LC Higher Level sample paper – 30 marks)

11. Outline the effects of rural to urban migration in a developing region that you have studied.
                                    (LC Higher Level – 30 marks)

12. (a) Name one city in the **developing world** that has grown rapidly in recent years.
    (b) State one reason why this city has grown rapidly.
    (c) Describe two problems caused by this rapid growth.
    (d) Explain one solution to one of the problems that you identified in (c) above.
                            (LC Ordinary Level – combined questions)

16 The Irish Republic's economy will continue to grow strongly over the coming 15 years as the population reaches 5.3 million by 2020. It is also forecast that one in five of the population, close to one million people, will be migrants. The total population is forecast to reach 6 million by 2050. The Irish Republic's present population is 4.04 million.

Year ending April	Natural change (000)	Immigrants (000)	Emigrants (000)
1987	29.0	17.2	40.2
1989	22.6	26.7	70.6
1991	22.0	33.3	35.3
1993	20.0	34.7	35.1
1995	17.2	31.2	33.1
1997	19.0	44.5	25.3
1999	21.2	48.9	31.5
2001	24.8	59.0	26.2
2003	31.9	50.5	20.7
2005	33.5	70.0	16.6

17 Population and migration estimates for Ireland

Higher Level Leaving Cert question, marking scheme and sample answer

The question

Migration, both internal and international, continues to play an important role in shaping the populations of states and regions. Examine one impact of population movement on donor countries and one impact on receiver regions.

(30 marks)

The marking scheme

Name impact on donor state or region	= 2 marks
Name impact on receiver state or region	= 2 marks
Examination: 13 SRPs at 2 marks each	= 26 marks
Total	**= 30 marks**

Note:
- Up to a total of 3 examples may be counted as SRPs.
- An answer based solely on donor or receiver regions can accrue credit for a maximum of 7 SRPs only.

Use the marking scheme to mark the sample answer given below.

International migration can provide an economic 'dividend' (advantage) for a donor state because it offers a safety valve for jobless migrants and provides them with the possibility of learning new work skills and of sending remittances home.

When unemployed people emigrate from a donor state, unemployment levels and demands for unemployment benefits are reduced in that state. This saves the state money and thus provides it with a better chance to develop economically. The economic 'safety valve' that emigration provides might even reduce the dangers of social or political unrest in the donor state. Such a 'safety valve' helped Ireland through periods of high unemployment in the 1950s and the 1980s. At that time, more than half a million people emigrated, mainly to England, in search of work.

Many emigrants send some of their income home to support their families. These 'remittances' represent a beneficial cash injection to the economy of a donor state. Emigrants may also eventually return home with new professional skills that they acquired abroad. These skills are part of the economic dividend that emigration can provide for a donor state.

International migration can also enrich the economies of host states.

Many host states suffer from labour shortages that are met by incoming migrants. This was the case in Ireland during the Celtic Tiger economic boom years of 1996–2008. At that time, rapid economic growth was made possible only by the arrival of hundreds of thousands of workers from Poland, Lithuania and other Central European countries. Such workers became the backbone of the construction industry on which the Celtic Tiger economic boom was largely based. Ireland's need for migrant labour was then so strong that in 2006 overseas workers filled two-thirds of all our job vacancies. Host countries also benefit economically from high-level and useful skills among some immigrants. In Ireland's case, these skills include those of Pakistani doctors and Philippine nurses. Migrant workers also pay taxes in their host countries and increase host countries' home markets for goods and services. These factors, too, help to balance the national budgets and nourish the economies of host states.

Site and situation of towns

Below are some questions to ask yourself when **describing the site and situation** of a town on an OS map.

Learn these questions and use some of them to help you describe the site and situation of towns.

Terms to know

- **Settlement**: a place where people live. Settlements can range in size from individual houses to large cities.

- ***Site**: the ground or 'actual spot' on which a settlement is built. Site characteristics are important in the initial establishment of settlements.

- ***Situation**: the location of a settlement in relation to surrounding features such as rivers, coastlines, mountains, communications or other settlements. Situation plays a vital role in the gradual development and growth of settlements.

- **Function**: the purpose or purposes for which a settlement was built and the *services* and activities that a settlement provides for its residents and for the people of its hinterland (surrounding land). Most settlements are *multifunctional*, which means that they have several functions.

*The term *location* is sometimes used to describe site and situation together.

Site

1. *Where is the town on the map?*
2. *At what altitude is it?* Refer to a spot height or contour.
3. *Is it on flat, undulating (gently rolling) or sloping land?*
4. *Is it at a 'wet point site' on the banks of a river?* In former times, the river would have been used to provide water for drinking and domestic purposes. In past times *wide* rivers may have also been used as transport routes.
5. *Is it at a 'dry-point site' that stays back from parts of the river?* In such cases, the river may be liable to flood.
6. *Does it occupy a bridge point or points?* Roads meet at bridge points. This stimulates traffic, business and the growth of settlements. The lowest bridge point on a river (the one nearest to the sea) is usually especially important because it controls busy coastal traffic.
7. *Is it at the meeting point of two rivers?* Bridges are often constructed near such **confluence points**.

Situation

1. *Is the town situated in a lowland area?* Such an area might be agriculturally productive and may have provided agricultural produce that helped the town to develop as a market centre.
2. *Is it at a route focus, where roads and/or rail routes meet?* People meet and business and settlements develop at such route foci.
3. *Do roadways link it with other towns?* Which towns?
4. *Is it on the coast?* Coastal locations may enable a town to develop as a port or as a tourist centre.
5. *Is it close to hills or mountains?* Mountains might provide shelter or recreational facilities for its inhabitants.

Sample question and answer
Question

Describe the site and situation of Letterkenny, using the OS map in Figure 1.

Site

Letterkenny dominates the eastern part of the map, for example at C 170 120. Contours show that it is sited on north-sloping land of between approximately 10 and 100 metres. This site gives the town a generally sunny south-facing aspect. Parts of the town (C 165 109) occupy a wet-point site on the banks of the River Swilly. In former times the river would have provided water for drinking and other domestic purposes. Most of the town, however, occupies a dry-point site somewhat back from the river (for example at C 170 111). This might indicate that the river is liable to flood the flat flood plain on its northern side. Letterkenny occupies what appears to be the lowest bridge point of the Swilly (Port Bridge at C 184 112). This bridge controls important coastal traffic and roads such as the N14 and the R250 meet close to it. Converging traffic stimulates business and urban growth in Letterkenny.

Situation

Letterkenny is situated between the flat-floored valley of the River Swilly to its south and higher ground of up to 336 metres at Gregory Hill (C 116 124) to its west and north. It is possible that this varied terrain could provide a variety of local agricultural produce that might have enabled Letterkenny to develop initially as a market centre. The town is at the focus of national primary and regional roads, such as the N14 and the R245. The convergence of these roads must stimulate business and therefore urban growth in Letterkenny. Low hills such as Gregory Hill and Croaghmore are a mere 4 kilometres to the west of the town. They provide Letterkenny with some limited shelter from westerly winds and might also provide townspeople with some limited opportunities for recreations such as hill walking.

> Describe the site and situation of Youghal using the map on page 85.

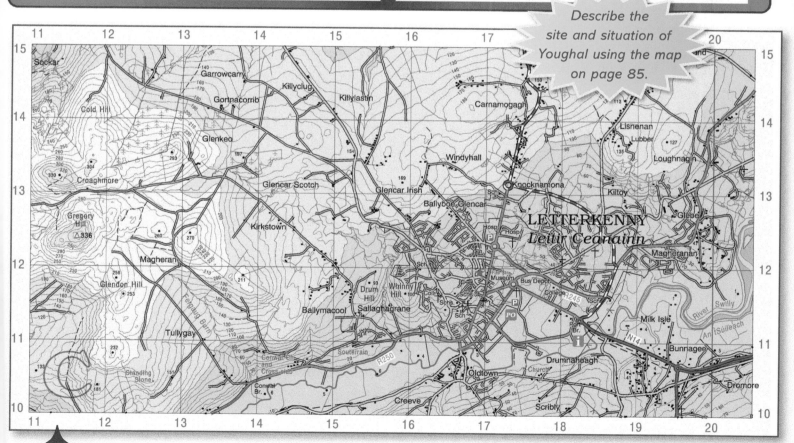

1   Letterkenny, Co. Donegal

Prehistoric and historic settlements

There is much evidence of prehistoric and historic settlement in Ireland. This evidence is widely recorded on **Ordnance Survey** maps. There follows a description and explanation of settlement in Ireland throughout selected prehistoric and historic periods.

The Middle Stone Age

People first arrived in Ireland about 8000 BC during the **Mesolithic** period or **Middle Stone Age**. With no permanent settlements, they moved from place to place in search of food. They used dogs and stone-headed spears and axes to hunt deer, wild pigs and other animals, and gathered berries, nuts and mushrooms. Many lived on coastlines, where they gathered crabs and shellfish such as periwinkles and limpets. **Middens** or ancient rubbish heaps provide evidence of the existence of Mesolithic settlements. (Middens are heaps of discarded bones and seashells: they indicate what people ate at that time.) See Figure 2.

The term **prehistoric** refers to times before the use of writing. Prehistoric times in Ireland came to an end with the Early Christian Period that began in the fifth century AD.

Antiquities such as middens, dolmens, etc. are all labelled in red and their location is shown with a red dot on Ordnance Survey maps. (See Figure 2.)

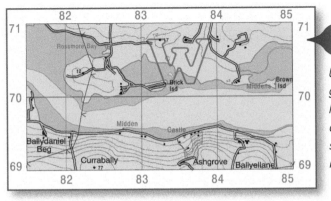

2

Use six-figure grid references to locate evidence of Mesolithic settlement on this map fragment

The New Stone Age

Ireland's first farmers arrived in the country around 4000 BC. They were called **Neolithic** or New Stone Age people because they used new, improved stone tools and weapons. Neolithic farmers settled permanently so that they could tend their cattle and their crops of wheat and barley. They often settled in areas with light soils that were less densely forested and therefore easier to clear and till. Nothing remains now of their flimsy, timber-framed, thatched dwellings, which were located close to fresh water supplies but at dry points that were not liable to flooding. But their large burial places provide plentiful evidence of Neolithic settlement. These burial places sometimes take the form of **barrows** or **burial mounds**. More often, they are **megalithic tombs** (meaning 'great stone' tombs) in which leaders or other important people were buried. The principal types of megalithic tomb are **court cairns**, **portal dolmens** (see photograph) and **passage graves**.

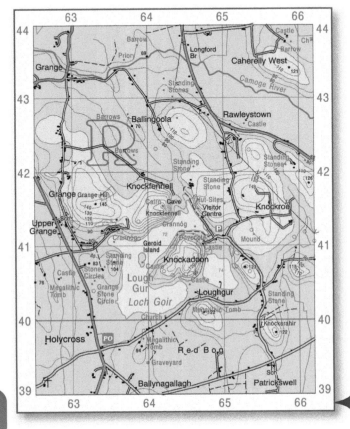

3

List the different clues to Stone Age settlement that can be found on this map fragment

A portal dolmen at Poulnabrone, Co. Clare.

Portal dolmens or **cromlechs** contain two or three upright **portal** stones with a single capstone or **dolmen stone** laid horizontally on the top. The cremated remains of important people were laid beneath the capstone and covered in a heap of smaller stones called a cairn. The remains of 16 people were discovered beneath this portal dolmen at Poulnabrone.

The Bronze Age

About 2000 BC, people arrived in Ireland who had discovered how to make sharp weapons and tools out of bronze.

- Bronze was made by mixing locally mined copper with tin imported from Cornwall. The presence on OS maps of a **copper mine** (in the form of an *antiquity*) might therefore indicate Bronze Age settlement.

- Wedge tombs and cist graves also indicate Bronze Age settlement. A **wedge tomb** rather resembles a portal dolman, but it gets its 'wedge' shape by being high and wide at one end and low and narrow at the other. A **cist grave** is a small rectangular pit lined with stone slabs.

- **Standing stones** are another sign of Bronze Age settlement. These mysterious stones are sometimes found on their own, but are sometimes arranged in lines or in circles. They may have been the sites of burials, sacrifices or other ceremonies.

- A **fulacht fiadh** was a Bronze Age cooking pit. A hole was dug in wet ground so that it would fill with water. Hot stones taken from a nearby fire were used to heat the water, which was then used to boil meat that was wrapped in straw.

A Bronze Age standing stone near Kealkill, Co. Cork

Celtic settlement

From about **600** BC a new people began to trickle into Ireland. These were the Celts, who brought the **Iron Age** to Ireland with their use of iron tools and weapons. The Celts lived in scattered settlements that were located close to water supplies and on land suited to grazing cattle. Apparently a warlike people, their settlements were designed to provide protection for themselves, their families and their cattle. Dwellings were surrounded by round defensive walls and are sometimes described generally as **ring forts**. There were various types of ring fort:

- A ring fort with an earthen defensive wall may be called a **rath** or a **lios**.
- A fort with a stone wall was usually referred to as **dún**, **caiseal** or **caher**. These stone forts are more common in stony landscapes in the West of Ireland.
- **Promontory** (headland) **forts** were built on the edges of sea cliffs or headlands for added protection.
- **Crannógs** were timber ring forts built on small natural or man-made islands within lakes. A crannóg had the surrounding lake as an extra defensive feature.

Ring forts are shown as small red circles on OS maps (see Figure 4). Their former existence can also be guessed at by the presence of place names that include words such as *Rath* (Rathmines), *Dún* (Dún Laoghaire), *Lios* (Lismore), *Caher* (Cahir) or *Caiseal* (Cashel).

Some ring forts had souterrains beneath their outer walls. A **souterrain** was an underground stone-lined passageway that was used as a hiding place or as an escape route if the ring fort was successfully attacked. Being a cool place, it was also probably used to store milk and butter.

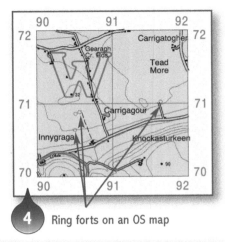

4 Ring forts on an OS map

A promontory fort at Slea Head, Co. Kerry

(a) *What special advantages did this location have for an Iron Age fort?*

(b) *What does the presence of forts such as this one suggest about life in Iron Age Ireland?*

Leaving Cert question and marking scheme

The question

'The OS map extract in Figure 5 shows evidence of a wide range of historic settlement.'
Examine the above statement using map evidence, with reference to any three different aspects of historic settlement.

(LC Higher Level – 30 marks)

Marking scheme

Mark three historic settlements at 10 marks each as follows:

Settlement feature named	= 2 marks
Settlement feature located by six-figure grid reference	= 2 marks
Examination (3 SRPs at 2 marks each)	= 6 marks

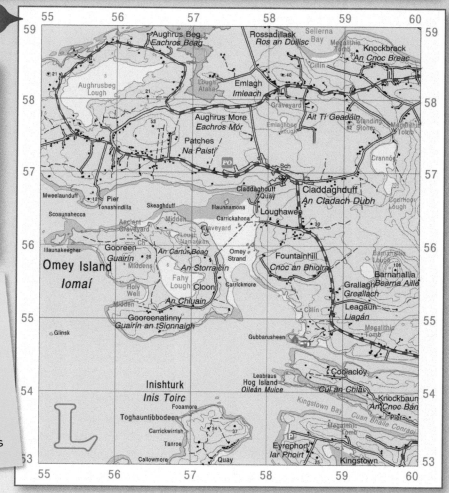

Note:

- 'Examination' must describe/explain settlement rather than give further map references.
- It is tactically best to choose three settlements/antiquities from three different periods of history.

Early Christian Settlement

From the fifth century AD, Christianity began to spread throughout Ireland. Many **monasteries** existed in early Christian Ireland. They were often located near rivers that provided the monks (or nuns) with fresh water and fish. Some were located in isolated spots such as islands or remote valleys, so that monks might escape from worldly distractions.

- Most monasteries were very small. They contained only a few thatch-roofed houses made of timber and mud. They would also have a tiny stone church called a **cillin**, the remains of which may still survive.
- Some monasteries grew into major centres of piety and learning. They were normally surrounded by circular defensive walls in the fashion of ring forts. The most important structures in such monasteries were made of stone, and many survive to this day. These structures included **round towers**, **oratories** (churches) and **high crosses**.

Place name evidence

Irish place names often provide evidence of possible early Christian settlement:

- 'Cill' is the Irish word for an oratory or a church. Place names that begin with 'kil' or 'kill' may therefore indicate a settlement's early Christian origins. Examples include Kildare and Kilkenny.
- Towns with '**mainistir**' or '**monaster**' in their names might also have early Christian origins. Examples include Monasterevin and Mainistir na Corann (Midleton).

Holy wells

Holy wells were a common feature of early Christian settlement. In pre-Christian times wells had already been revered as places in which gods and spirits dwelt. In Christian times some wells became 'Christianised', often as places of devotion to local saints. Many holy wells have survived and some continue to be places of devotion to the present day.

A round tower at Rattoo, Co. Kerry.

Some large early Christian Irish monasteries had round towers. A tower could be up to 40 metres tall. It was used as a belfry to house the bell that called monks to prayer. It was also used for storage and as a safe hiding place if the monastery came under attack. In order to prevent attackers from gaining entry, the door of the tower was high above the ground and could be reached only by a (removable) ladder.

Norman or medieval settlement

The Normans first arrived in Ireland in 1169 and they gradually settled throughout the country. Their earliest settlements were concerned mainly with **defending** the lands that they had captured from the native Irish.

- The earliest type of Norman defence structure was the **motte–bailey** fortification. This consisted of a steep and high mound of earth (the motte), on top of which a round timber fortification was erected. The motte was surrounded by a courtyard (the bailey), which was protected by a high, circular timber wall. The remains of mottes are marked on OS maps.
- Motte–bailey fortifications were replaced gradually by sturdier stone **castles**. Norman castles were often sited on easily defended rocky knolls or at the sides of rivers that helped to provide natural defensive moats. Larger castles consisted of tall rectangular towers called **keeps**. The keeps were surrounded by courtyards, which were protected by high outer walls with battlements. Smaller castles or 'tower houses' consisted of sturdy rectangular towers, usually without protective courtyard walls.

Norman **towns** often developed around important castles. Some towns were surrounded by defensive **walls**, **towers** and entrances called **gates**. These towns became centres of trade and commerce and were outposts of Norman culture in Ireland. The remains of **castles** are still to be found in such towns.

Abbeys and **priories** are another sign of Norman settlement. The Normans encouraged orders of monks such as the Cistercians and friars such as the Augustinians to settle in Ireland. These monks and friars provided alms for the poor, medical care for the sick, education for the young and shelter for travellers. The existence of such services often encouraged the growth of settlements in the vicinity of important abbeys.

Place name clues

● Place names such as **Abbeyleix** and **Abbeyfeale** might provide indirect evidence of the presence or the former presence of a Norman abbey in a town.

● **Grange** is another place name that indicates the former presence of an abbey. Monastic lands near towns were referred to in medieval times as 'granges'.

6

Trim, Co. Meath.

This OS map fragment and aerial photograph contain evidence of Norman settlement. Name, locate and examine three examples of such evidence.

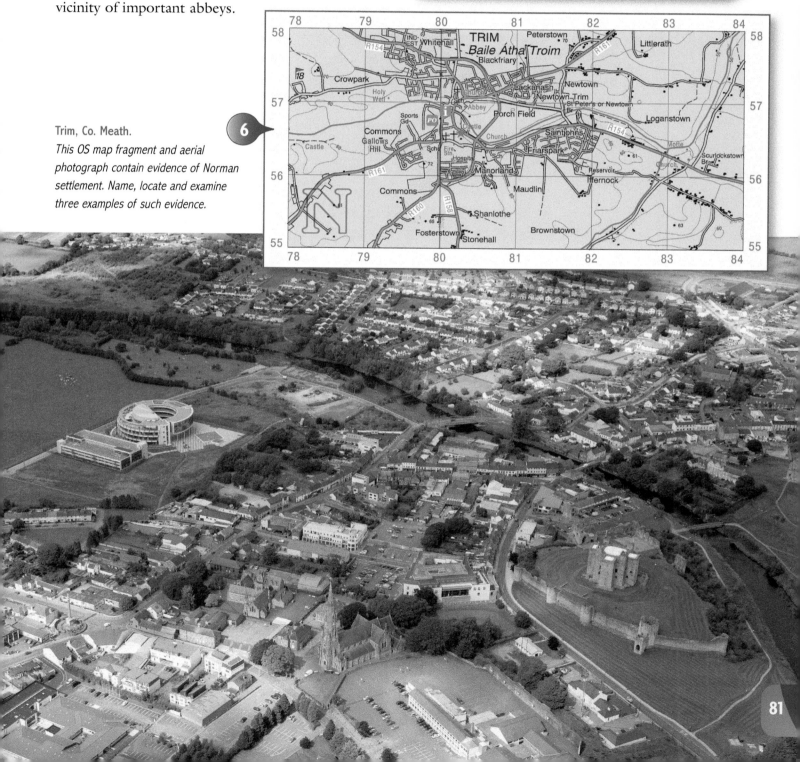

Plantation settlements

Several plantations took place in Ireland during the sixteenth and seventeenth centuries. In these plantations large tracts of land were taken from their Irish owners and given to English or Scottish 'planters' or 'settlers'. These settlers then became a new ruling Protestant landlord class.

The building of **planned towns** was often a feature of the plantations. Some individual landlords also sponsored the planned development of towns or villages. These towns or villages might be identified on OS maps or aerial photographs by the presence in their centre of regularly shaped **squares**, **market greens** or **triangular areas** and of **wide straight streets** with **right-angled street intersections**.

Many planters were preoccupied with their safety in the 'hostile' land that they occupied. Some lived in **fortified houses**, which were large houses that included defensive features such as towers. Fortified houses are sometimes shown on OS maps.

Place names can also provide clues to plantation settlements:

- Rural place names such as **Williamstown** might refer to the name of a landlord, while place names such as **Deerpark** might refer to part of a landlord's estate. The presence of the word **demesne** also signifies a landlord's estate.
- A planter's land was sometimes referred to as a **'lot'** or **'lott'**. Place names such as 'Smyth's Lot' or 'Creminslott' are therefore clues to plantation settlements.

Kenmare, Co. Kerry –
a plantation town.

7

(a) What evidence can you find from the OS map fragment and aerial photograph that Kenmare is a planned town?

(b) Use the map and photograph together to state the number of the road labelled **X** on the photograph.

(c) In what direction was the camera pointing when the photograph was taken?

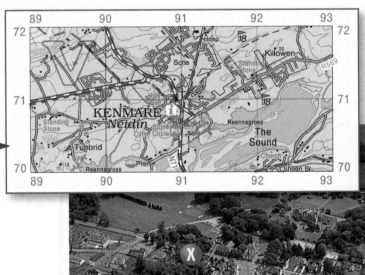

Case Study:
Youghal – the historic development of an Irish town

Youghal, Co. Cork is one of Ireland's oldest and most historic towns. The timeline in Figure 10 gives a brief idea of some of its history. The account that follows will focus on three aspects of the historic development of Youghal.

8 Location of Youghal

Medieval Youghal

By the fourteenth century, Youghal had become an important medieval Norman town and port. A defensive wall with at least ten towers then surrounded the town (see Figure 9). The wall contained three guarded entrances or gates: the Southern Gate; the North Gate; and the Water Gate, which controlled access to the busy harbour. The town grew so quickly at that time that an extra 'base town' (complete with its own outer gate) was added to Youghal's southern end.

The Normans usually encouraged the setting up of abbeys and priories in their medieval towns. Two large abbeys – South Abbey and North Abbey – were built just outside the town walls, while a Benedictine priory thrived within the walled town.

Youghal was one of Ireland's leading trading ports in the Middle Ages. It traded with ports in England, northwest Europe and the Mediterranean. It exported local wool, wood, fish and agricultural products and imported wine, spices and salt. So important was the port of Youghal that it was declared to be one of Ireland's 'cinque ports' (five great ports) in 1462.

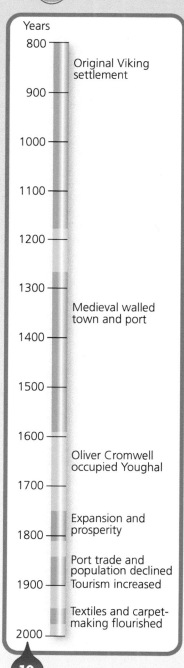

Years

Years	
800	Original Viking settlement
900	
1000	
1100	
1200	
1300	Medieval walled town and port
1400	
1500	
1600	Oliver Cromwell occupied Youghal
1700	
1800	Expansion and prosperity
1900	Port trade and population declined / Tourism increased
2000	Textiles and carpet-making flourished

10 A timeline of Youghal

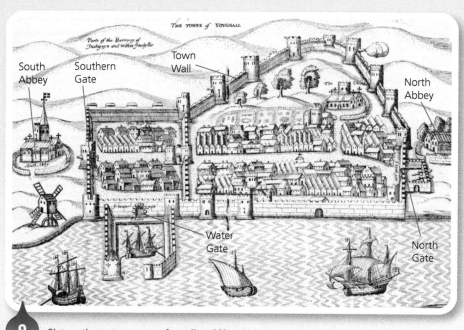

9 Sixteenth-century map of medieval Youghal.

How does this map support the view that 'defence, trade and religion were important aspects of medieval towns'?

Eighteenth-century prosperity

The eighteenth century was a time of prosperity and growth for Youghal. Increasing sea trade with foreign ports such as Bristol and Bordeaux demanded greater port facilities. This demand was met with the building of the town's **quays** (see Figure 11) and the **spread of the town** beyond the old walls. The quays were then great centres of activity, with wheat, oats and meat being loaded for export and imports such as sugar, fruit and coal being unloaded in great quantities.

Prosperity from trade caused several **notable buildings** to be erected at that time. One such building was the **Clock Gate** (which replaced the old medieval Southern Gate). Another notable building was the **Mall House** (now the Town Hall), which contained several assembly (meeting) rooms. The Mall House was reported at the time to be an attraction for Youghal's earliest **tourists** who were then beginning to visit Youghal in summer 'for the benefit of the salt water'.

Youghal's prosperity at that time was reflected in its population growth. The population of the town grew from 4,000 in 1764 to more than 10,000 by 1821.

The Mixed fortunes of Victorian Youghal

The development of Youghal suffered several *setbacks* during the reign of Queen Victoria (1837 to 1901).

- The town's sea **trade declined** dramatically. Larger ships and increased silting in Youghal harbour caused the port to lose out to rival ports such as Cork and Waterford.
- Between 1821 and 1900 the **population** of Youghal decreased by more than 40 per cent to about 6,000. This was owing to increased emigration, particularly during and after the Great Famine of 1845–49. The Famine affected Youghal so badly that bread shops were attacked and serious food riots occurred in the town.

Youghal's Water Gate.
In medieval times the Water Gate led directly to the harbour. Land on the seaward side of the ancient gate has since been reclaimed and built on.

Youghal's Clock Gate.
This gate was built in 1777 to replace the old Southern or 'Trinity' Gate. The Clock Gate was originally used as a prison. United Irishman prisoners were hanged from the windows of the gate during the 1798 uprising.

There were, however, some *positive developments* in Victorian times.

- In 1832, the estuary of the River Blackwater was **bridged** at Youghal for the first time. This bridge and later replacement bridges greatly improved access to Youghal and so facilitated its growth.

- **Tourism** increased steadily in importance throughout the second half of the nineteenth century. This was helped by the opening in 1860 of a Cork–Youghal rail link, which allowed city visitors much more easy access to the seaside town. Youghal's railway station was situated to the south of the town and this encouraged the growth of the town in a southerly direction.

Day-trippers from Cork arrive at Youghal railway station in the 1950s. *Rail access stimulated tourism in Youghal up to the closure of the Cork–Youghal passenger railway service in the 1960s.*

Youghal, Co. Cork.

 11

(a) Draw a sketch to half the length and half the breadth of this OS map. Show and name the following features in your sketch.
- The coastline.
- The estuary of the River Blackwater.
- A national primary road.
- Youghal town.
- One piece of evidence that Youghal was a medieval town.
- Youghal's (eighteenth-century) quays.

(b) Youghal's old bridge across the Blackwater Estuary was located at X 101 804. State the location of the present Youghal Bridge. Which of the two locations do you think was the more suitable? Explain.

(c) Prior to the bridging of the Blackwater estuary, an old ferry service offered the only access to Youghal from the east. Give a six-figure map reference for the likely location of this ferry service. Why was the location you chose suitable for a ferry service?

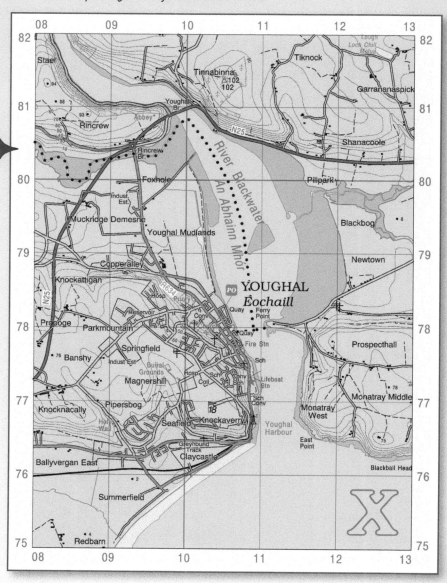

Rural settlement patterns

The arrangement of rural dwellings may form different shapes or patterns.

The principal **rural settlement patterns** are:

- **dispersed** settlement
- ribboned or **linear** settlement
- **nucleated** or clustered settlement
- an **absence** of settlement.

Rural settlement patterns were introduced on page 149 of your Changing World core textbook.

Dispersed settlement

Dispersed settlement consists mainly of isolated dwellings that are spread out in the countryside. An example is farmhouses.

12 Dispersed settlement

Explanation of dispersed settlement

- Dispersed settlement is common in agricultural areas where each **individual farm** contains its own farmhouse.
- Houses are located deep within farm holdings and at the end of **private lanes**.
- Dispersed settlement first became usual during the **agricultural revolution** of the eighteenth century, when 'common' land was enclosed into individual farms, each with its own house. This enclosure system began in England, but it also applied to Ireland, which was by then under English control.
- There are many large **farms** in the east and southeast of Ireland. Dispersed farmhouses in these areas tend therefore to be relatively far apart from each other. In the west and northwest, where farm holdings are generally small, dispersed farm dwellings tend to be somewhat closer together.

Ribboned (linear) settlement

Ribboned or linear settlements are long and narrow in shape. Buildings form a line, usually along the side of a road, along a coastline or at the foot of a steep hill.

Ribboned settlement 13

Explanation of ribbon settlement
- Most ribbon settlement developed **along roads**. Such settlement became very common in Ireland between the 1960s and the 1990s. There were a number of reasons for this.
  - Many roads were serviced with electricity and telephone lines and with water and sewage mains. People wished to build homes where these **services** were readily available.
  - It was particularly convenient for people to live close to the **approach roads** to towns or villages, in which shops, schools and other facilities are located.
  - Roadside locations especially suited businesses that rely for their prosperity on **passing trade**, such as petrol stations and guesthouses.
  - Some **farmers** responded to market demand by selling roadside sites for individual houses.
- Ribbon development sometimes occurs along **coastlines**. This is especially so in scenic areas where coastline dwellings enjoy picturesque sea views
- Linear housing is also common at the **foot of steep hills**, where building is easier and less expensive than on hill slopes.

Nucleated settlement

Nucleated settlements include buildings that are clustered together, such as at the meeting point of roads. Many **villages** are nucleated in shape.

Explanation of nucleated (clustered) settlement
- Clustered villages often develop **where roads meet**, for example at the **bridging points of rivers**. *Businesses* such as shops and pubs and *services* such as schools and churches are frequently located at such meeting points and they often form the nuclei of villages. In the days before piped water schemes, rivers provided some villages with domestic *water supplies*.
- Some old nucleated settlements grew up around castles that provided protection in times of war. Other settlements developed close to **monasteries**, **abbeys** or **priories** that once provided local people with health care, education and alms.
- Some small nucleated settlements in the west of Ireland are remnants of an ancient farming system called the **rundale** system. Farmers lived in small housing clusters called **clochans** and worked the surrounding land.

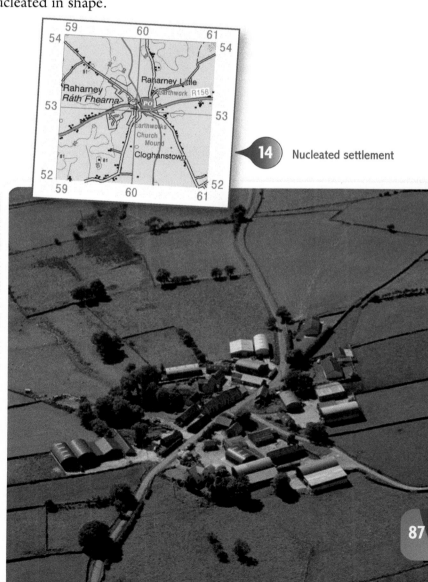

14 Nucleated settlement

Absence of settlement

Some areas contain no settlement because they are unsuited to building, to agriculture or to human habitation.

15 Absence of settlement

Explanation of absence of settlement

Human settlement may be absent from **upland or highland areas** for the following reasons:

● Places of **high altitude** may be so **cold** that they are unsuited to agriculture or to human habitation. Temperatures decrease by about 1°C for every 150 metres of altitude – a factor known as the **lapse rate**. Elevated areas are also likely to be windier than lowlands. Exposure to wind further reduces temperatures by as much as 10°C in winds of 50 kilometres per hour – this is called the **chill factor**. These factors help to explain why very few people in Ireland live at high altitudes.

● **Steep slopes** make the building of houses and access roads difficult and expensive. They also hinder profitable agricultural practices such as arable farming or cattle rearing.

● Settlement may also be absent from flat low-lying **flood plains** close to 'old' or 'mature' rivers. Such areas are liable to flood when river levels rise following periods of heavy rain. Land drainage and the building of houses on Ireland's river basins have contributed to increased river flooding in recent times.

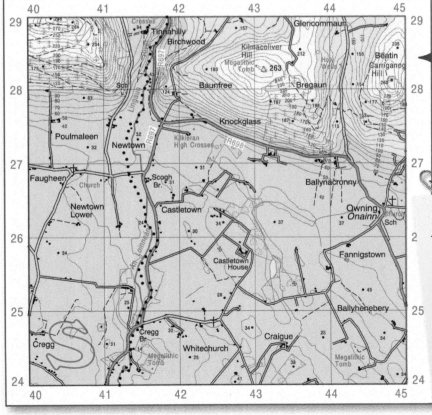

16 LC Higher Level question:
Examine the OS extract in Figure 16.
Using map evidence to support your answer, identify and explain three patterns of rural settlement.   *(30 marks)*

Marking scheme

Three patterns at 10 marks each:

● Pattern identified   = 2 marks

● Six-figure map reference   = 2 marks

● Explanation:
3 SRPs at 2 marks each   = 6 marks

Tip:
Try to exceed 3 SRPs in each of your explanations.

Sum Up

- **Site** refers to the actual ground on which a settlement stands. **Situation** refers to the location of a settlement in relation to its wider environment.
- Evidence of **historic settlement** can be found on **OS** maps:
  - *Middens* (ancient rubbish heaps) are a sign of **Middle Stone Age** settlement.
  - *Barrows*, *burial mounds* and *megalithic tombs* signify **New Stone Age** settlement.
  - The **Bronze Age** left Ireland with *wedge tombs*, *standing stones* (including *stone circles*) and *fulachta fia*.
  - The **Celts** left us with **ring forts** of various types. A ring fort might be a *rath*, *lios*, *dún*, *caiseal*, *caher*, *promontory fort* or *crannog*. *Souterrains* are also of Celtic origin.
- Small **early Christian** monasteries usually contained tiny stone churches called *cillíns*. Some larger monasteries had *round towers*, *oratories* and *high crosses*. *Holy wells* may be another sign of early Christian settlement.
- **Norman** settlements featured *mottes*, *castles* and medieval towns with *walls*, *towers* and *gates*. *Abbeys* and *priories* are other signs of Norman settlement, as are place names containing 'abbey', 'castle' or 'grange'.
- **Plantation** settlements included old *planned* towns, *fortified houses* and English-sounding names such as Deerpark or Smyth's Lot.
- **Youghal** was an important medieval town and trading port. It was surrounded by a defensive wall with towers and gates and had a priory and two large abbeys. Eighteenth-century prosperity resulted in the spread of the town beyond its walls. It also resulted in the building of quays and notable buildings such as the Mall House. The sea trade and population of Youghal declined during Victorian times. But Youghal's first bridge and growing tourism assisted prosperity.
- **Rural settlement patterns** include the following:
  - *Dispersed* settlement, such as in areas of scattered farmhouses.
  - *Ribboned* settlement, such as along roads, coastlines or at the base of steep slopes.
  - *Nucleated* settlements, such as where roads meet at the bridge points of rivers.
  - An *absence* of settlement, such as in steep highland areas or on some flood plains.

Test Yourself **eTest.ie**

Each of these activities relates to the Wexford Harbour OS map on the next page.

Activities

1. Describe the site and the situation of Wexford town.
2. Using evidence from the Wexford Harbour map, describe and explain three different examples of historic settlement.
   (Based on frequently asked Higher and Ordinary Level LC questions)
3. Identify, locate and explain three patterns of rural settlement to be found on the Wexford Harbour map.
   (Based on commonly asked Higher and Ordinary Level L.C. questions)

LC marking scheme:
3 historic settlements at 10 marks each:
- Settlement identified = 2 marks
- Settlement located = 2 marks
  (6-figure grid reference)
- Explanation:
  3 SRPs at 2 marks each = 6 marks

Tip: try to exceed 3 SRPs in each explanation.

LC marking scheme:
Use the marking scheme shown on page 88.

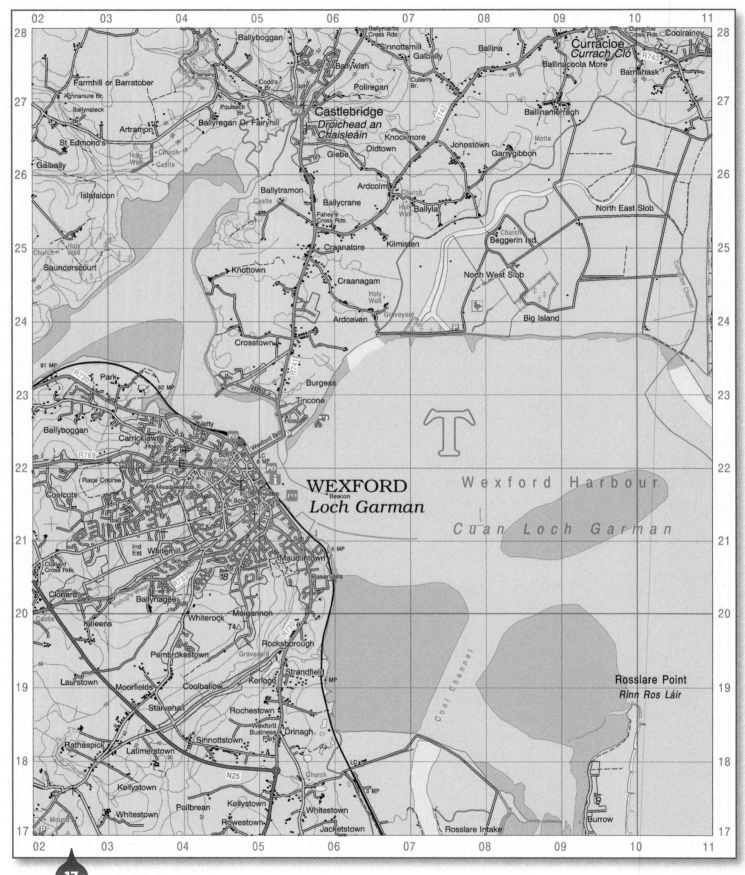

17 Wexford Harbour OS map extract

Rural Planning Strategies

The importance of planning strategies for rural settlement

The population of rural Ireland has been increasing since the 1970s. This increase resulted partly from **counter-urbanisation** or the migration of people from urban to rural areas. Counter-urbanisation around cities such as Dublin has created ever-increasing demands for rural housing. It has also robbed some rural villages of their unique identity as they grew into larger, soulless commuter settlements for nearby cities. These pressures have created an urgent need for careful settlement planning strategies in rural areas, which are laid down by a combination of **National Development Plans** and **County Development Plans**.

National Development Plans (NDPs)

The Irish government drew up an NDP for the years 2000 to 2006 and another to span the years 2007 to 2013. The current NDP states its support for 'orderly and sustainable rural development'. This means that rural settlement policies should meet local people's genuine need for housing, but at the same time protect the environment from inappropriate development.

Some aspects of NDP policies on rural settlement

One-off housing

A great number of one-off (stand-alone) houses have been built in rural Ireland in recent decades. National development planners generally **discourage the building of one-off houses** for a variety of environmental reasons (see box on next page). Exceptions are often made in the cases of rural people seeking permission to build homes for themselves in their own local area or in an area in which they work. **Urban-generated housing** (houses built in rural areas for urban people) are actively discouraged as they tend to be built as holiday homes or as 'investment properties' rather than out of genuine housing need.

A one-off house in a scenic rural area.

(a) Why might planners discourage the building of houses such as this? (After answering, check the column on the next page.)

(b) What arguments might be made in favour of building such houses?

Why planners discourage one-off housing

1   One-off houses require individual sites of up to half an acre (0.2 of a hectare) of *land*. This can be a wasteful use of the nation's finite land resources.

2   Building one-off houses can lead to the destruction of many ditches and other *wildlife habitats*.

3   One-off houses lead to more *traffic* on country roads. Individual entrances can also lead to traffic hazards.

4   Scattered one-off houses give rise to huge numbers of ESB and telephone *poles* crisscrossing the countryside. This is costly and wasteful and is a source of visual pollution.

5   Some large houses look out of place and *ugly* in scenic rural areas.

6   Individual (septic tank) sewerage schemes can sometimes malfunction and allow *sewage* to seep into groundwater. This can endanger human and animal health.

Ribbon development

Ribbon development happens when many one-off houses are built along the sides of public roads. This type of development is especially common along the approach roads to towns and villages, where local landowners have made large profits from selling building sites to people who work in the towns and villages.

Planners now **discourage ribbon development** for the following reasons:

●   Long ribbon development can encourage *car dependency*. This leads in turn to increased fuel use and to air pollution.

●   It deprives road users of views of the countryside. It can therefore sometimes be a *visual pollutant*.

●   Ribbon development also creates the *problems* associated with one-off housing listed in the column on the left.

Donegal town.

(a) *Locate the ribbon development on this photograph.*

(b) *Describe some possible causes and consequences of ribbon development.*

Village clusters

Planners usually prefer rural settlement to take the form of **clusters of houses** in or on the fringes of villages or small towns. Clustered dwellings require relatively small land banks, can tap into existing public sewerage and water mains and require the use of fewer electricity and telephone poles. They also tend to reduce car dependency and they have less visual impact on the countryside.

Planners' preference for housing clusters is reinforced by the **village renewal schemes** that are encouraged by Ireland's NDP. Village renewal schemes provide public money for upgrading water and sewerage schemes in villages, for improvements to footpaths and street lighting and for providing amenities such as playgrounds and village parks.

A clustered housing scheme.

(a) Why have Ireland's National and County Development Plans favoured the establishment of clustered housing schemes such as this one?

(b) What evidence can you find in the photograph to suggest that this village has benefited from a village renewal scheme?

Too much of a good thing.

Throughout the Celtic Tiger economic boom, 'developers' received planning permission to build large numbers of housing schemes in many of Ireland's small villages. These schemes sometimes swamped villages with too many new residents and thus altered the old and unique character and atmosphere of the original village. Following the economic crash of 2008, many overpriced houses failed to sell, leaving some villages with largely uninhabited and sometimes unfinished 'ghost estates'. By 2010 there were more than 2,800 ghost estates in Ireland.

County Development Plans (CDPs)

Each Irish country has its own CDP, which usually supports the policies of Ireland's NDP. County councils use CDPs to promote sustainable housing development in their county. They try to grant planning permission for the building of enough houses to meet local needs, while protecting rural areas from inappropriate building or other environmental damage.

Case Study
Rural settlement and Waterford's CDP

The **overall rural settlement policy** of the Waterford CDP is as follows:

- To grant permission, where appropriate, for the building of enough houses to meet the genuine needs of local rural people and their families.
- To steer profit-driven and other housing developments into villages that are already serviced with water, sewerage, electricity and telephone supplies.

Figure 1 shows that the Waterford CDP identifies **three main types of rural area** in the county. Rural settlement policies vary somewhat between these three types.

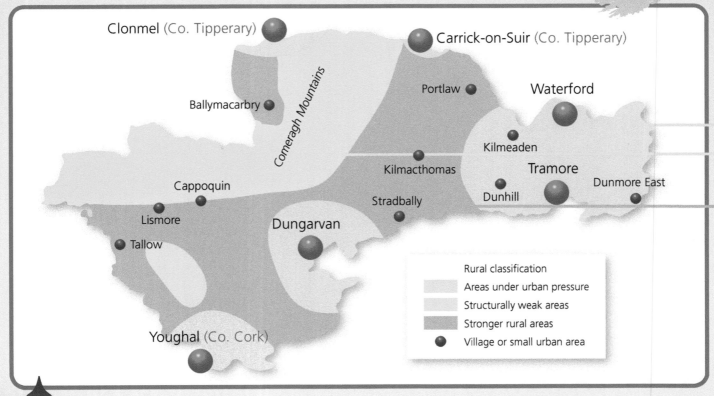

Rural classification
- Areas under urban pressure
- Structurally weak areas
- Stronger rural areas
- ● Village or small urban area

1 Rural area types in Co. Waterford

Areas under urban pressure

Description:

There is strong demand for building in these areas because they are close to large urban centres.

Settlement strategy:

- To facilitate the genuine one-off housing requirements of local people,* subject to the suitability of sites and of house designs.
- To direct urban-generated and other housing into nearby towns or villages.

An 'area under urban pressure' near Waterford City

Structurally weak areas

Description:

Many of these economically weak areas experience population decline. Areas such as the Comeragh Mountains are high scenic and amenity areas.

Settlement strategy:

- Where appropriate, to encourage clustered housing development in or near villages or at some cross road sites.
- Where appropriate, to allow the building of one-off houses in areas that suffer from population decline.
- To discourage the indiscriminate construction of one-off rural housing in scenic areas.

A 'structurally weak area' in the Comeragh Mountains

Stronger rural areas

Description:

These relatively prosperous agricultural areas tend to enjoy stable population levels.

Settlement strategy:

- Where appropriate, to allow for the building of enough one-off houses to satisfy genuine local* need.
- To give priority to housing development in villages or other existing clustered settlements.

A 'stronger rural area' in Co. Waterford

*Local people are defined as those who live within 7 kilometres of the proposed new building.

Sum Up

- Rising rural population creates a **need for rural planning strategies** in Ireland.
- Ireland's **National Development Plan (NDP)** supports 'orderly and sustainable rural development'.
- NDP planners **discourage one-off rural houses**, though exceptions are often made in the cases of local people's genuine housing needs.
- Planners also **discourage ribbon development**, for example along approach roads to towns.
- Planners favour the development of housing clusters in or on the fringes of villages or towns. The building of those clusters has sometimes been excessive.
- Local authorities use **County Development Plans (CDPs)** to promote sustainable settlement development.
- The **Waterford CDP** generally facilitates genuine local needs for one-off housing. But it discourages one-off housing in scenic areas and favours the development of clustered housing in or near villages or towns.
- Waterford's CDP distinguishes between **three types of rural area**: areas under urban pressure; structurally weak areas; and stronger rural areas.

Activities

1. Describe and explain the rural settlement planning strategies of Ireland's National Development Plan.
2. With reference to one named Irish County Development Plan, explain how local authorities in Ireland seek to promote the orderly development of rural settlement.
3. The OS map in Figure 2 shows part of Co. Waterford. Examine the three simulated planning permission applications related to different parts of the OS map. In the case of each application, state whether or not Waterford County Council is likely to grant or to refuse planning permission. Give reasons for your answer in each case.

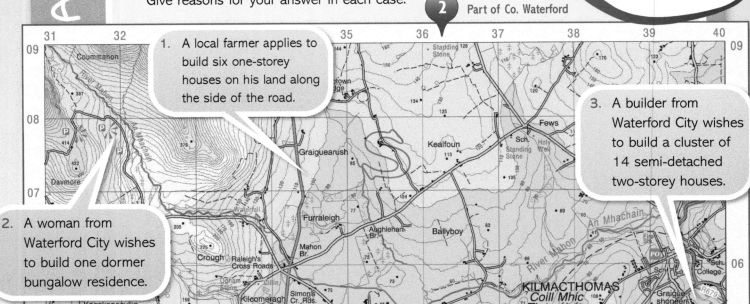

2 Part of Co. Waterford

7 Urban Hierarchy and the Central Place Theory

Urban Hierarchy

All urban settlements can be described as **central places** because they provide shops, businesses and other services and functions for their surrounding trading areas or **hinterlands**. But some settlements are more important than others. An **urban hierarchy** exists in which settlements are classified according to size, function and extent of hinterland.

Hinterland (trading area): The area surrounding an urban centre that trades with and uses the services of that centre.

The pyramid in Figure 1 provides a theoretical **model of urban hierarchy**. The place occupied by any individual settlement within the urban hierarchy depends on the following factors:

- *Population size:* the larger a settlement's population, the higher it will be in the urban hierarchy.
- *Services:* the greater a settlement's range of services, the higher it will be in the urban hierarchy.
- *Hinterland:* the larger a settlement's hinterland, the higher it will be in the urban hierarchy.

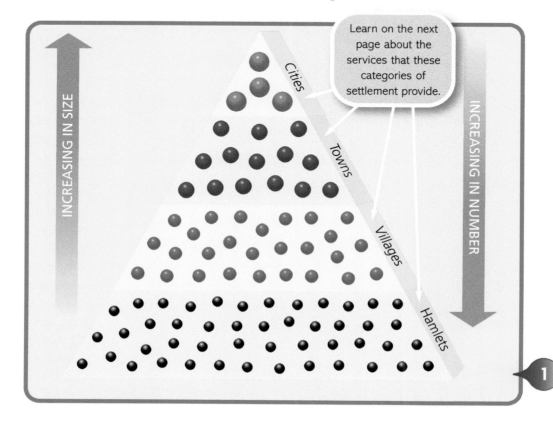

Learn on the next page about the services that these categories of settlement provide.

INCREASING IN SIZE

INCREASING IN NUMBER

Cities
Towns
Villages
Hamlets

1 Urban hierarchy

97

Some settlement categories within the urban hierarchy

Hamlet

Hamlets are small villages or rural housing clusters. A hamlet might provide a few low-order services such as a bar, a filling station or a small shop.

Village

A village will provide several low-order services as well as one or two medium-order services such as a post office, a school or a pharmacy.

Town

A town provides a full range of low-order and medium-order services. It might also provide some high-order services such as jewellery shops, solicitors' offices and department stores. Most towns are important market and service centres for their local hinterlands.

City

A city provides a full range of low-, medium- and high-order services. Such services might include very widely spaced high-order services such as theatres, a university or an airport.

Orders of services and goods

- **Low-order services** provide 'everyday' goods such as food items, newspapers and petrol. These low-order goods are bought frequently, but people are usually not prepared to travel long distances to acquire them. Low-order services are therefore widely available.

- **Middle-order services** include supermarkets, pharmacies and doctors' surgeries. They are required less often than low-order services, so people are prepared to travel somewhat further to acquire them.

- **High-order services** include law courts, universities, hospitals, large department stores and specialist shops such as jewellers. The goods and services they provide are of high value and are needed only occasionally. Customers are therefore willing to travel long distances to acquire them.

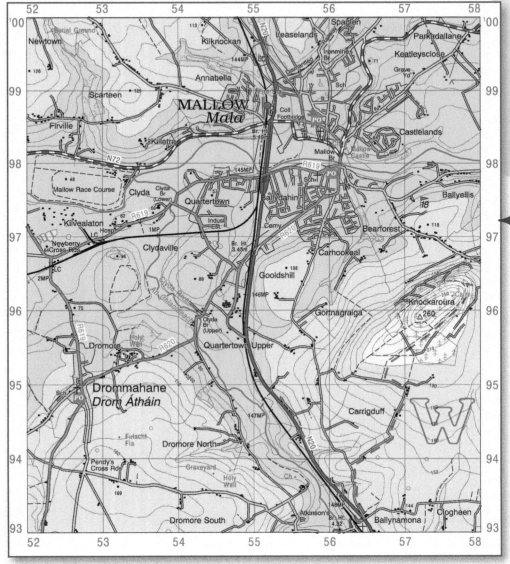

2 The Mallow area.

(a) List the following three settlements in rank order and categorise them according to their place in the urban hierarchy (city, town, village, etc.): Ballynamona, Dromahane, Mallow.

(b) Which of these three settlements has the largest hinterland and which has the smallest hinterland?

(c) Using map evidence, contrast the level of services provided by the largest of the three settlements with those provided by the smallest of the three settlements.

(d) Why is Mallow an important urban centre? Refer in your answer to size, transport routes and services/functions.

Central place theory

Central place theory is a geographical model that tries to explain *patterns in the numbers, the spacing and the functions of different categories of urban settlement.* The theory is also called the **Christaller theory** because a German geographer named Walter Christaller formulated it in 1933.

Christaller based his theory on two main concepts or ideas. They are the concept of *range* and the concept of *threshold*.

- **Range** is the maximum distance that people are prepared to travel in order to purchase a particular product or service. Low-order services such as village shops have small ranges. High-order services such as car dealerships have larger ranges because people are prepared to travel longer distances to avail of them.

- **Threshold** is the minimum population that is needed to make a particular service profitable. Low-order services (such as village shops) provide frequently bought products and so can function profitably on small thresholds. High-order services (such as car dealerships) need larger thresholds because most people purchase cars only rarely.

Terms to know

- **Central place:** a settlement that provides services and goods to an area larger than itself.
- **Geographical model:** a simplified way of presenting a complicated geographical truth. Because models are idealised, they provide only general and abstract views of reality. They seldom reflect the reality that exists in any particular geographical area.
- **Low-order and high-order services and goods:** see the box on page 98.

Three services.

*Identify the **range**, the **threshold** and the **order** of each of the three services shown in these photographs.*

Christaller classified a **hierarchy of settlements** or 'central places' according to their size and according to the range and the threshold of the services they provide. According to his central place theory:

- The bigger the settlement, the more (and higher-range) services it will provide.
- The bigger the settlements, the fewer in number they will be.
- The bigger the settlements, the further apart they will be.
- The bigger the settlement, the larger the trading areas it will have.

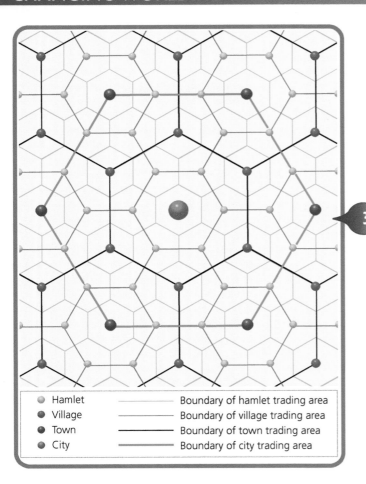

Legend:
- ◯ Hamlet — Boundary of hamlet trading area
- ● Village — Boundary of village trading area
- ● Town — Boundary of town trading area
- ● City — Boundary of city trading area

Christaller theorised that, under perfect geographical conditions, various categories of settlement would be positioned as shown in Figure 3. Each settlement would trade within a hexagonal-shaped trading area. The trading areas of larger settlements would also incorporate those of smaller surrounding settlements.

3 The location of settlements according to the central place theory.

(a) Examine carefully on this diagram the trading area of a city, a town, a village and a hamlet. Which of these trading areas is the largest and which is the smallest?

(b) How many cities, towns and villages are shown on this diagram? How do those numbers support Christaller's theory?

(c) Which of the following types of settlement are spaced closest to each other: towns, villages or hamlets?

Criticisms of the central place theory

Christaller based his theory on a number of theoretical assumptions that seldom exist in reality. These assumptions are contrasted with real-life situations in the grid below.

Like all models, the central place theory is a simplification of reality. It helps people to understand some general principles relating to the spacing of settlement. It does not however fit perfectly into any real-life situation.

Christaller's assumptions	Reality
● The countryside is a flat plain and served by only one form of transport	Very few places are perfectly flat and many are served by a variety of transport links.
● Transport is equally cheap and accessible everywhere	Motorways, rail connections and other transport links make some urban settlements more easily accessible than others.
● Population and natural resources are equally distributed throughout the countryside	Population and natural resources are almost never equally distributed.
● People have equal purchasing power	People do not have equal purchasing power: wealth is distributed unequally in most countries.
People purchase at the nearest centre available to them	Some people may have personal preferences for centres that are not the nearest to them. 'Sales' or 'special offers' in centres further away may make extra travel worthwhile.

Sum Up

- There is a **hierarchy of urban settlement**. The place of any settlement within this hierarchy depends on its population size and on its variety and order of services.
- **Low-order** services provide day-to-day goods to local people. **High-order** services provide high-value, seldom-bought goods to people in a large trading area. Small settlements mostly provide low-order services, while big settlements provide high-order as well as low-order services.
- **Christaller's central place theory** is a model that tries to explain patterns in the numbers, the spacing and the functions of different categories of settlement.
- The central place theory is based on the concept of **range** (the maximum distance that people will travel to access goods) and the concept of **threshold** (the minimum population that is needed to make a service profitable).
- The theory states that **large settlements** are fewer in number, are further apart from each other and have larger trading areas than smaller settlements.
- Like all models, the central place theory is a **simplification of reality**. It does not fit perfectly into any real-life situation.

Test Yourself
eTest.ie

Activities

1. Explain each of the following geographical terms as used in this chapter: *central place; hamlet; hinterland; low-order services; range; threshold; urban hierarchy.*

2. The diagram in Figure 4 depicts a hierarchy of settlements of varying categories.
   (a) Identify each of the settlement categories labelled **A–C** on the diagram.
   (b) Name two Irish examples in each category that you identify.
   (c) Explain how services in settlement A would differ from those in settlement C.

3. Examine the diagram in Figure 5, which shows Christaller's central place theory. Explain what you understand by this theory.
   (LC Higher Level – 30 marks)

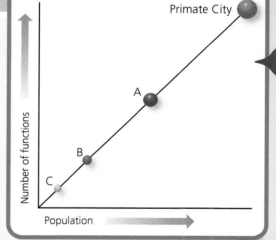

Number of functions
Population
Primate City
A
B
C

4

Primate city: a city that has at least twice the population of any other city in its country.

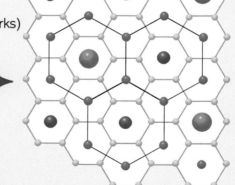

5

Key
● City
● Town
● Market Town
● Village
— Boundaries

Leaving Certificate marking scheme
Count 15 SRPs at 2 marks each.

Note:
Up to two examples can count as SRPs.

8 Urban Functions

The **functions** of an urban area are the activities, employment and services that it provides for its inhabitants and for the inhabitants of its hinterland. Most settlements are **multifunctional**, which means that they have more than one function. Some common urban functions are examined in this chapter.

> *You may be required to recognise and describe (usually three) functions of an urban area shown in an Ordnance Survey map or on an aerial photograph. Name each function, give its location and describe it using at least four SRPs.*

Revise the following in your *Changing World* core textbook:

- The development of towns (pages 150–151).
- Factories and industrial activities in towns (pages 154–155).
- Towns as centres of economic activities (pages 156–157).

Residential

Most town buildings are residential in character, with older dwellings generally located nearer to town centres and newer housing estates occupying outer urban fringes. Many people choose to live in towns to be close to facilities such as shops, schools and places of entertainment. Others live there to be near industrial or commercial workplaces that can be found in towns. Most County Development Plans and planning authorities have favoured the development of urban rather than rural housing development and this has contributed to the growth of urban housing estates.

Clues on maps and photographs
- Housing estates.
- Apartment complexes (on *photographs* only).

Market

Most Irish towns developed as agricultural market towns where, up to the 1960s, livestock and produce were traded at agricultural fairs or markets. The *surrounding countryside* can provide clues to the types of produce available in a former market town. The presence of *converging roads* and a *railway station* might have assisted the movement of cattle to and from fairs.

All towns continue to have market functions in that they are *shopping hubs* for people in their hinterlands.

Clues on maps and photographs
- Flat flood plains might provide dairy cattle.
- Flat or gently sloping lowlands might provide a variety of tillage crops and cattle.
- Highlands typically provide sheep.
- Town squares or diamonds were often used for fairs or markets.

Port

The presence of a sheltered deep-water *harbour* (not completely sandy) along with *piers, docks* and some *fishing trawlers* would be signs of a **fishing port**. A nearby *lighthouse* might provide supplementary evidence. A minority of coastal towns might also provide clues of some **commercial port** activities. Such clues might include *large docks, portside cranes* (lifting equipment) or *cargo ships.*

Manufacturing

Many towns are manufacturing centres. Describe the advantages that a town possesses regarding factory *sites, transport* access, local *labour* force, possible local *raw materials* and (in the case of industrial estates) possible *linkages* with other factories.

Clues on maps and photographs
- Industrial estates or individual factories.
- Large housing estates (source of local labour).
- Large, flat *sites* for industry.
- Good transport facilities (major roads or port or airport facilities).

Tourism and recreation

Most Irish towns offer some tourist or recreational functions. Seaside towns in particular attract tourists with *sandy beaches* (for sunbathing or swimming), *sheltered harbours* (for boating, sailing and fishing) and *sea cliffs* (for walking and sightseeing). Other tourist and recreational facilities might include *tourist information centres, golf courses, caravan parks* and nearby *mountains* for hiking and scenic views. *Antiquities* such as old castles might provide added tourist attractions. *Good transport facilities* increase tourist access to a town.

Clues on maps and photographs
- Harbours, sandy beaches, sea cliffs, piers, picnic sites, caravan parks, campsites, golf courses, antiquities, scenic viewing points, mountains.
- Tourist offices, youth hostels, walking routes (usually on *OS maps* only).
- Town parks, playgrounds, sports grounds, and pitch and putt courses (usually on *photographs* only).
- Transport networks for access (roads, rail, airport, seaport).

Clues on maps and photographs
- Sheltered harbours, piers, docks, lighthouses.
- Trawlers, cargo boats, portside cranes *(on photographs only).*

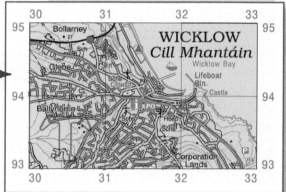

Wicklow Town.

Describe the functions of Wicklow Town as revealed by the photograph and/or the OS map fragment in Figure 1.

Other tertiary services

Most large towns have a wide variety of tertiary services.

- **Educational** services include *schools, colleges* and third-level institutions such as *institutes of technology* or *universities.*
- **Medical** services include *hospitals.*
- **Commercial** services such as shops, offices and hotels are common in town centres.
- Other services might include **Garda stations** and **post offices.**
- **Transport** services (a *railway station,* converging principal *roads*) stimulate the services mentioned above.

> **Clues on maps and photographs**
> - Schools, colleges, universities, institutes of technology, hospitals.
> - Converging main roads, railway stations.
> - Shops, offices, hotels, etc. (on *photographs* only).
> - Garda stations, post offices.

Religious

Most towns have religious functions in that they contain *churches.* A *cathedral* indicates that a town is the headquarters of a diocese. *Old abbeys, monasteries, priories* or *round towers* in or very near a town might indicate a **former** religious function. Orders of monks or friars once provided alms for the poor, medical care for the sick and education for the young. Some larger abbeys and monasteries were established in old Norman towns, the original monks and friars having accompanied the Normans to Ireland.

> **Clues on maps and photographs**
> - Churches, cathedrals, monasteries, convents.
> - The remains of old monasteries, etc.
> - Place names that include 'Abbey' or 'Monaster' might indicate a religious function.

Defence (former function)

A town might include **antiquities** such as a *castle*, a *motte* (an early type of wooden castle on an earthen mound), a *tower*, a *town wall* or a *town gate*. They provide evidence that the town was once a defence settlement, probably of the Norman period during the Middle Ages. Defence features such as the above provided protection for townspeople in times of war or unrest. Castles also provided employment. Some castles were sited by the sides of rivers that served as natural moats.

> **Clues on maps and photographs**
> - Castles, mottes, town walls, town gates.
> - Place names that include the word 'Castle'.

Exam training
Question, marking scheme and sample answer (using an OS map)

The question

Study the OS map of the Carlow area in Figure 2. Examine any three functions of Carlow town, using evidence from the map to support your answer.

(LC Higher Level-type question)

The marking scheme

Three functions at 10 marks each. Allocate each 10 marks as follows:
- Naming the function = 2 marks
- Six-figure map reference = 2 marks
- Examination:
  3 SRPs at 2 marks each = 6 marks

Tip:

Try to write at least four SRPs in each examination.

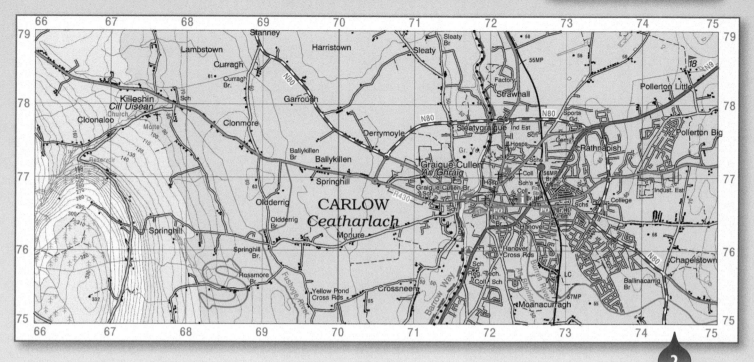

Sample answer

1   It is very likely that Carlow was once an agricultural market town. The flat low-lying flood plain of the River Barrow, for example at S 730 753, was likely to provide dairy cattle and dairy produce for fairs and markets that probably took place in Carlow in the past. Slightly higher, gently sloping land (for example at Clonmore (S 68 77)) might have produced cattle and a variety of tillage crops. Steep-sided hills to the west (S 667 753) may have provided sheep and wool for market. Converging roads assisted the modality of Carlow as a market town and the presence of a railway station meant that cattle could have been moved between Carlow and other parts of Ireland.

2   Carlow is a manufacturing town, evidence for which is the industrial estate at S 724 777. This industrial estate is located on flat land, which makes the building of factories easier and cheaper. Converging roads such as the N80, the R430 and an unnumbered national primary roadway, combined with a railway line and a railway station (S 728 771) could facilitate the movement of raw materials, finished products and workers to and from the factories. A plentiful local labour supply might be recruited within nearby large housing suburbs such as that at S 735 754. There is also the possibility that linkages might exist between factories located within the industrial estate.

3   A tourist information centre (with regular opening) at S 724 767 and an independent holiday hostel at S 717 760 suggest that tourism and recreation is a function of the town. The River Barrow might provide opportunities for angling, while boating activities near Graigue-Cullen Bridge confirm that the river is used for recreational purposes. The Barrow Way waymarked walk must be another recreational/tourist attraction. The railway station and converging roads such as the N80 and the R430 help to make Carlow a nodal town to which tourists would have easy access.

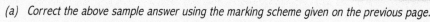

(a) Correct the above sample answer using the marking scheme given on the previous page.

(b) Examine three functions of Wexford town, supporting your answer with evidence from the OS map on page 90. Be guided by a similar marking scheme to that on page 104.

Question and sample answer (using an aerial photograph)

The question

Examine the aerial photograph of Ballina. Examine any three functions of the town, using evidence from the photograph to support your answer.

Ballina

Sample answer

Mark this sample answer using the marking scheme given on page 104.

1   The photograph suggests that Ballina was probably once an agricultural market town. Gently sloping lowlands shown on the background of the photograph seem to contain fertile pasturelands and croplands. Such lands would have provided abundant beef and dairy cattle and other agricultural produce for the local market. Agricultural fairs (which were once common in most Irish country towns) could have been held in the wide principal street that runs diagonally across the centre foreground of the photograph. Two bridges suggest that Ballina is a nodal point at which several roads converge. Such nodality would have facilitated the gathering of cattle and agricultural produce in Ballina and so have enhanced the town's suitability as a market town.

2   Ballina's commercial function is especially apparent in the centre foreground of the photograph where the old CBD (central business district) of the town appears to be situated. The wide street that runs diagonally across the centre foreground appears to be the main street of the town and several of its mainly three-storey buildings contain ground-floor shops. Several parked vehicles indicate on-street parking facilities, which would tend to facilitate commercial activity on this street. The CBD area is at the convergence of two principal streets. Such convergence points are ideal for commercial activity because many people meet at them.

3   Ballina also has an industrial function. An industrial estate can be seen on the right middleground of the photograph. A large, flat site facilitates the building of factories there and offers plenty of room for factory expansion. The nearby town and the housing estates on the right middleground/ background have the potential to provide a very convenient workforce. Straight roads appear to pass through and by the industrial estate and these provide easy access for the transportation of raw materials, finished products and workers. Several different factories appear to be situated together in this estate and it is therefore possible that industrial linkages might exist between some of them. One factory, for example, might provide production materials for another.

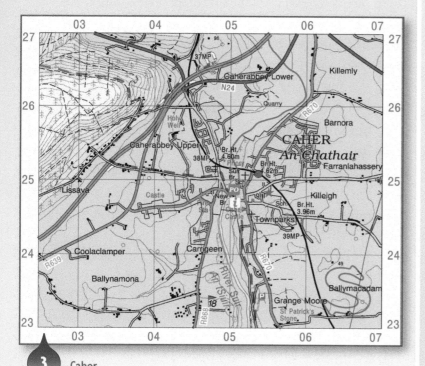

3

Caher.

Discuss how the presence of a river and nodality influenced the development of Caher.

Extra!

Why towns developed at their present locations

Some examination questions ask why a town shown on an OS map or in a photograph developed at its present location. A description of town functions will usually suffice to answer such a question. You could, however, also refer to the following points.

A river:

A river that flows through a town might affect the town's location and development in the following ways.

- In times before piped water supplies the river might have provided **water** for domestic purposes such as washing clothes.
- A *wide* river might have once been used as a **transport or trading** route. (Piers, quays, slipways or docks might provide clues to this.)
- If a river is liable to flood its flat flood plain, a town might occupy a *dry-point site* on higher ground a small distance from the river.
- A town is very likely to be located on a **bridge point** of a river. Roads (and therefore people) converge to cross bridges. Trade develops and towns grow where people converge.

Nodality:

Most towns are **nodal points** or *route centres* where several *roads meet*. The presence of a *railway station* or (less likely) a ferry port or airport adds to the nodality of a town. Nodality contributes greatly to various urban functions. For example, it assists the transport of cattle to an agricultural market town; the transport of raw materials, finished products and workers to an industrial town; the transport of customers to a commercial town and of tourists to a tourist town.

Case Study:
How the functions of Cork City changed over time

The functions and services of urban centres change over time. Cork City provides an example of this. This case study will focus particularly on the city's *port, industrial* and *educational* functions.

Cork City's docklands – once the site of large industries such as those of the Ford and the Dunlop companies.
Account for the decline of port traffic at these docks.

The Apple computer facility at Hollyhill Industrial Estate.
This facility manufactures Macintosh computers and serves as a large customer service support centre. By 2010 the facility employed approximately 2,800 workers and was one of Cork's largest employers.

Port function

Changing port functions played an important role in the development of Cork over time. The **Vikings** established a settlement at the site of the city in the ninth century and sea trade was a function of that settlement. From 1170 onwards, the **Normans** began to develop Cork as a port for exporting agricultural produce such as wheat, beef and cheese and for importing luxury goods such as spices, wine and French cloth. The city's port function developed further in the **eighteenth century**, for example with the building of a Custom House in 1724. Port activities reached their height in the twentieth century when large **dockside industries** such as Ford (tractors and motors) and Dunlop (tyres) contributed to port trade until these companies closed in the 1980s. Port activities have now **declined** hugely in the city. The increasing size of ships has forced most port traffic to relocate seawards from the city to wider and deeper harbour facilities at Ringaskiddy.

Industrial function

Manufacturing has been a function of Cork City since the **Middle Ages**. Cork, like any other Norman town, then contained small-scale manufacturers such as blacksmiths, shoemakers and potters. Medieval Cork was also noted for the manufacture of woollen cloth.

Throughout the **nineteenth century**, manufacturing thrived in Cork. Most industries – such as brewing and distilling – used locally produced agricultural raw materials.

Manufacturing increased further in importance in the early and mid-twentieth century with the building of dockside branch-plants by big foreign companies. These companies included Ford and Dunlop, which employed thousands of Cork City workers until they closed in the 1980s, followed by the collapse of other big **traditional industries** such as the Sunbeam Wolsey textile plant near Blackpool.

Traditional industry has been replaced by **high-tech industries** that manufacture computers, computer software and pharmaceuticals. Computer plants range from a large Apple facility at Hollyhill Industrial Estate in the north side of the city to small locally owned companies such as PC Pro at Southside Industrial Estate. Multinational pharmaceutical factories, such as the large Pfizer plant at Ringaskiddy, have been situated mainly in greenfield sites* outside the city itself.

Education function

Cork City originated as a **monastic settlement** when, in the early seventh century, St Finbarr founded a monastery near where St Fin Barre's Cathedral stands today. The education of young men was a function of such monasteries. This educational function must have increased after the **Normans** took over the city in the eleventh century. The Normans introduced European religious orders to the city and these orders set up abbeys such as the Red Abbey (Augustinian) and St Francis Abbey (Franciscan).

The number of **primary and post-primary schools** in Cork grew dramatically throughout the nineteenth and twentieth centuries. This was due partly to the setting up of the *National Schools System* in 1831 and partly to the spread of *Catholic religious teaching orders* throughout the city. These religious orders included the Presentation, Mercy and Loreto Sisters, who established schools for the education of girls, and the Christian Brothers and Presentation Brothers, who dedicated themselves to boys' education. The building of numerous post-primary *technical schools*, *community schools* and *community colleges* also enhanced the city's educational function.

Cork became a university city in 1845 when Queen's College Cork was founded. This is now *University College Cork* (UCC), which caters for more than 19,000 students. Cork's function as a hub of **third-level education** was enhanced greatly in 1973, when a regional technical college was established in the Bishopstown area of the city. This college is now *Cork Institute of Technology* (CIT) and it educates up to 17,000 full-time and part-time students.

> *** Greenfield site:** land that has not been previously used for urban or industrial development

Cork City's coat of arms.
The Latin motto on this coat of arms emphasises the importance of the city's port function. It translates as 'A safe harbour for ships'.

University College Cork (UCC).
UCC is now one of Ireland's leading universities. Its motto is, 'Where Finbarr taught, let Munster learn'.

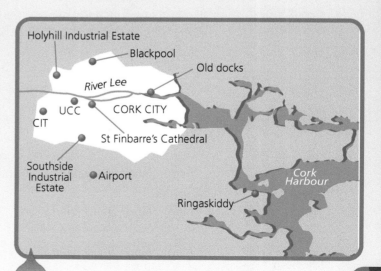

Some of the places referred to in this case study

- Most towns are **multifunctional**, which means that they provide a variety of services for people who live in them or in their hinterlands:
    - Most urban buildings are residential. County Development Plans encourage urban rather than rural housing.
    - Most Irish towns developed as **market** towns.
    - Fishing or commercial **ports** developed in some sheltered, deep harbours.
    - **Manufacturing** functions are assisted by suitable *sites, access, labour supply, raw materials* and *linkages* between factories.
    - Many towns have **tourist and recreational** functions.
    - **Other tertiary functions** include educational, medical, commercial, transport, etc.
    - Antiquities such as old monasteries indicate former **religious** functions. All towns continue to have churches that provide religious services.
    - **Defence** (usually provided by castles, town walls, etc.) was a former function of some old towns.
- Towns may also develop because of:
    - The presence of a **river** that might have formerly provided *water* for domestic purposes or (in the case of a wide river) a *transport route.* Some towns occupy *dry-point sites* above rivers that are liable to flood. Most towns are built on or very near to *bridge points.*
    - **Nodality,** which happens *where roads converge* and therefore where people meet and business thrives. A *railway station* can contribute to a town's nodality.
- The **functions of Cork City** have changed over time:
    - Its **port function** began with the Vikings and continued with the Normans. It reached its height and later declined in the twentieth century.
    - **Manufacturing** existed in medieval Cork and thrived in the nineteenth century. Traditional industries such as textiles have now been replaced by high-tech industries such as computer manufacturing.
    - Cork's **educational function** originated with *monastic* education. *National primary schools* and post-primary schools run by *Catholic teaching orders* multiplied in the nineteenth and twentieth centuries. UCC and CIT have made the city a hub of *third-level* education.

Test Yourself
eTest.ie

Activities

1. Explain two functions of an urban area studied by you. Clearly state the name of the urban area in your answer.
   (LC Ordinary Level)

2. Study the *aerial photograph* of Carrick-on-Suir on the next page. Examine any three functions of Carrick-on-Suir, using evidence from the photograph to support your answer.
   (Frequently asked LC Higher Level question)

3. Study the *OS map* of the Carrick-on-Suir area on the next page. Using map evidence to support your answer, explain three reasons why Carrick-on-Suir developed at its present location.
   (Frequently asked LC Higher and Ordinary Level question)

4. With reference to one urban centre that you have studied, examine how its functions have changed over time.
   (LC Higher Level)

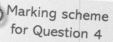

Marking scheme for Question 4

Name the urban centre	= 2 marks
Name two functions at 2 marks each	= 4 marks
Examination: 12 SRPs at 2 marks each	= 24 marks
Total	**= 30 marks**

Tip: you must make references to *time* in your answer.

Carrick-on-Suir

Tips for answering questions like questions 2 and 3 on the previous page.

In the case of each function or reason that you refer to:

● Name the function or reason.

● Refer accurately to a specific location.

● Include four SRPs in the explanation or examination.

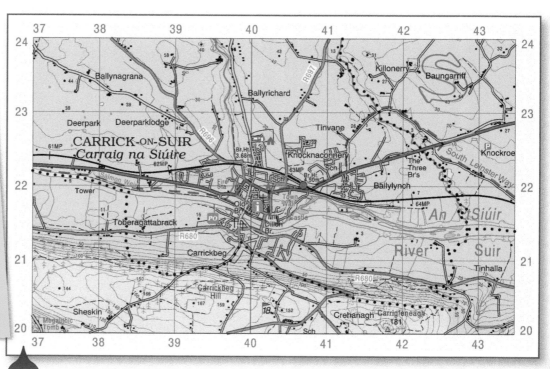

4 OS map of Carrick-on-Suir

9 Land Use Zones in Urban Areas

Every town or city has within it many different land uses, such as those related to housing, commerce, recreation and industry. These different land uses tend to develop in different urban areas, sometimes with the assistance of city council or county council urban planning. This tendency helps to create different **land use zones** in individual towns and cities.

Common urban land uses
- Commercial
- Industrial
- Residential
- Open space and recreational
- Transport
- Educational
- Religious

Commercial

Commercial land use zones contain shops, offices, banks and a wide variety of services ranging from hairdressing salons to restaurants.

- The most important commercial zone in any urban area is the **Central Business District (CBD)**. This is usually located at the heart of the town or city, where the most important streets intersect.
- Shops and other services can also form ribbon patterns along **principal streets or urban exit routes** that are accessible to motorists.
- Large shopping centres are sometimes located on the **fringes of urban areas.** Such places enjoy cheaper land values, ample room for large car parks and access to urban ring roads or other important roadways.

Industrial

- Most factories are now located on or close to the **edges of urban areas**. These locations often have large and relatively cheap industrial sites, along with congestion-free roads that connect factories to country-wide supplies or markets. Many light industries are located in *industrial estates* where they may enjoy linkages with adjacent industries.
- A few **old factories** are still to be found close to the centres of urban areas or close to railway stations or old docks.

Grafton Street: part of Dublin's commercially busy CBD

112

Residential

Residential areas make up the largest single land use in urban areas.

- These areas vary in **density**. High-density housing (multi-storey apartments and terraced houses) tend to be found near urban centres where land values are extremely high. Low-density dwellings (detached houses with gardens) tend to be confined mainly to the edges of towns and cities.
- Residential areas also vary in **age**. Older dwellings are typically (thought not always) found closer to urban centres. Newer housing estates are usually found on the fringes of urban areas.
- Residential zones may also vary in the **quality** of their dwellings. Some consist mainly of relatively low-cost local authority housing. Other zones are dominated by large, expensive detached private houses.

Open space and recreational

Outdoor recreational areas are **favoured by urban planners** because they are important to the mental and physical well-being of urban dwellers. These areas can include large city **parks,** smaller green areas, river or canal walks, sports fields, ornamental gardens and children's playgrounds. Phoenix Park in Dublin is an example of an exceptionally large urban open space.

Transport

Transport land use zones consist of roads, railway lines and railway stations, airports, navigable rivers and canals.

Educational

Educational land uses consist of all kinds of **schools and colleges**. They may sometimes be recognised on aerial photographs because of the playing fields or playgrounds attached to them.

Religious

Churches – sometimes with cemeteries – are to be found in all Irish towns and cities.

Can you name examples of similar land uses in another Irish city?

Low-density private housing in Killiney, Co. Dublin

High-density public authority apartments in Dublin city centre

Some examples of land use zones in Dublin

Commercial:	
CBD	*Grafton Street*
Suburban shopping centre:	*Dundrum*
Industrial:	
Old city-centre factory:	*Guinness (St James's Gate)*
Suburban industrial estate:	*Sandyford*
Residential:	
High-density, local authority:	*Crumlin*
Low-density, private:	*Foxrock*
Older housing:	*Glasnevin*
New housing:	*Portmarnock*
Open space/recreational:	*Phoenix Park*
Transport:	*M50 ring road*
Educational:	*Trinity College*
Religious:	*Pro-Cathedral*

Very frequently asked Leaving Cert question

You may be asked to do the following in your Leaving Cert examination:

● Draw a sketch map of the aerial photograph accompanying the examination paper. This sketch map may have to be half the length and half the breadth of the aerial photograph provided.

And:

● Show and name several prescribed features on your sketch map.

Or:

● Show and name three or four different zones of urban land use.

Important!
Revise pages 164 and 165 of your Changing World *core textbook.*
These pages explain how to draw a sketch map of an aerial photograph and how to show and name some prescribed features on your sketch map.

Activity 1

Examine the aerial photograph of Fermoy on the next page. Draw a sketch map half the length and half the breadth of the photograph. On it show and name each of the following:

● *the river*
● *a weir*
● *two interconnecting roads or streets, one of which crosses a bridge*
● *a church*
● *a playing field*
● *two adjoining pasture fields that might be prone to flooding by the river.*

Activity 2

First, carefully examine Figure 1. It shows a sketch map of the aerial photograph of Fermoy that is on the next page. It also shows and names four different urban land use zones in the town of Fermoy.

Then draw a sketch map of the *aerial photograph of Carrick-on-Suir that appears on page 111*. Make your sketch the *full* length and breadth of the photograph. On it show and name four different land use zones. You need not colour the land use zones.

Land use key

1	Residential suburbs
2	Recreational
3	Commercial (CBD)
4	Manufacturing or warehousing

1 Sketch map of Fermoy, Co. Cork showing four urban land use zones

Fermoy, Co. Cork

Changing land uses in urban areas

As urban areas develop, different activities compete for space in them.
This causes land uses in urban areas to change over time.

City centre land use

City centres tend to undergo considerable land use changes.

- City-centre **Central Business Districts** (CBDs) are ideal for commercial activity because many people converge at them. This high 'footfall' (presence of people) makes land in the CBD extremely valuable and in high demand. Buildings in the CBD tend therefore to be taller than buildings in other parts of a city, with commercial activities 'stacked' in multi-storey buildings to maximise the use of valuable ground space. Older CBD buildings in cities such as Hong Kong have now been replaced by **high-rise** 'skyscrapers'.

- A wide variety of commercial and residential land uses once occupied the CBDs of cities such as Dublin, where small family-run shops and poor housing existed in or close to the city centre. But very high land values now result in CBD areas being occupied mostly by those who can afford to pay very high rents or purchase prices. These **occupiers** include specialist and 'chain' retail stores, as well as some banks, offices and wealthy residents of exclusive city-centre apartments.

Industrial land use

Industrial land use in most cities has changed dramatically over time.

- *In former times*, factories were often situated **close to city centres**. Many were built near railway stations or old city docks for the convenient transport of raw materials and finished products. They were also near old residential areas, so that people could walk to work. The Guinness brewery at St James's Gate is a surviving example of such a factory in Dublin.

- Very few factories now remain in traffic-congested, high-value inner city sites. Most industry is now located in industrial estates on the **perimeter (fringes) of cities and towns**. Larger and cheaper sites are available there and nearby major roads provide factories with easy access and efficient transport facilities. Examples of such industrial estates include those at Sandyford in Dublin and Hollyhill in Cork.

- When old factories or warehouses abandon inner city areas, these areas are often **redeveloped** for other purposes. When Jacob's biscuit factory off Camden Street in Dublin was closed in 1975, the site was later converted to house the National Archives Building. Redevelopments such as this are often part of the planned transformation of decayed inner city areas.

Residential land use

As cities grow outwards, *new housing estates* – interspersed with green areas and shopping centres – tend to occupy expanding **urban fringes**. The age of urban housing thus decreases generally as one moves outwards towards the fringes of a city. But new housing developments also occur in **inner city areas**. Older or decayed housing has been *renewed** in places such as the Liberties and Fatima Mansions in the Dolphin's Barn area of Dublin. Urban *redevelopment** has created new and expensive high-rise apartments in the Albert Street area of Cork. Urban planners favour the renewal and redevelopment of decaying inner city areas because such projects help to *regenerate** and repopulate those areas. They also help to reduce commuting in and out of the city.

A modern high-rise CBD emerges from London city.

(a) Why are buildings so high in such city centre areas?

(b) Who is likely to occupy the new CBD buildings shown?

Terms to know

- **Urban renewal:** the replacement or refurbishment of old dwellings and the improvement of urban environments mainly for the benefit of existing inner city residents.

- **Urban redevelopment:** the demolition of old houses and other buildings and their replacement by shops, offices, apartments or other buildings. Redevelopment is often profit-driven rather than undertaken for the benefit of existing local inhabitants.

- **Urban regeneration:** any planned, sustainable measures to improve the quality of (usually decayed) urban areas. Urban regeneration can refer to urban renewal or to urban redevelopment.

The National Archives Building, which was once the site of Jacob's biscuit factory

AN CHARTLANN NÁISIÚNTA THE NATIONAL ARCHIVES

Theories of urban land use

Geographers have devised **theories** or **models** to try to describe and explain the growth and layout of a 'typical' city. This chapter will examine three urban land use theories:

- concentric zone theory (Burgess)
- sector theory (Hoyt)
- multiple nuclei theory (Harris and Ullman).

The concentric zone theory: E.W. Burgess

E.W. Burgess based his concentric zone theory on studies of *Chicago* that he made in the 1920s. According to Burgess:

- The **CBD** lies at the centre of any city.
- The city grows outwards in all directions from its centre. The **oldest buildings** are therefore in or near the centre.
- **Housing standards** improve (and the wealth of their inhabitants increases) with distance from the city centre.
- **Housing densities** decrease with distance from the city centre.

The diagram in Figure 2 illustrates the Burgess model. It shows that this model divides the city into *five concentric circular zones*, labelled 1 to 5.

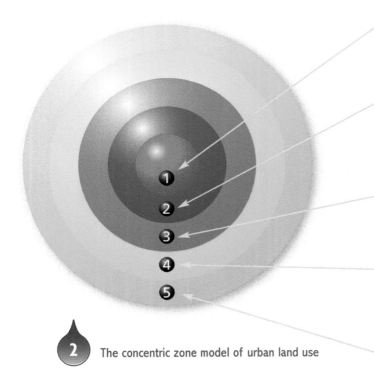

2 The concentric zone model of urban land use

Zone 1 is the *Central Business District*.

Zone 2 is called the *zone of transition*. This zone contains old, multi-storey houses that have degenerated into slum apartments occupied mainly by poor immigrants. This zone is also an industrial area.

Zone 3 consists mainly of *working-class terraced* houses. The occupants of these houses are low-income but are better off than the people in Zone 2.

Zone 4 contains many *semi-detached* houses that are occupied by *middle-income* families.

Zone 5 is a *high-income* residential area that contains many large and expensive *detached houses*. Some of these houses are located in commuter towns that can be up to an hour's journey from the city.

How relevant is the Burgess theory to modern cities?

Some aspects of the Burgess Model are relevant to many cities of today:

- CBDs are typically located in city centres and most cities expand outwards over time. Older suburbs are usually closer to city centres, while newer suburbs tend to be located in urban fringes.

Dublin's CBD is at the heart of the city. Older suburbs such as Terenure are closer to the city centre than are newer suburbs such as Darndale.

But the Burgess model contains many weaknesses:

- The model of 'concentric circle' urban growth is based on the assumption that the land on which cities are built is flat and featureless. This does not allow for the fact that hills, rivers and coastlines can greatly affect the growth and shape of cities.

Dublin Bay prevents the eastward expansion of Dublin, while the Dublin mountains hinder the city's expansion to the south.

- The model takes no account of how road and rail routes can influence the growth and shape of cities.

Motorways such as the M4 and N3 have helped to stimulate the westward spread of Dublin, while the DART has been a factor in the southward coastal development of the city.

- The wealth of urban dwellers does not now always increase with distance from city centres. Redeveloped inner-city areas now often contain exclusive expensive apartments, while some low-income local authority estates are located on urban fringes.

Dockland developments near the city centre now house many high-income residents. Urban fringe areas such as West Tallaght contain many local authority housing estates.

- Older, inner-city housing is not always of higher density than housing developed more recently near urban fringes.

The tower-block apartments built during the 1960s in the outer suburb of Ballymun were of much higher density than older dwellings in inner suburbs such as Drimnagh.

- Suburban industrial estates, business parks and shopping centres did not exist when Burgess developed his model. They are, however, important features of urban development today.

The Sandyford Industrial Estate and the Dundrum Shopping Centre have played significant roles in the growth of modern Dublin.

The sector theory: Homer Hoyt

Homer Hoyt developed his sector model of urban land use in 1939. He supported the Burgess concentric zone model to some degree. Unlike Burgess, however, he recognised that particular urban land use zones can develop *outwards along major routeways*. This gave rise to the **wedge-shaped 'sectors'** in his model, as shown in Figure 3.

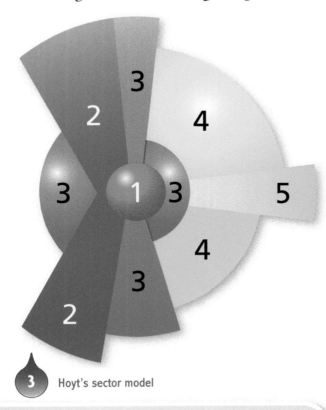

3 Hoyt's sector model

1   **Zone 1** is the *Central Business District*. It lies at the heart of the city.

2   **Zone 2** follows railway lines or navigable waterways. This wedge-shaped sector is dominated by wholesale warehouses and by *manufacturing industry*.

3   **Zone 3** is a *low-income residential sector*. Many people who live here work in the nearby industrial zone. The environment in Zone 3 might be polluted by nearby industries. This allows for low rents, which 'working-class' people can afford.

4   **Zone 4** consists of *middle-class housing*. It is further removed than Zone 3 from the polluted industrial sector.

5   **Zone 5** is the city's *high-income residential sector*. This is the most desirable part of the city, perhaps because it has fine views or is sited alongside a pleasant river. It is also furthest removed from industrial and low-income sectors. Only rich people can afford the high house prices that this zone commands. Zone 5 can extend quite far from the city centre because its rich inhabitants can afford to commute relatively long distances.

Some strengths and weaknesses of Hoyt's model

Strong points
- Unlike Burgess, Hoyt based his model on an investigation of a *large sample* of 142 cities
- Hoyt recognised that important *routeways* could influence the shape of urban growth.

Weak points
- Like all models, the Sector Theory is very *generalised*. It is unrealistic, for example, to say that any zone would be occupied entirely by middle-class housing.
- Hoyt (like Burgess) assumed that residential areas would be *segregated* strictly on the basis of people's income. That is no longer always the case.
- Hoyt based his theory on studies of *US cities only*. He gave no consideration to the structures of cities anywhere else in the world.

The multiple nuclei theory: Harris and Ullman

- C.H. Harris and Edward Ullman developed their multiple nuclei theory in 1945. They recognised that modern cities have *more complex structures* that those outlined by either Burgess or Hoyt. They believed that **cities grow not from one CBD alone but also from several smaller centres or nuclei**. Not all nuclei will have exactly similar functions – one might be mainly administrative, while others might be mainly commercial or industrial. Nevertheless, growth occurs outwards from each of these centres until they all merge into a single large urban area.

- The multiple nuclei model suggests that *activities of a similar kind attract each other* to some growth centres. A manufacturing industry, for example, might be attracted to a large industrial suburb in the hope of forming linkages with other industries there.

- The model also theorises that *some contrasting land uses repel each other*. High-income housing, for example, is likely to be located well away from zones containing heavy industry.

- Like Burgess and Hoyt before them, the founders of the multiple nuclei theory assumed that strong *social stratification* exists in cities. This means that people of different 'social classes' tend to live in different parts of a city.

The multiple nuclei theory is illustrated in Figure 4 below.

See question, marking scheme and sample answer on pages 132 and 133.

The relevance of the multiple nuclei model

The multiple nuclei theory is quite relevant to the growth of modern cities such as Dublin. The administrative, commercial and financial CBD of Dublin is located at the core of the city. The old dock area was once a mainly industrial centre, while places such as Rathmines and Dún Laoghaire were smaller commercial and residential centres in their own rights. These and other nuclei expanded and merged together over time to form the large urban area that is now Dublin.

As Dublin expanded more recently to its west, nuclei developed rapidly in areas such as Tallaght, Lucan and Blanchardstown. The multiple nuclei model suggests that these and other centres will continue to merge into an ever-growing Dublin City.

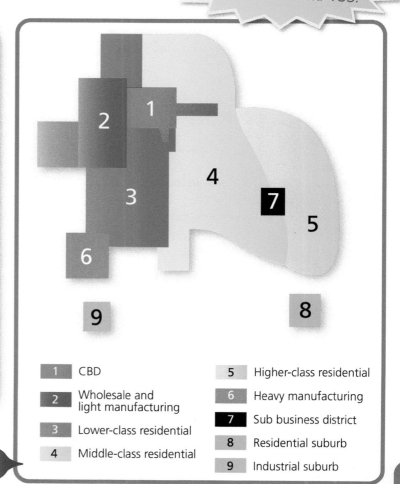

1	CBD
2	Wholesale and light manufacturing
3	Lower-class residential
4	Middle-class residential
5	Higher-class residential
6	Heavy manufacturing
7	Sub business district
8	Residential suburb
9	Industrial suburb

Harris and Ullman's multiple nuclei model 4

Terraced local authority housing in north Dublin

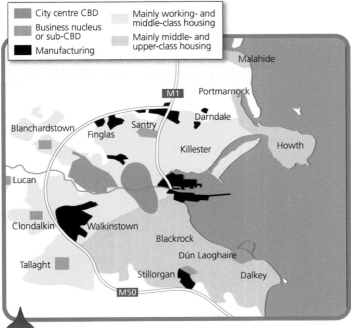

■ City centre CBD	Mainly working- and middle-class housing
■ Business nucleus or sub-CBD	Mainly middle- and upper-class housing
■ Manufacturing	

Malahide
Portmarnock
Darndale
M1
Blanchardstown
Finglas Santry
Killester
Howth
Lucan
Clondalkin Walkinstown
Blackrock
Dún Laoghaire
Tallaght
Stillorgan Dalkey
M50

5 Social stratification in Dublin.
Describe the general patterns shown.

Contrast this house in South Dublin with the houses shown at the top of the page

Social stratification in cities

There is a tendency for people of similar economic backgrounds to cluster together in the same areas of a city. This tendency results in **social stratification**, or the separation of residential areas according to income or so-called 'social class'. Richer people tend to monopolise those parts of a city that are considered to be most 'desirable' and in which property prices are highest.

● The quality, size and design of **housing units** usually reflect social stratification in urban areas. Many 'working-class' urban zones are dominated by multi-storey, local authority apartment blocks or by modest terraced or semi-detached houses of uniform design. Coolock in Dublin and Knocknaheeny in Cork are examples of such areas. High-income areas, on the other hand, are usually characterised by larger semi-detached or detached houses, some of which are individually designed and many of which include generous gardens. Such housing can be found in Foxrock, Dublin and in Rochestown Road, Cork.

● Access to **third-level education** is another symptom of social stratification. In Ireland it is estimated that children from 'upper' or 'middle-class' backgrounds are on average seven times more likely to attend third-level colleges than children of 'working-class' backgrounds.

● Social stratification can sometimes also be partly **age-based**. New housing estates in urban fringe areas such as Tallaght in Dublin and Mahon in Cork tend to be inhabited initially by young couples with children. A larger proportion of elderly people are to be found in older 'settled' urban areas such as Terenure in Dublin and Middle Parish in Cork's inner city. Clusters of young adults can be found in rented accommodation close to universities such as UCD and UCC.

The building by **local authorities** of massive 'corporation' estates in areas such as Coolock (Dublin), Churchfield (Cork) and Ballinacurra (Limerick) contributed in the past to social stratification within cities. But this trend has been reversed somewhat because local authorities are now helping lower-income families to rent houses in middle-income estates. The Celtic Tiger economic boom years up to 2008 also helped to reduce social stratification. Some residents of low-income estates made enough money in the economic boom to upgrade or extend their houses or to move into new homes in middle-income areas.

Social stratification in cities outside Ireland

Social stratification has been and is still a feature of urban areas in many parts of the world.

- Models of urban land use by people such as Burgess and Hoyt are based largely on social stratification. They show that such stratification was very common in **US cities** in the 1920s and 1930s.

- The shantytowns or *bustees* of Indian cities such as **Kolkata** are a symptom of large-scale social stratification.

- The black *townships* located outside urban areas in **South Africa** are relics of enforced, racist* social stratification in the past (see box).

Revise bustees in Kolkata, pages 31–32.

South Africa's townships — relics of enforced social stratification

Between 1948 and 1994 South Africa was ruled by a racist, white minority government that stratified society according to colour. The white governments of that period enforced on South Africa a system of **apartheid** or strict racial separation. Under apartheid, the country's black majority was denied the right to reside freely in the 'white' areas that made up 87 per cent of South Africa. These 'white areas' included all major cities. Urban blacks were forced to live in huge, poverty-stricken '**townships**' *outside* the cities in which they worked. One township of Johannesburg – a sprawling area named Soweto – contained more than one million black people.

White rule and the apartheid system finally collapsed in 1994. But South Africa's townships still remain as a legacy to its racist past.

***Racism:** a false belief that some ethnic groups are naturally superior to others. Racism has often entailed discrimination against black people.

Part of a township in South Africa

Land values in cities

The value of land varies greatly within cities. Value trends are generally as follows.

- The most valuable land is in the city centre, where business customers are most numerous.
- Land values (and the number of business customers) tend to decline from the city centre outwards.
- Secondary peaks in land values occur in suburban shopping centres or business parks.

A principle called the **bid-rent theory** seeks to explain variations in land values and related land uses within urban areas. This theory states that in a free market the best city locations will be sold or rented to the highest bidder. This will be the person or the company that will profit most from property in that location. People who cannot pay the highest prices or who do not need to be in the best location tend to locate elsewhere.

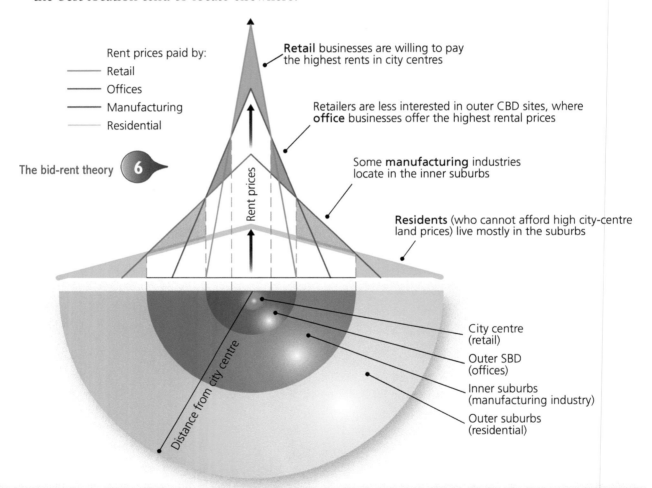

Rent prices paid by:
- Retail
- Offices
- Manufacturing
- Residential

The bid-rent theory 6

Rent prices

Distance from city centre

Retail businesses are willing to pay the highest rents in city centres

Retailers are less interested in outer CBD sites, where **office** businesses offer the highest rental prices

Some **manufacturing** industries locate in the inner suburbs

Residents (who cannot afford high city-centre land prices) live mostly in the suburbs

City centre (retail)

Outer SBD (offices)

Inner suburbs (manufacturing industry)

Outer suburbs (residential)

Weaknesses of the bid-rent theory

Like all theories or models, it is very generalised. It suggests, for instance, that retail businesses or offices occupy all CBD land. This is not the case. The CBD of Dublin, for example, includes Trinity College.

Some details of the bid-rent theory are out of date. For example, very few manufacturing industries now inhabit sites close to the CBD. Neither does the theory take account of the fact that large suburban shopping centres now create many localised 'secondary peaks' in urban land values.

Land values and land use in urban areas today

The city centre

The city centre attracts huge numbers of people because important streets and other routes converge there. The city centre is therefore the ideal location for a wide variety of economic activities and this creates lots of competition for city centre land. Competition drives prices up, so the value of city centre land is higher than in any other part of the city.

Retail chain stores, such as Debenhams and Brown Thomas, and specialist retail stores, such as jewellery shops and fashion boutiques, tend to occupy city centre sites at the heart of the CBD. These retail stores are best able to afford very high rents. They also benefit most from the huge number of customers who visit city centre areas.

High land values also result in the building of multi-storey, **high-rise** buildings in the city centre. Business activities can thus be 'stacked' on many floors and so make maximum use of the valuable ground space available.

Up to half a million people a week pass through Grafton Street in the heart of Dublin's CBD. Some leading retailers paid rents of up to €5,000 per square metre in Grafton Street at the height of the Celtic Tiger economic boom in 2006.

The edges of the CBD

Office owners cannot usually afford to pay very high city centre rents. Unlike retailers, offices do not need ground-floor shop fronts. Offices owned by law firms, doctors and accountants tend therefore to occupy buildings at the edges of the CBD, where rents are somewhat lower than in the city centre. Other offices are located in the slightly less expensive upper floors of tall city centre buildings.

The suburbs

Suburban areas traditionally attract fewer customers than city centre areas. The price of suburban land tends therefore to decline with distance from the city centre. In the past, **manufacturing industry** tended to occupy sites outside but close to the CBD.

Most suburban land is occupied by **residential** owners and tenants, who cannot normally compete for land in the city centre.

Manufacturing industry now tends to locate in city fringes, where urban land is normally cheapest. Most modern factories require large sites and such sites are more usually available and affordable in urban fringes. Factories also benefit from being located far from inner city traffic congestion and close to ring roads and motorways on the edges of cities.

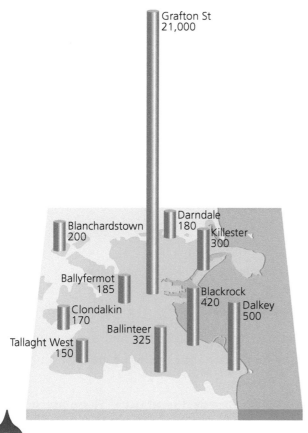

7 Property values in various parts of Dublin. (Values are given in euros per square metre and are based on a 2010 survey.)

(a) *Which area shown has the highest property values? Why?*

(b) *'Property values in Dublin's southeastern suburbs tend to exceed those in the west and north of the city.'*
To what extent does the information in this map support this statement?

Suburban shopping centres

Some city suburbs and urban fringes now contain **major shopping centres** such as those at Dundrum (Dublin) and Douglas (Cork). These centres were built in suburban locations to access growing numbers of suburban customers and to take advantage of land that was cheaper than land in the city centre. Once suburban shopping centres are established they raise the value of the land in which they are sited. This creates localised secondary peaks in suburban land values. These peaks are not accounted for by the bid-rent theory, which was devised before the creation of suburban shopping centres.

Urban land uses – some Dublin examples

- *City Centre retail streets:* Grafton Street, O'Connell Street.
- *Edge of CBD office areas:* Spencer Dock, Merrion Square.
- *Inner suburb manufacturing:* Guinness in St James's Gate.
- *Residential suburbs:* Terenure, Artane.
- *Suburban shopping centres:* Dundrum, Liffey Valley.
- *Suburban industrial estates:* Sandyford, Park West.

List similar examples in the city that is located closest to you.

Liffey Valley Shopping Centre on the outskirts of Dublin.
What effect does this large retail centre have on local land values?

How expanding cities pressurise rural land uses

Cities throughout the world have expanded rapidly, especially since the mid-twentieth century. Dublin City, for example, now occupies more than four times the area it occupied at the beginning of the nineteenth century.

The expansion of cities has led to huge **pressures on rural land uses**. These pressures have in turn had **negative impacts** on the social, cultural, economic and environmental lives of rural or former rural areas.

1 Social and cultural impacts

- Expanding cities **surround former rural villages** such as Dundrum in Dublin and Douglas in Cork. These villages may lose their unique social and cultural characteristics as they are swallowed up by large and rather soulless city suburbs.

Factors that contribute to the expansion of cities

- **Rural to urban migration** has caused both the populations and spatial sizes of cities to expand rapidly. This is especially so in the cases of Third World cities such as Mumbai and Kolkata in India. The effects of inward migration on city expansion is boosted by the fact that many in-migrants are young adults who are most likely to contribute to urban birth rates and to resulting population growth.
- Urban expansion in economically developed countries is partly due to the improvement of **suburban roadways** and to rapid growth in **car ownership**. As roads improve and as car numbers increase, city suburbs tend to expand outwards into the countryside.
- Building shopping centres on the fringes of cities also encourages urban expansion. The facilities and services provided by shopping centres such as Dublin's Liffey Valley help to stimulate local residential growth.

- Some rural villages and small towns, such as Monasterevin in Co. Kildare, suffered when busy urban **commuter roads** were built through them. Heavy traffic on such roads disrupted access between different parts of these villages and so damaged their social and environmental wellbeing. Most of these settlements (including Monasterevin) are now bypassed by main roads.
- As cities expand into rural areas, old country **place names** are often replaced by culturally meaningless housing estate names. Old Irish place names are sometimes replaced by new English-sounding names such as 'The Cotswolds' or 'The Dales'. This dilutes the cultural identity of Irish suburban areas.
- Developers have been accused of interfering with important **historic sites** when they built commuter roads that serve expanding cities. Controversy surrounded the building of the N3 roadway through the Skryne Valley in Co. Meath. Some environmentalists believe that this road runs too close to the Hill of Tara, which is one of Ireland's most important historical and archaeological sites.

The Hill of Tara.

(a) Why might some environmentalists have opposed the close to building of the M3 motorway close to this location?

(b) Why might some people have favoured the building of this motorway?

Urban sprawl expanding on to fertile agricultural land

2 Agricultural impacts

- As cities expand outwards, more and more city suburbs are built on what was formerly **agricultural land**. This trend has reduced Ireland's agricultural land bank in areas such as north Co. Dublin, where fertile tillage land has made way for city suburbs such as Coolock and for urban satellite towns such as Rush and Swords. The reduction of our agricultural land bank contributes to diminishing food production in Ireland and to an increase in Ireland's food imports.

- Some farms were rendered unworkable when major **roads** such as Dublin's M50 ring road were built through them.

- In recent years, some farmers have sought to increase the size of their farms in order to make them financially viable. The rezoning of agricultural land for residential use makes this process almost impossible. When agricultural land is rezoned for other uses, its **price can increase** more than tenfold as developers seek to buy it. Local farmers cannot compete with such price increases and so cannot expand their farms.

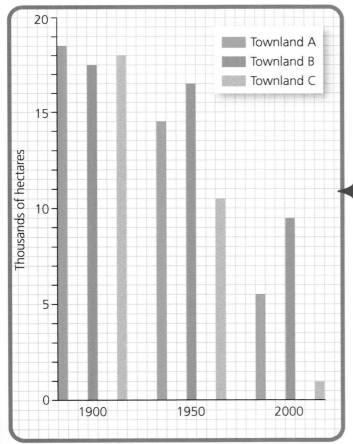

8 Skills work

Imagine that these bar graphs represent the amounts of agricultural land that existed in three townlands in the years 1900, 1950 and 2000. These townlands are located on the fringes of an expanding city.

(a) How much agricultural land existed in townland A in each of the years given?

(b) How much agricultural land was lost in townland B between 1900 and 2000?

(c) Which of the three townlands appears to have been most affected by urbanisation between 1900 and 2000?

(d) Do you think that the city expanded more between 1900 and 1950 than it did between 1950 and 2000? Explain your answer.

(e) State two likely effects of the trends shown in the bar graphs.

3 Environmental impacts

Urban expansion can have the following environmental impacts on rural or former rural areas.

- As agricultural land is built upon, large areas of **hedgerow** are destroyed. Hedgerows are the habitat (natural environment) of a wide variety of plants and animals ranging from wrens to hedgehogs. Hedgerows also provide a kind of 'highway' for small animals to move freely across the countryside. This improves the genetic pools of individual species by allowing members of the species to mate over a wide area. When hedgerows are destroyed or disrupted, the number and the genetic strength of these animal species are diminished.

- When **wetlands** are 'developed' for urban expansion they are usually converted to drylands by being drained and infilled with earth and rubble. Wetlands provide unique habitats for plants such as sphagnum moss and bog cotton, and for animals such as frogs and dragonflies. The destruction of wetlands threatens the welfare – if not the very survival – of some of these plant and animal species.

- The expansion of cities on river **flood plains** can result in flooding. When flood plains are paved over, rainwater can no longer soak slowly into the ground but is instead directed rapidly into rivers. This rapid water input can cause river 'flash floods' in times of heavy rain.

- Commuter roads to growing cities sometimes damage environmentally important **woodlands**. The widening of the Dublin–Wexford N11 roadway, for example, entailed the destruction of part of an ancient deciduous forest at the Glen of the Downs in Co. Wicklow.

A wren in a hedgerow.
Why are hedgerows important to species such as the wren?

The 'urban fox' – a victim of urban expansion.

The expansion of urban areas into the countryside has deprived foxes and other animals of their natural habitats. This deprivation has been so severe that some foxes have been forced to scavenge for food in the expanding urban areas.

- **Land use zones** in cities include:
  - *Commercial* zones such as in the CBD, along important exit routes and in urban fringes.
  - *Industrial* zones, which are now mainly in urban fringes.
  - *Residential* zones, in which houses can vary in density, age and quality.
  - *Recreational* zones, such as city parks.
  - *Transport* land uses such as roads, railway lines and airports.
  - *Educational* land uses that include schools and colleges.
  - *Religious* land uses that include churches and cemeteries.
- **Land uses change over time** in urban areas:
  - High-rise commercial buildings have come to dominate central *CBD* areas.
  - Most *manufacturing* industry has moved from inner-city to urban fringe locations.
  - Some inner city areas have been *regenerated* for residential or commercial purposes.
- There are several models or **theories of urban land use** in a 'typical' city.
  - E.W. *Burgess* devised the **concentric zone theory**. He assumed that the typical city is developed on flat featureless land. His land use zones consist of concentric circles around a central CBD. Housing zones become newer, less dense and increasingly high-income with distance from the centre.
  - Homer *Hoyt* recognised that particular land uses could develop outward along major routeways. His **sector theory** shows wedge-shaped land use sectors radiating outward from the city-centre CBD.
  - *Harris and Ullman* developed the **multiple nuclei theory**. This model states that cities develop when the CBD and other smaller nuclei (centres) grow and merge together.
- The above models of urban land use are very theoretical and are somewhat out of date. However, they continue to have **some relevance** to the reality of urban land use.
- **Social stratification** in cities refers to people of similar backgrounds clustering together in certain parts of cities. High-quality housing and access to third-level education is most common in high-income urban areas. Stratification can also be age-based.
- Social stratification has been and still is common in many countries. Enforced racial segregation led to extreme stratification in **South Africa** during the years of apartheid.
- The **bid-rent theory** seeks to explain variations in land values and related land uses within cities.
- **Retail** businesses tend to occupy the most valuable and sought-after **city-centre** locations. Tall multi-storey buildings make most use of expensive land in these locations.
- **Offices** are often located on slightly less expensive land at the **edge of CBDs**.
- **Suburban** areas are occupied mainly by **residential owners** who cannot afford high city-centre property prices.
- **Manufacturing** has migrated from inner-city sites to spacious, convenient and less expensive **urban fringe** locations.
- **Suburban shopping centres** and business parks create **'secondary' land value peaks** where they are located.

- **Expanding cities** have various **negative impacts** on rural areas:
  - *Social and cultural impacts* include the 'swallowing up' of unique villages, the spread of culturally meaningless place names and possible interference with historic sites.
  - *Agricultural impacts* include the reduction of agricultural land banks, the dissection of farms by new roads and dramatic increases in land prices.
  - *Environmental impacts* include the destruction of hedgerows, wetlands and woodlands, along with increased flooding on river flood plains.
- Rural to urban **migration**, increasing **car ownership** and the building of urban-fringe **shopping centres** have all contributed to the expansion of cities.

Activities

1. Draw a sketch map of the *aerial photograph* of Carrigtwohill shown below.
   On your sketch map show and name and four different zones of urban land use.

   Or:

   Draw a sketch map of the *aerial photograph* of Carrigtwohill shown below.
   On your sketch show and name the following:
   - A church with a graveyard
   - A small industrial estate
   - An open-air recreational area
   - A residential area
   - The CBD or main street
   - A major road

   Test Yourself eTest.ie

   (Based on frequently asked LC Higher and Ordinary Level questions)

Carrigtwohill, Co. Cork

2. Examine the aerial photograph of Carrigtwohill shown on the previous page.
   (a) State the location on the photograph of a small industrial estate or business park.
   (b) Do you think that this industrial estate or business park is suitably located? Give three reasons for your answer, referring to the photograph in each case.

   Or:

   Imagine that you have been given the task of locating a new housing estate somewhere in the area represented by the photograph.
   (a) Name the location of your choice (use terms such as 'left background' or 'right middleground', etc.).
   (b) Explain clearly one reason in favour of this location and one reason against it.

   (Based on an LC Ordinary Level question)

3. Describe and explain the land zones in any city that you have studied.

   (LC Higher Level question)

4. With reference to an example that you have studied, describe and explain changing land uses in urban areas.

   (LC Higher Level question)

5. The diagram in Figure 9 refers to the *bid-rent theory*, which seeks to explain variations in land values and related land uses in urban areas. Describe the main points of the bid-rent theory and examine their accuracy in relation to any one city of your choice.

6. 'As cities expand they impact on the surrounding rural areas.'
   Discuss this statement with reference to examples that you have studied.

   (LC Higher Level question – 30 marks)

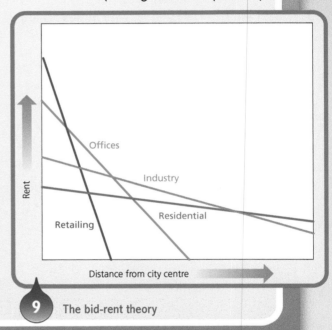

9 The bid-rent theory

Exam training: Leaving Cert question, marking scheme and sample answer

The question

Examine the two urban land use models from Hoyt and Burgess shown in Figure 10 on the next page. Explain two main differences between the two models.

(LC Ordinary Level question)

Leaving Cert Marking Scheme
Two differences at 20 marks each marked as follows:

- Difference stated   = 5 marks
- Difference explained by 5 SRPs at 3 marks each   = 15 marks

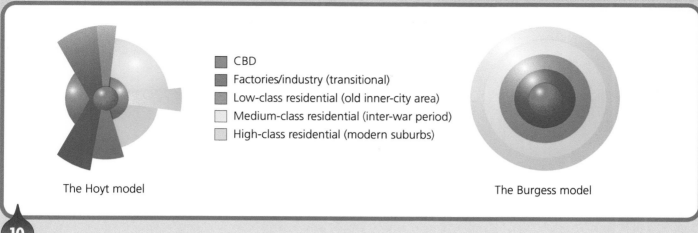

CBD
Factories/industry (transitional)
Low-class residential (old inner-city area)
Medium-class residential (inter-war period)
High-class residential (modern suburbs)

The Hoyt model

The Burgess model

10

Use the marking scheme given on the previous page to correct and mark this sample answer.

Sample answer

1   One difference between the two land use models is that the Burgess model is designed completely around concentric circles. In contrast, Hoyt's model also contains some wedge-shaped land use 'sectors'. This is why the Burgess model is called the concentric zone model, while Hoyt's theory is called the sector model. Burgess assumes that the 'typical' city develops on flat and featureless land. Hoyt, on the other hand, recognises that important routeways influence the shape of urban growth. Burgess places his industrial 'transitional' zone in a circle around the CBD. Hoyt's industrial zone follows a major railway line or a navigable waterway. This runs along a long narrow wedge or 'sector' that radiates out from near the CBD.

2   Burgess places his 'low-class residential' zone in a circular, old inner-city area. He claimed that the wealth of urban dwellers increases with distance from the city centre, with high-income families occupying modern, 'high-class' residences in the outer suburbs. Hoyt, on the other hand, placed his 'high-class residential zone' along a wedge of land extending to the outer suburbs.

   Burgess assumed that all inner-city residential areas are old and low-income zones and that high-income families inhabit the urban fringe only. In Dublin, however, regenerated inner-city areas now contain many new and 'exclusive' apartment residences. Urban fringe developments, on the other hand, include working-class, local authority housing in places such as Darndale.

   Hoyt's idea of a wedge-shaped sector of high-income residential land use seems to be more relevant today. A sector of such land use exists, for example, along south Dublin's coast between Blackrock and Dalkey.

10 Urban Problems

Urban decay in inner-city areas

The term **inner city** usually means the area that surrounds a city's CBD. Inner-city areas include the Liberties in Dublin and Blackpool in Cork.

As cities expanded outwards over time, some inner-city areas fell into *social, economic and population decline*. This decline is referred to as **urban decay**. It happened, for example, in Dublin and other Irish cities between the 1930s and the 1980s, when it was associated with the following occurrences:

- **People** migrated to the suburbs, where some were rehoused in big new 'corporation' (city council) housing estates such as in Ballyfermot (Dublin), Churchfield (Cork) and Ballybeg (Waterford). Suburban houses offered bathroom, garden and playground facilities that were not widely available in old inner-city housing.

- Manufacturing **industries** and warehouses abandoned their ageing inner-city buildings. They relocated to outer suburbs where there was more space, cheaper land and less traffic congestion. The loss of inner-city industrial employment forced more people to migrate to the suburbs.

- As more people migrated to the suburbs, inner-city shops, schools and other **services** began to close. The loss of such services also contributed to a spiral of out-migration from inner-city areas.

This chapter will examine the following urban problems:
- Urban decay
- Urban sprawl
- Absence of community
- Traffic congestion.

Revise
Urban decay on page 268 of your Changing World core textbook.

Inner-city decay in Dublin in the 1980s. Most formerly decayed inner-city areas have now undergone urban regeneration.

Poverty: the main problem of urban decay

Poverty has been the greatest overall problem associated with inner-city decay. This poverty has had many interrelated facets:

- As industry migrated to the suburbs, many inner-city areas became **unemployment** 'black spots'.

- Out-migration resulted in the closure of shops, schools and other important services. These closures **undermined community spirit** and encouraged even more people to abandon city centre areas. This contributed to a *spiral of out-migration and decay*.

- Many enterprising young adults migrated from inner-city areas. Remaining inner-city populations therefore contained large proportions of **older**, **poorly educated** or **poorer people**, many of whom were less well equipped to cope with mounting inner-city problems.

- **Old run-down buildings** blighted the environment in many inner-city areas. Vacated buildings fell into disrepair. Some were boarded up and abandoned for many years before being resold by speculators for 'development' purposes.

- Some decayed buildings were demolished and replaced by **large local authority apartment blocks** such as Fatima Mansions in Dublin and in Blackpool, Cork. Some of these apartment blocks were of such poor quality that they, in turn, eventually had to be demolished.

- As poverty and decay deepened in inner-city areas, so did some residents' feelings of alienation and despair. These feelings contributed sometimes to **drug abuse, anti-social behaviour and crime**.

1 A cartoonist's idea of inner-city decay.

(a) *Which facets of urban decay are illustrated in this cartoon?*

(b) *Are these facets of decay typical of Irish inner-city areas today? Explain.*

Urban regeneration

Urban regeneration has been widely used to reverse the problems of urban decay. Regeneration can take the form of urban *redevelopment* or urban *renewal*.

- **Urban redevelopment** involves demolishing old inner-city buildings and rehousing their inhabitants in suburban areas. Valuable inner-city sites are then used mainly for new commercial buildings. The development of the International Financial Services Centre in the *Custom House Quay* area is an example of redevelopment in Dublin.

- **Urban renewal** involves refurbishing or rebuilding decayed houses and apartments, mainly for existing inhabitants. It also involves providing shops and other social services that might encourage people to remain in their old neighbourhoods. Regeneration in the *Liberties* is an example of urban renewal in Dublin's inner city. The regeneration of *Ballymun* is an example of urban renewal in Dublin's northern urban fringe (see pages 136–137).

Case Study
Ballymun – from 'faulty towers' to urban regeneration

Ballymun's 'Faulty Towers'

In 1966, hundreds of Dubliners were moved from decayed inner-city areas to new tower-block apartments in Ballymun on the northern fringe of the city. Ballymun's seven tower blocks were then a source of great excitement and national pride. Soaring above other buildings, they were seen as a symbol of Ireland's social and economic development. They were, however, a colossal failure.

The new tower block apartments were of poor quality. Substandard insulation left them noisy, cold in winter and sometimes uncomfortably hot in summer. Their vandalised lifts often malfunctioned, forcing some residents to carry children and shopping up fifteen storeys of stairwells. A shortage of work and of basic services such as local shops contributed to feelings of stress and depression. Ballymun gradually degenerated into a decayed area of high unemployment, drug abuse and petty crime.

Ballymun's former apartment tower blocks

The regeneration of Ballymun

In 1997, Dublin City Council launched a long-term plan for the **urban regeneration of Ballymun**. The Council set up a company called *Ballymun Regeneration Ltd* to carry out this plan with the advice and approval of the local community. The ongoing regeneration programme includes the following successful strategies.

- Old high-rise tower blocks were demolished and their residents were rehoused in comfortable, well-insulated **low-rise dwellings** of one to four storeys. A total of up to 3,500 new homes are planned for Ballymun. There will be a 50:50 split between public and private housing in order to avoid social stratification in the area.
- Ballymun's new houses will be part of a new town of up to 30,000 people. The **town centre** will include a half-kilometre long Main Street that will provide a variety of shops, banks, restaurants, cafés and other services.
- The new town will be divided into **neighbourhoods**, each of which will provide day-to-day facilities such as playgrounds, parks and corner shops.
- The town will provide a full range of educational and recreational **services**, including schools and sports facilities such as playing fields and swimming pools. It will also be well serviced by public bus routes and eventually by Dublin's planned metro system.
- A **technology park** has been developed near the Ballymun exit from the M50 motorway. This is ideally located to attract industries and other businesses that will help to provide employment for the new town.

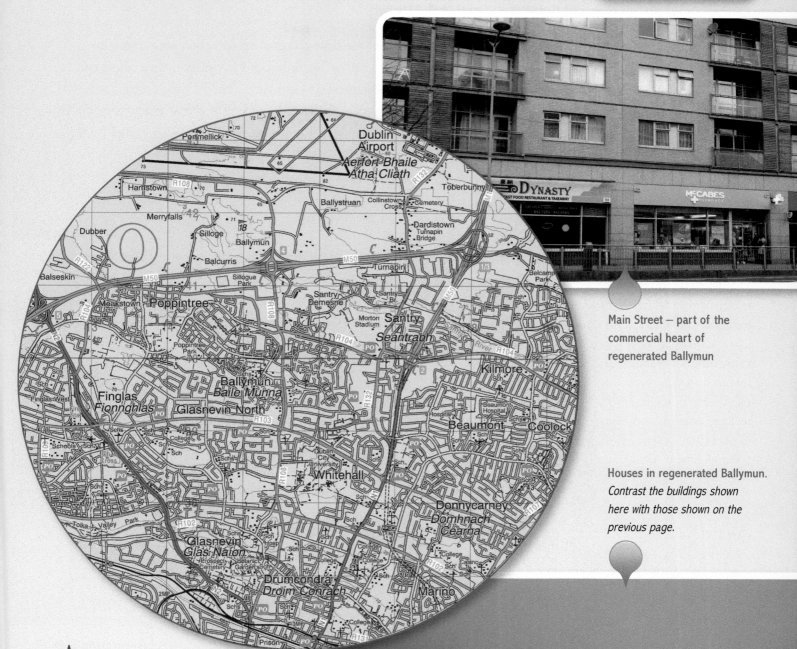

Main Street – part of the commercial heart of regenerated Ballymun

Houses in regenerated Ballymun. *Contrast the buildings shown here with those shown on the previous page.*

2

Ballymun and other north Dublin areas.

(a) Describe the location of Ballymun. Refer to a grid reference, to major roads and to neighbouring urban areas.

(b) Explain in detail why this is a suitable location for a technology park or industrial estate.

(c) How might the presence of green areas assist the regeneration of Ballymun? Be specific in your answer.

Revise
- Pages 266–267 of your *Changing World* core textbook.
- Pages 126–129 of this book.

Urban sprawl

Urban sprawl is the excessive outward growth of urban areas into the surrounding countryside. It has been especially common since the mid-twentieth century and has affected Irish cities. Dublin, for example, now sprawls more than 20 kilometres from Darndale in the north to Shankill in the south. In 2006 the European Environmental Agency identified Dublin as one of the worst cities in Europe for urban sprawl.

Some causes of urban sprawl

1 Rural to urban migration

Rural to urban migration has caused the population and the spatial size of cities to expand rapidly. This is especially so in the case of Third World cities such as Mumbai and Kolkata in India; but it is also true of urban areas such as Dublin, the population of which grew by 70 per cent between 1961 and 2011. The effect of rural to urban migration is magnified by the fact that many migrants are young adults who are most likely to contribute to urban birth rates and therefore to resulting urban expansion.

2 Increased car ownership

Increased personal wealth resulted in a rapid rise in car ownership in First World cities throughout the second half of the twentieth century. This allowed increasing numbers of better-off city people to migrate out into the suburbs and to commute to and from their work in the cities. Suburbs thus grew larger and larger until they eventually took the form of full-blown urban sprawl. Middle-class migration to the suburbs also increased poverty and urban decay in some inner-city areas. This prompted even more outward urban migration and so contributed further to a spiral of urban sprawl.

Sprawling Los Angeles. The US city of Los Angeles contains one of the world's largest urban sprawls. This is partly because of people's excessive reliance on cars as a means of transport. The presence of large multi-lane highways in the heart of the city is a sign of this reliance.

Facts

In 2007 the Irish Urban Forum warned that **Dublin's urban sprawl** was growing so rapidly that it might eventually equal that of Los Angeles.

3 Planning strategies

Urban planning strategies in countries such as Ireland sometimes contribute to urban sprawl. These strategies are usually formulated in response to popular demand.

- Increasing car numbers create demands for new or improved **access roads** in cities. The development of major access roads such as the M50 in Dublin and the N25 'South Ring' in Cork have been developed in response to these demands. But such roads encourage even more commuting and therefore more suburban growth.

- Urban sprawl also creates a demand for suburban or **out-of-town shopping centres,** business parks and industrial estates. But building such facilities at places such as Liffey Valley in Dublin, Douglas in Cork and Dooradoyle in Limerick creates suburban hubs that may in turn stimulate even more suburban sprawl.

- Most Irish urban dwellers prefer one- or two-storey houses with gardens to multi-storey apartment buildings. In response to this preference, our city suburbs are made up almost entirely of middle-density or **low-density** housing estates. Such housing takes up a great deal of space and so contributes hugely to urban sprawl.

- Large **local authority housing estates** have been built in places such as Darndale (Dublin), Knocknaheeny (Cork) and Ballybeg (Waterford). They were built on urban fringes and so contributed to outward urban growth.

Urban sprawl in Waterford. Identify and locate three items or features in this photograph that might contribute to urban sprawl. Explain how the items you identify contribute to urban sprawl.

Some effects of urban sprawl

1 Damage to rural environments

- Urban sprawl has 'swallowed up' unique **rural villages** such as Dundrum in Dublin and Douglas in Cork and has surrounded them with large, monotonous and sometimes poorly serviced suburbs.

- **Farmland** is rezoned for residential, commercial or other urban purposes. This has happened in places such as Rush and Swords in north Co. Dublin, where a great deal of fertile land has been lost to agriculture.

- **Rural ecosystems** are harmed by urban sprawl. The destruction of *farmlands and hedgerows* deprive a wide variety of plants and animals of their habitat and force some animals such as foxes to forage for survival in expanding urban areas. The expansion of urban areas into *wetlands* damages the unique habitat of plants such as sphagnum moss and animals such as frogs.

- Increased building on river **flood plains** can contribute to rapid run-off and thus to the occurrence of flash floods following periods of heavy rain. Such floods have caused serious damage to residential and commercial property in urban areas such as Cork and Clonmel.

2 Increased commuting

As cities expand outwards, commuting times and distances tend to increase within them. The US city of Los Angeles has now grown so large that commuters spend an average of two hours a day travelling to and from work. Increased commuting has also led to the overuse of cars within the Greater Dublin Area. It is feared that this may increase heart disease, obesity and social isolation among commuters. It may also increase air and noise pollution in urban areas.

3 An absence of community

Absence of community has been a problem in some new suburban areas: see the page opposite.

River flooding in Cork City, November 2009.
How might increased urbanisation in the Lee river valley contribute to flooding such as this?

Absence of community

Many old inner-city areas once enjoyed such tightly knit communities that they were described as 'urban villages'. Neighbouring families often inhabited the same street for several generations. Shared memories, loyalties and values helped to bind these families together as close-knit communities. This led to the development of mutual support networks that might include child minding, borrowing and lending household items and assisting neighbours in need.

From the 1930s onwards, many people were moved from inner-city areas and rehoused in new, sprawling suburban schemes. This led to improved housing conditions for many. It contributed, however, to a loss of community both in suburban and inner-city areas.

- People who moved to the **suburbs** were often separated into different housing estates where they did not know their neighbours. With the loss of family and old neighbourhood support systems, they suffered from prolonged feelings of social isolation and alienation. Such feelings sometimes led to anti-social behaviour, drug-taking or even crime.

- As mainly young people moved to the suburbs, older people who **remained in inner-city area**s began also to suffer from an absence of community. Deprived of their children and grandchildren, they felt the loss of schools, shops and other services that give vitality to neighbourhoods. Feelings of loneliness and isolation were sometimes mixed with fear as crime and anti-social behaviour accompanied the decay of depopulated inner-city areas.

Responding to an absence of community

Urban renewal is the process of regenerating city areas so as to encourage people to remain in their old neighbourhoods. Urban planners use *mixed development schemes* as an aspect of urban renewal. These schemes provide housing, services and employment within the same neighbourhood. Some affordable housing is usually included within those schemes to ensure that they attract people from a variety of social backgrounds.

Revise *urban renewal on page 135.*

A memory of inner Dublin

I remember, in the mid 1930s, when the new corporation housing schemes were completed in Crumlin, Kimmage and Drimnagh, some of our neighbours with large families, cooped up in single rooms, were dispatched to the wilds.

Within days they had returned, almost demented, trying to get their rooms back. They complained that the 'air was too strong' in the schemes, that they couldn't live next door to strangers, that they were too far away from the Mammy, that there were no shops. And worst of all, there was no one to 'borry' a bit of tea or sugar from. 'You could be got dead out there and the devil a wan id know – or care.'

It was this 'caring' within the old communities that made them special. There was never any problem about getting somebody to mind the 'babby' or to keep an eye on the sick old granny or to get someone to run to the shops for a few messages – and you were never stuck if you needed 'the lend of a loan'.

From Marian Johnston in the Irish Times.

What does this newspaper extract tell us about community life in Dublin in the 1930s?

Inner-city Dublin in the 1930s.
Do you think the people shown here would wish to he rehoused in the suburbs? Explain your answer carefully.

Responding to the problems of urban sprawl

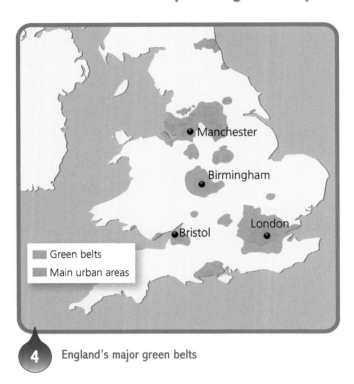

4   England's major green belts

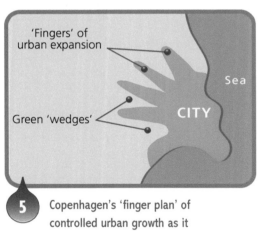

5   Copenhagen's 'finger plan' of controlled urban growth as it was first outlined in 1947

Revise page 267 of your Changing World core textbook.

1   Green belts and wedges

Green belts are preserved areas of countryside that surround large cities. Building is severely restricted within green belts so that the countryside there is preserved for farming and recreation. Green belts were first established in England in 1947 in order to check uncontrolled urban sprawl from cities such as London and to prevent large urban areas merging together. More than 10 per cent of England now consists of green belt areas that surround cities such as London, Manchester and Bristol (see Figure 4).

A variation of the green belt concept is the provision of '**green wedges**' that radiate outwards from inner suburbs. These preserved green areas get wider as they expand outwards and many urban planners believe that they are more achievable and effective than green belts. Copenhagen in Denmark uses such green wedges to control urban sprawl. They form part of what is called Copenhagen's 'finger plan' of expansion, in which 'fingers' of urban growth are allowed to develop between preserved 'green wedges' (see Figure 5).

2   New Towns

New towns such as Tallaght, Blanchardstown and Lucan-Clondalkin have been built on the western fringes of Dublin. The purpose of these new towns is to house some of Dublin's overspill population and thus to stem the city's uncontrolled urban sprawl.

3   National Spatial Strategy

The uncontrolled growth of Dublin has adversely affected the development of other Irish urban centres. To counteract this unbalanced development, the government launched a National Spatial Strategy in 2002. This strategy encourages the development of 'gateways' and 'hubs', which are urban growth centres outside the capital.

Traffic congestion

Many city streets and access roads now suffer from severe traffic congestion. Traffic jams are especially common on busy city routes during morning and evening *peak traffic periods,* when most people commute to and from their workplace.

More than nine-tenths of all goods and passenger movements in Ireland are by road.

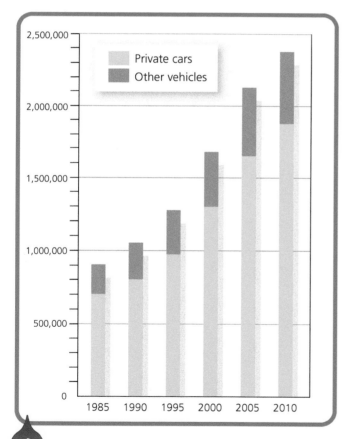

6 Motor vehicles in Ireland in selected years.

(a) *State the number of private cars in Ireland in 1985.*

(b) *What was the total number of motor vehicles in 1995?*

(c) *By how much did the number of private cars increase between 1985 and 2010?*

(d) *Describe and account for the changes in total motor vehicle numbers between 1985 and 2010.*

Causes of traffic congestion

1 Increasing numbers of motor vehicles

Rapid growth in motor vehicle ownership has been a major cause of urban traffic congestion in countries such as Ireland.

- Private **car** ownership in Ireland increased dramatically from the 1960s onwards. Between 1996 and 2008, for example, the number of cars in Ireland almost doubled. This was largely owing to increased incomes and to a consumerist 'borrow and spend' culture that accompanied the Celtic Tiger economic boom years. By 2008, a large proportion of Irish families possessed two or more cars and the number of cars in Ireland exceeded 1.9 million.

- The Celtic Tiger economic boom also resulted in a huge increase in Ireland's number of trucks and other **heavy goods vehicles** (HGVs). Heavy vehicles can have a particularly negative impact on traffic congestion. They did so in places such as Dublin's quay areas prior to the opening of the Dublin Port Tunnel in 2006.

- The Irish government and local authorities have tried hard to match rising vehicle numbers with better **road facilities** such as the Jack Lynch Tunnel in Cork and the M50 ring road in Dublin. It has proved impossible, however, to meet the demands of increased traffic in all urban areas. The streets and access roads of Dublin, for example, now have to cope with more than half a million vehicles each day. Traffic congestion, especially during peak traffic hours, is an inevitable result of this.

The world's worst traffic jam.
The world's worst traffic jam happened on the outskirts of Beijing, China in August 2010. It stretched for 100 kilometres and moved as slowly as two kilometres a day. The congestion took more than two weeks to clear. Stranded motorists passed the time by playing cards and chess.

2 Urban design

- The **old streets** of many urban areas were built long before the invention of motor vehicles. Many of these streets are too narrow to accommodate more than one lane of cars or trucks. This led to serious traffic congestion that was eased only with the introduction of one-way traffic systems and strict parking restrictions. Such narrow streets include South Frederick Street in Dublin and lanes such as Drawbridge Street, which joins Patrick Street in Cork.

- Important **routes often converge** close to the centre of cities. The meeting of such routes can create traffic bottlenecks, such as at O'Connell's Bridge in Dublin and Patrick's Bridge in Cork.

- Irish cities tend to consist largely of middle- to **low-density housing**, such as terraced or semi-detached dwellings with front and back gardens. This low-density urban design has caused Dublin to sprawl outwards for up to 14 kilometres from its centre. Urban sprawl forces people who live in outer suburbs to commute relatively long distances to and from the city centre. In the absence of a highly developed and fully integrated public transport system, such commuting is done mainly by car. This situation has contributed greatly to traffic congestion in cities such as Dublin.

A suburb on Howth Road in Dublin.

(a) *Does this photograph show high-density or low-density housing?*

(b) *How can housing density affect urban traffic congestion?*

Some effects of traffic congestion

Health and safety

- Traffic congestion contributes to many minor **accidents** on overcrowded roads or streets. Such accidents often result in personal injury and financial loss for those involved.
- Traffic congestion contributes to long commuting periods that may damage the **physical and mental wellbeing** of motorists. Some workers spend more than three hours a day commuting between Dublin and towns in counties such as Wexford and Westmeath. Some long-distance commuters may become prone to obesity because they have neither the time nor the energy to take sufficient physical exercise. They may also be subject to harmful mental stress while in congested traffic.

Environmental effects

Excessive motor traffic can be environmentally unsustainable on a number of counts:

- When motor vehicles idle in congested traffic they continue to emit benzene fumes, hydrocarbons and gases such as carbon monoxide and nitrogen oxides. Prolonged doses of these **air pollutants** can aggravate human respiratory illnesses such as asthma and bronchitis. They may also contribute to heart disease and to the growth of cancerous tumours. These pollutants are believed also to damage the world's ozone layer and to contribute to the occurrence of acid rain.
- Idling car engines continue to burn petroleum, which is a valuable and **finite resource** that will be seriously depleted in the course of this century.
- **Noise** pollution can be a concern for the residents of busy city streets such as South Douglas Road in Cork and Harold's Cross in Dublin.
- Local authorities build new roads, widen existing roads and create more car parks in efforts to reduce traffic congestion. These facilities use up large amounts of valuable **urban space**. More than a third of the urban space of Los Angeles is now taken up with private driveways, roads, parking spaces and other car-related facilities.

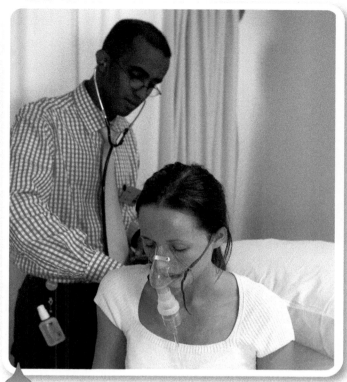

A hospital patient suffering from severe asthma.
How might excessive motor traffic contribute to illnesses such as asthma?

The Red Cow roundabout on the M50 in west Dublin.
Increasing amounts of land are now being devoted to roads and other vehicle-related facilities.

145

Solutions to traffic congestion

1 Traffic management techniques

A variety of techniques are employed to improve traffic flow and to reduce traffic congestion in urban areas.

Revise
*page 167
of your
Changing World
core textbook.*

The following strategies are used to assist **traffic flow and road safety**:

- Traffic flow is often assisted by the use of marked *traffic lanes, one-way street systems, roundabouts* and *ring roads* or *bypass roads.*

- Traffic flow is also helped by the operation of on-street parking restrictions. *Single or double yellow lines* painted on the edges of streets may signal these restrictions. Single yellow lines indicate that parking is prohibited during business hours. Double yellow lines mean that parking is never allowed. *Yellow boxes* are sometimes painted on streets at important junctions or outside fire brigade or Garda stations. These painted grids indicate that motorists should not enter a 'box' unless they are sure they can drive through it without interruption.

- Parking restrictions need to be compensated for by the provision of ample *parking places* on the sides of selected streets or in off-street open-air or multi-storey *car parks.*

- Traffic flow is now sometimes assisted by the use of centrally controlled closed-circuit TV (*CCTV*) *cameras* that monitor traffic flow and that direct clamping company operatives to illegally parked vehicles.

- The use of *traffic lights* and *pedestrian crossings* further promote traffic flow and road safety.

- *Cycle lanes* and *pedestrian streets* improve safety by filtering cyclists and pedestrians away from motor traffic.

Carlow Town.
Describe the traffic management features visible in this photograph.

2 Promoting public transport

A well-filled bus can transport as many passengers as are normally carried by dozens of cars. A train has even more carrying capacity than a bus. It is clear, therefore, that improved public transport is a major key to reducing traffic congestion in urban areas.

Government and local authority initiatives have improved **Dublin's public transport system**:

- Street lanes called **quality bus corridors** are reserved for buses and taxis. This initiative has helped to speed up bus transport and to increase public transport usage throughout the city.

- The **Luas** consists of two electrified light railway lines that link the southern and southwestern suburbs and fringes of Dublin to the city centre. These lines are supported by five 'park-and-ride' stations at places such as the Naas Road and they carry a total of up to half a million passengers a week. It to now planned to integrate the two existing lines into one unified Luas system.

- The **DART** railway system serves the coastal area between Malahide in the north and Greystones in the south. An integrated ticketing system has been introduced, which allows passengers to use a single ticket to access Luas, DART and Dublin Bus services.

- Dublin's **bike-rental scheme** is a new and novel mode of public transport throughout the inner city (see the box on the next page).

- A **metro** system between St Stephen's Green and Dublin Airport has been planned. Much of this rail system would run underground or on elevated over-ground tracks. Work was due to begin on the system in 2011 but was postponed because of a shortage of funds.

The Luas

The DART

A quality bus corridor in Dublin

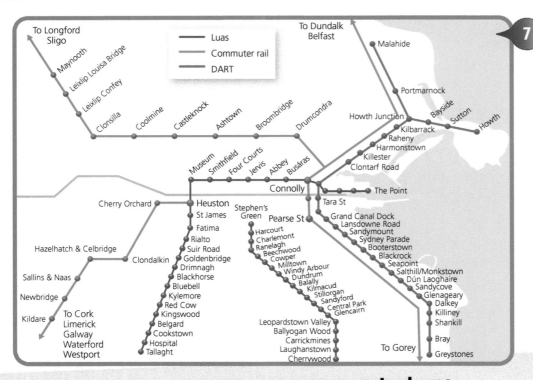

Luas
Commuter rail
DART

To Longford
Sligo
Maynooth
Leixlip Louisa Bridge
Leixlip Confey
Clonsilla
Coolmine
Castleknock
Ashtown
Broombridge
Drumcondra
To Dundalk
Belfast
Malahide
Portmarnock
Howth Junction
Kilbarrack
Raheny
Harmonstown
Killester
Clontarf Road
Bayside
Sutton
Howth
Museum
Smithfield
Four Courts
Jervis
Abbey
Busáras
Connolly
The Point
Cherry Orchard
Heuston
St James
Fatima
Rialto
Suir Road
Goldenbridge
Drimnagh
Blackhorse
Bluebell
Kylemore
Red Cow
Kingswood
Belgard
Cookstown
Hospital
Tallaght
Stephen's
Green
Pearse St
Harcourt
Charlemont
Ranelagh
Beechwood
Cowper
Milltown
Windy Arbour
Dundrum
Balally
Kilmacud
Stillorgan
Sandyford
Central Park
Glencairn
Leopardstown Valley
Ballyogan Wood
Carrickmines
Laughanstown
Cherrywood
Tara St
Grand Canal Dock
Lansdowne Road
Sandymount
Sydney Parade
Booterstown
Blackrock
Seapoint
Salthill/Monkstown
Dún Laoghaire
Sandycove
Glenageary
Dalkey
Killiney
Shankill
Bray
Greystones
Hazelhatch & Celbridge
Clondalkin
Sallins & Naas
Newbridge
Kildare
To Cork
Limerick
Galway
Waterford
Westport
To Gorey

7

Some public transport networks in Dublin in 2010.

(a) Explain how you could use the transport networks shown here to travel from Clondalkin in west Dublin to Killiney on the coast.

(b) What advantage does an integrated ticketing system provide for somebody who is making the journey outlined in question (a) above?

The speedy success of Dublin's bike rental scheme

Dublin's bicycle rental scheme began in September 2009. A total of 550 bikes were then made available in 50 bicycle stations that surround the city centre.

People can access bikes by registering for an annual fee of €10. Registered persons can borrow a bicycle from any station and deposit it in any other station. Bike usage is free for the first half-hour and comes at a nominal cost of 50 cent for each successive half-hour.

The scheme is paid for through advertising. A French advertising company pays for and maintains the system in return for being allowed to erect large advertising hoardings throughout the city. The company generates profit for itself by renting spaces on the hoardings to local businesses.

Within a year of its launch, Dublin's bike rental scheme had 47,000 registered users and claimed more than a million individual rentings. Dublin City Council has described the scheme as the most successful of its kind in Europe.

Bicycles at a renting station in **Temple Bar**

Sum Up

- **Urban decay** happened in inner-city areas when people and industry migrated from inner cities to suburbs.
- Causes of **poverty** associated with urban decay include *unemployment, damaged community spirit, derelict buildings, poor housing* and feelings of *alienation* that can lead to *drug abuse* or *anti-social behaviour*.
- **Urban regeneration** reverses urban decay. Urban *redevelopment* replaces old dwellings with new commercial buildings. Urban *renewal* refurbishes inner-city areas for existing inhabitants.
- People from Dublin's inner city were once unsuccessfully rehoused in apartment tower blocks in **Ballymun**. The regeneration of Ballymun now features 'low-rise' dwellings, a town centre, ample services and a technology park.
- **Urban sprawl** is the excessive outward growth of urban areas.
- **Causes** of urban sprawl:
  - *Rural to urban migration*, which increases the spatial size of cities.
  - *Increased car ownership*, which allows people to commute from ever-expanding suburbs.
  - *Planning strategies* that include the building of new urban access roads, suburban shopping centres and low-density housing estates.
- **Effects** of urban sprawl:
  - *Rural environmental damage* that includes the swallowing up of villages and farmland, damage to rural ecosystems and increased river flooding.
  - *Excessive commuting*, which can damage human health and lead to increased air and noise pollution.
  - An *absence of community* in monotonous new suburbs.
- **Solutions** to urban sprawl include:
  - *Green belts and wedges* that restrict building in areas around or within cities.
  - *New towns* that house the overspill populations of cities.
  - A *National Spatial Strategy* that develops smaller urban 'gateways' and 'hubs' so as to counteract the overdevelopment of cities such as Dublin.
- Urban **traffic congestion** has been **caused** by:
  - An increase in the number of *motor vehicles,* especially during times of economic boom.
  - *Urban design* that includes old *narrow streets, route convergence* in city centres and *urban sprawl* that leads to increased commuting.
- Traffic congestion can have the following adverse **effects**:
  - It can lead to road *accidents* and can contribute to *health problems* such as obesity and mental stress.
  - It can cause air and noise *pollution* and contribute to the overuse of petroleum.
- **Solutions** to traffic congestion include:
  - A variety of *traffic management* techniques that range from using lane markings to providing pedestrianised streets.
  - The promotion of *public transport*, such as DART and Luas services in Dublin.

1. (a) What is *urban decay*?
    (b) Examine one problem of and one attempted solution to urban decay in relation to a city that you have studied.

2. (a) Explain the term *urban sprawl*.
    (b) Explain two causes of and one problem resulting from urban sprawl in any city studied by you.
    (LC Ordinary Level – 30 marks)

3. Explain fully two reasons why it is important to preserve green belts within towns and cities. (LC Ordinary Level – 30 marks)

4. Examine two of the main problems created by the continued pace of urban growth in a region you have studied.
    (LC Higher Level – 30 marks)

5. (a) Explain the term 'traffic congestion'.
    (b) Explain two methods of overcoming traffic congestion. Use examples you have studied in your answer. (LC Higher Level – 30 marks)

6. (a) Explain two causes of traffic congestion in any city studied by you. Clearly state the name of the city in your answer.
    (b) Explain in detail one solution to this traffic congestion.
    (LC Ordinary Level – 40 marks)

7. *Cities are places of opportunities but also have problems.*
    Examine this statement, with reference to a city or cities of your choice.
    (LC Higher Level – 30 marks)

Marking Scheme for Question 4

Two problems named	= 2 + 2 marks
One urban region or city named	= 2 marks
Examination of problems: At least 12 SRPs (6 SRPs for each problem) at 2 marks each	= 24 marks
Total	**= 30 marks**

Hint:

The examination of both problems must be tied to the same urban region or city.

Leaving Cert question, marking scheme and sample answer

The question

(a) Examine the *aerial photograph of Galway on the facing page*. Locate two areas where traffic congestion can create problems. Use the usual notation (e.g. right background, etc.).

(b) Select one area in part (a) and using evidence from the photograph explain why traffic congestion might occur at that location.

(c) Examine in detail one possible solution to this traffic congestion.
(LC Ordinary Level – 40 marks)

The Marking Scheme

Two suitable locations given at 3 marks each	= 6 marks
Evidence explained: 5 SRPs at 3 marks each	= 15 marks
Solution named	= 4 marks
Solution examined: 5 SRPs at 3 marks each	= 15 marks
Total	**= 40 marks**

Galway

Sample answer

(a) Traffic congestion might create problems:

1   At the street junction just to the left of the centre foreground.

2   Along the narrow street in the right foreground and centre foreground.

Use the marking scheme provided to mark this sample answer.

(b) Traffic congestion might occur at place (1) in answer (a) above. At least three streets meet at this place and where streets meet traffic converges. At least one of these streets appears from the photograph to have some commercial function, so the street in question might experience quite heavy traffic. The presence of a well-filled car park (on the right foreground) close to the junction also supports my belief that traffic might be heavy. The converging streets are quite narrow and this would increase traffic congestion. So would the fact that two of the streets meet at an acute angle. This angle would make it more difficult for traffic to negotiate the junction corner between these two streets.

(c) More public transport would help to solve traffic congestion problems.

A well-filled bus can carry as many passengers as are normally carried by dozens of cars. It follows, therefore, that improved public bus services could help to take many cars off the streets and so reduce traffic congestion. The provision of traffic lanes called 'quality bus corridors' that are reserved for buses and taxis only has reduced traffic congestion in Dublin. The same might also be provided in Galway. The provision of a suburban rail service similar to Dublin's DART system might also be useful. Such a system might, however, be too expensive for a city of Galway's modest size. A bicycle rental scheme, on the other hand, might prove both inexpensive and effective. Dublin's bike rental system is funded entirely by advertising.

Air, Water and Waste – Environmental Issues in Urban Areas

Air quality in cities

When fossil fuels* are burned, a cocktail of gases such as carbon dioxide, chlorine and oxides of nitrogen are emitted into the atmosphere. Sunlight causes some of these gases to react chemically with each other, greatly increasing their harmful effects on human health, plant growth and other aspects of the environment.

The burning of fossil fuels in homes, in places of industry and in motor vehicles has therefore been a major cause of air pollution in urban areas. *Smog*, *acid rain* and *greenhouse gases* are all associated with this pollution.

- **Smog** is a mixture of smoke and fog that appears most typically over densely populated areas in times of calm winter weather. In such weather conditions, cold heavy air becomes trapped beneath a layer of warmer air above it – an occurrence called *temperature inversion*. With no wind to blow them away, chimney smoke, car emissions and other pollutants soon build up in the cold air and create brown or yellowish smog. Smoke is the most visible but by no means the only pollutant in smog. There is also likely to be a cocktail of harmful gases and chemicals such as ozone, sulphur dioxide and oxides of nitrogen. These pollutants irritate people's lungs, throat and eyes and are particularly harmful to people who suffer from asthma or other breathing complaints.

- Smog severely affects cities such as Los Angeles (USA) and Milan (Italy). These large cities contain vast numbers of cars, frequently experience calm weather conditions and are surrounded by highlands – factors that all favour the occurrence of temperature inversion and the formation of smog.

Smog over Milan

Fossil fuel emissions such as sulphur dioxide and nitrogen oxides sometimes combine with moisture in the air to form acids. These acids may be carried great distances before eventually falling to the earth as **acid rain**. Acid rain can kill trees, reduce soil fertility, discolour and damage buildings and contribute to human illnesses such as bronchitis.

Urban pollution also contributes to the **greenhouse effect**. Greenhouse gases such as carbon dioxide allow short-wave sunrays to pass in through the earth's atmosphere. But they hinder the outward movement of long-wave heat radiated from the earth. As these gases increase, the temperature of the atmosphere tends also to increase – an occurrence known as *global warming*. Global warming has the potential to lead to climate change, crop failures and sea-level rises that could threaten the wellbeing of our entire planet.

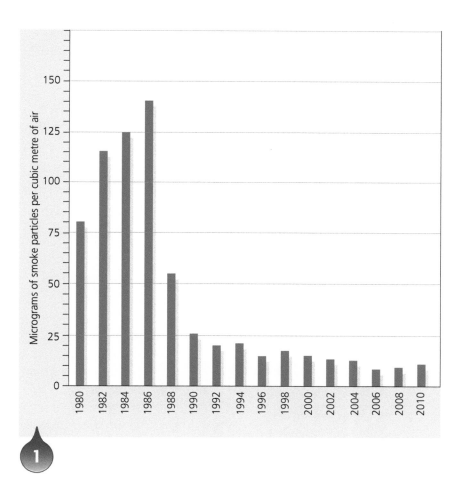

1

Smoke levels in a Dublin suburb between 1980 and 2010.

(a) *Describe the general trends shown.*

(b) *Offer one possible explanation as to why smoke levels rose in this suburban area between 1980 and 1986.*

(c) *Attempt to account for the dramatic decline in smoke levels between 1986 and 1990.*

Combating air pollution in Irish cities

Up to the late 1980s, severe air pollution and smog were common in Irish cities. This was mainly because of the widespread burning of coal as a household fuel. Air pollution diminished dramatically in Irish cities following the **Air Pollution Act 1987**. The Act permitted the use of smokeless coal only, initially in Dublin and later in all Irish cities. Within a year, air pollution levels fell by nearly 70 per cent in the areas affected by the Act.

The Environmental Protection Agency (EPA) has revealed that motor vehicles are the fastest-growing contributors to air pollution in Ireland. But some successful steps have already been taken to help **reduce motor pollution**. Petrol that contains lead is now no longer sold in Ireland. Greater public transport facilities have reduced the need to use private cars in Dublin, Limerick and Cork cities. Such facilities in Dublin now include the DART, the Luas, the Port Tunnel and numerous quality bus corridors. Limerick and Cork benefit from commuter rail links such as those that connect Limerick to Ennis and Cork to Midleton.

Government regulations, incentives and public awareness campaigns have led to improved standards of **insulation** in people's homes. This has reduced the need for home heating in many houses.

Water quality

It is the responsibility of local authorities such as city councils to provide urban areas with clean water supplies. Failure to do so can result in serious health risks. In 2007, for example, many people in **Galway City** became ill because a harmful parasite infected their water supplies. The source of this bug was animal waste and human sewage that had infiltrated the city water supplies from nearby Lough Corrib. Galway people then had to drink bottled water and pre-boil the water they used for cooking. This went on for several months until adequate water treatment was put in place.

The **Dublin area** benefited from the setting up of a sophisticated wastewater treatment system in 2003. This system was part of a project called the **Dublin Bay Project** and it includes the following elements:

- A big wastewater **treatment plant** operates at Ringsend near the city's southern docklands. This treatment plant cost €300 million to build and is one of the most sophisticated in Europe. The plant treats up to 300 million litres of Dublin's sewage and wastewater every day – enough to fill a swimming pool about every two minutes!

- Four large, sunken **pipelines** carry raw sewage into the plant from all parts of the city and another large pipeline pumps treated water from the plant into Dublin Bay.

- **Pumping stations** operate at places such as Sutton and Dún Laoghaire. They assist movement through the pipelines.

It costs about €10 million a year to run the Ringsend treatment system. But the system provides the following **benefits**:

- It ensures that *pollution-free water* enters Dublin Bay.
- It helps to ensure pollution-free *beaches* at places such as Dollymount and Seapoint (which have both won 'Blue Flag' status since the treatment system went into operation).
- Its valuable by-products include *methane gas* and a *fertiliser* called biofert.

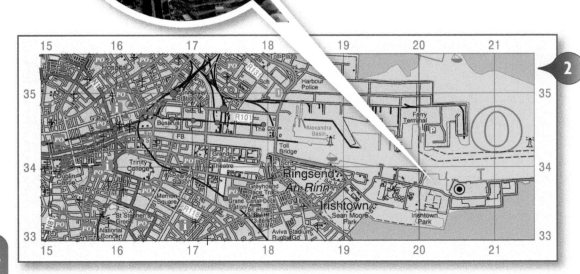

2 The wastewater treatment plant at Ringsend.

(a) Use the OS map provided to identify the building labelled **X** and the green area labelled **Y** on the photograph.

(b) Is the treatment plant suitably located? Explain your answer.

The wastewater treatment processes at Ringsend

1. Wastewater (toilet waste, sink waste, rainwater, etc.) is pumped through large pipes **to the treatment plant**.

2. The wastewater passes through tight **screens** that remove plastics, paper and other foreign objects from the sewage.

3. **Primary treatment** takes place in *settlement tanks*. Heavier sewage sinks to the bottom of the tanks, where it forms *sludge*.

4. The water then passes to **secondary treatment** tanks. *Bacteria* are used to remove ammonia, nitrogen and organic matter.

5. In **tertiary treatment**, *ultraviolet light* is used to disinfect the water. This removes **95** per cent of the original pollutants and makes the water as clean as good-quality river water.

6. Clean water is **pumped into Dublin Bay**.

Useful by-products:
- The *sludge* is heat-treated to kill germs. It is then sold as a fertiliser called **biofert**.
- **Methane** gas emerges from the sludge and provides 55 per cent of the energy that is needed to work the treatment plant.

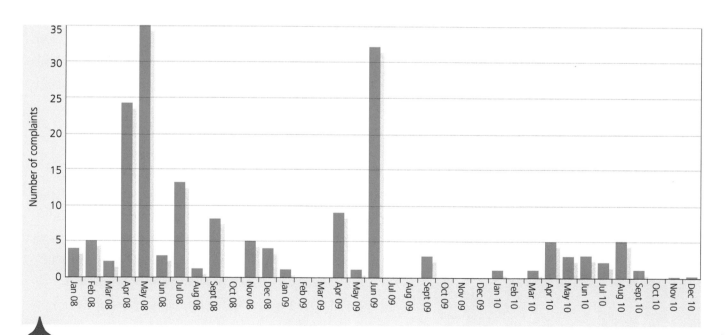

3 Complaints of odours from the Ringsend Wastewater Treatment Plant, January 2008 to October 2010.

(a) Name in rank order the three months in which complaints were most frequent and estimate the number of complaints that were made in each of those months.

(b) In how many months were no complaints made?

(c) Do these graphs support the statement that odour management improved over time at the Ringsend treatment plant? Refer in your answer to information provided by the graph.

Waste management

Waste management presents a major challenge for city councils and other local authorities. It involves overseeing the management and disposal of household, garden, industrial and construction waste. In Ireland, the average household produces 1.2 tonnes of household waste each year.

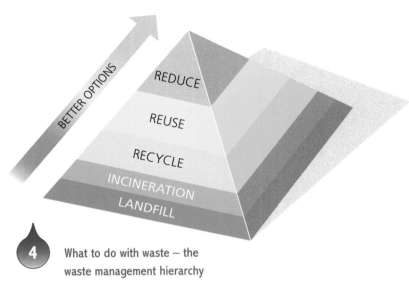

4 What to do with waste – the waste management hierarchy

The pyramid in Figure 4 shows the **options available** in managing waste. It illustrates a *waste management hierarchy*. The options near the top of the pyramid have least environmental impact and therefore should be pursued as much as possible. Options near the base of the pyramid should be minimised because they cause most environmental damage. Waste management in Ireland has traditionally been based on the options at the base of the pyramid.

Landfill

Landfill has been the traditional means of waste disposal. Landfill sites vary enormously in size and quality. They range from smouldering mountains of rubbish in Third World cities such as Manila (the Philippines) to carefully managed, enclosed First World sites in which rubbish is buried. The Kinsale Road landfill in Cork City is an example of such a carefully managed site.

Landfill is regarded as the least favoured waste disposal option because it tends not to be environmentally friendly. **Toxic materials** can seep out of landfill and damage soil and groundwater. Landfill waste can also produce **methane** – a greenhouse gas that contributes to global warming. Another problem with landfill sites is that they quickly become filled with rubbish. Dublin City's two municipal sites, for example, were filled almost to capacity by 2012.

'Smokey Mountain' rubbish dump in Manila.

(a) What environmental hazards might result from this dump?

(b) What do you think the people are doing on the dump?

(c) How might this Third World waste dump contrast with a landfill site in Ireland?

Incineration

In order to reduce landfill, three huge privately owned incinerators have been proposed for **Poolbeg** in Dublin and **Ringaskiddy** near Cork. These huge furnaces would burn domestic waste and (in the case of one Ringaskiddy furnace) toxic waste. The waste would be burned in a controlled environment at more than 850°C.

Incineration companies such as *Indaver* and *Covanta* say that the incineration process can reduce waste to 75 per cent of its original weight and that some of the ash that results from the process could be used in road construction or making concrete. The heat generated by the process could also be used to generate a limited amount of electricity.

Many people oppose incineration on environmental and health grounds. Some of their arguments are outlined in the box.

Some arguments against incineration

- The incineration of waste can produce deadly airborne **dioxins** and other microscopic particles. When these particles accumulate in the bodies of people or animals they can weaken the immune system and cause serious reproductive disorders, breathing difficulties and cancers.
- The incineration process releases **greenhouse gases** that contribute to global warming and climate change.
- Incineration, like landfill, is one of the least favoured waste management options The promotion of incineration instead of landfill is therefore an outdated and essentially **lazy waste strategy**. What is needed is to minimise landfill by reducing, reusing and recycling waste.

Members of CHASE (Cork Harbour Alliance for a Safe Environment) protest against proposed incinerators at Ringaskiddy

Reduce, reuse, recycle

Any sustainable waste strategy must aim especially at reducing, reusing and recycling waste. Only 30 per cent of Dublin's waste is currently recycled, while the figures for Cork and Limerick are 31 and 23 per cent respectively. Dublin hopes eventually to recycle 59 per cent of its total household waste. The following measures might go some way towards achieving this difficult goal.

- A *charge-by-weight* collection system will encourage householders to reduce the amount of rubbish that they generate.
- A *tax at source* on waste might encourage manufacturers and stores to reduce unnecessary packaging on the goods that they produce and sell.
- Separate bins are being used to collect *different categories* of waste. This encourages householders to facilitate recycling by 'sorting' the waste that they generate.

- The burning of fossil fuels is a major cause of **air pollution** in urban areas. *Smog* can harm human health, while *acid rain* can also reduce soil fertility and damage buildings. Air pollution is also associated with greenhouse gases that can contribute to *climate change.*

- Air pollution in Irish cities has been **reduced** by the *Air Pollution Act,* which led to a ban on the use of smoky coal. Improved *public transport* networks and the sale of *lead-free petrol* only has reduced pollution by motor vehicles. Improved *insulation* has reduced fossil fuel consumption in homes.

- The provision of **clean water** is an important function of municipal (urban) authorities. Contaminated water led in 2007 to human illness in *Galway.* The *Dublin Bay Project* provided Dublin with a big water treatment plant at Ringsend, along with associated pipelines and pumping stations. This system treats sewage and other wastewater so that only clean water enters Dublin Bay. By-products of the treatment process include biofert (fertiliser) and methane gas.

- Household and other **waste** should be reduced, reused and recycled rather than incinerated or buried in landfill sites. Ireland needs to do more in this regard.
  - **Landfill** waste can damage soil and groundwater. It also emits methane gas.
  - Big waste **incinerators** have been proposed for Poolbeg in Dublin and Ringaskiddy near Cork. They would reduce landfill and produce limited amounts of energy. But incinerators might pollute the air with greenhouse gases and deadly dioxins.
  - More needs to be done to **reduce, reuse and recycle** waste. If the disposal of waste were charged by weight and if wasteful packaging were taxed at source the volume of waste would be reduced. The separation of waste into different bins encourages recycling.

Test Yourself
eTest.ie

1. Explain each of the following briefly but clearly: *smog; acid rain; the greenhouse effect; the Air Pollution Act of 1987; the Dublin Bay Project; the waste management hierarchy.*

2. The bar graphs in Figure 5 show the waste management options used in 2010 by a selection of EU countries. The graphs are labelled A–G.
   (a) By what percentage does landfill in country **A** exceed landfill in country **G**?
   (b) In 2010 Germany disposed of slightly less than one-fifth of its waste in landfill and recycled almost 60 per cent of its waste. Which of the labelled graphs represents Germany?
   (c) In your opinion, which country employs the best and which country the worst waste management strategy? Explain your opinions by reference to Figure 5.

3. Evaluate the strategies used in one named city to respond to the environmental challenges of our time.

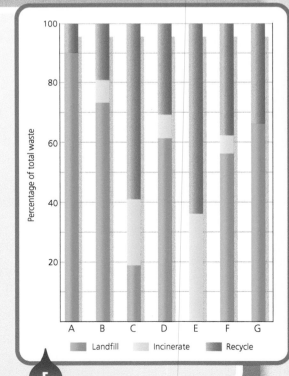

Figure 5

5

12 Heritage Issues in Urban Areas

When urban areas are redeveloped, sites or buildings of historical or archaeological importance may be destroyed. This has led to serious controversies between those who wish to develop urban areas and their infrastructures and those who wish to preserve urban heritage. Examples of such **controversies** in the Dublin area have included the following.

- Throughout the 1960s and the 1970s many fine **Georgian buildings** were demolished to make way for new development projects. The demolition of buildings in places such as Hume Street led to bitter controversy between developers (described as 'cultural vandals' by their opponents) and conservation groups such as the Irish Georgian Society (described by their opponents as 'belted earls').

- Huge controversy erupted in the 1970s when the building of Dublin Corporation's civic offices caused the destruction of a rich archaeological site at **Wood Quay**. This four-acre site included part of Dublin's medieval walls and the remains of an even older Viking settlement. Developers bulldozed some of the site before archaeologists could complete their excavations.

- The remains of an important medieval **castle at Carrickmines** in Co. Dublin were destroyed to make way for the building and development of the M50 motorway that skirts Dublin City. The controversy surrounding this was brought to the Supreme Court between 2004 and 2006.

The 'Battle of Hume Street'.
The so-called Battle of Hume Street took place in 1969 when protesters tried to prevent a developer from demolishing some Georgian houses on that street. Although those houses were destroyed, further demolitions on Hume Street were prevented.

Dublin's civic office buildings at Wood Quay.
These buildings (on the left of the picture) stand on the site of part of Dublin's medieval walls and of the ancient Viking settlement that marked the beginning of Dublin.

159

Some well-known listed buildings in Irish cities:

1 The GPO, Dublin

2 Shandon Church, Cork

3 St Mary's Cathedral, Limerick

4 Lynch's Castle, Galway

The **Urban Renewal Act 1986**, the **Planning Act 2000** and **National Monuments Acts** have all tried to bridge the gap between the need to preserve our heritage and the need to develop the country. These Acts have created the following rules and guidelines to encourage **culturally sensitive development**:

- Important *heritage sites* should if possible be avoided when roads or other vital structures are being built. When it is impossible to avoid them, the heritage sites should be excavated and their contents recorded before building work commences.

- All parts of *listed buildings* (and not just their outsides) are protected. Such buildings may be altered or demolished only under exceptional circumstances and with specific planning permission.

- *Local authorities* are required to play an active role in trying to ensure that listed buildings do not fall into decay.

- Planning permission for the development of a culturally sensitive area might require the *developer* to carry out an archaeological excavation and recording of the site before any development can take place.

Test Yourself
eTest.ie

Sum Up

- **Controversies** may arise between developers and those who wish to preserve cultural heritage. Such controversies in Dublin surrounded the demolition of *Georgian buildings*, the erection of civic offices over a Viking site at *Wood Quay* and the destruction of the ruins of *Carrickmines Castle*.

- Acts such as the Urban Renewal Act, the Planning Act and National Monuments Acts all encourage culturally **sensitive development**. Development projects are required to avoid or at least to excavate and record heritage sites. Local authorities must list and usually must protect buildings of archaeological or historical importance.

Activities

1. Examine how heritage issues have impacted on urban development in the case of any city that you have studied.

2. *'Urban development needs to be balanced with respect for urban heritage.'*
   Examine the above statement with reference to urban development in Ireland.

13 Urbanisation and Urban Problems in the Developing World

Urbanisation – or the growth of cities – is especially rampant in the developing world. This is shown by the fact that urban populations in the South now increase by approximately 4 per cent a year. It is also reflected in the fact that eight of the world's ten most populated cities are now in the South.

There are two main **reasons for rapid urbanisation** in the developing world:

- Massive *rural to urban migration* continues to swell city populations. Most migrants are pushed from the countryside by extreme rural poverty that can result from crop failure, hunger, a lack of medical care and sometimes even civil strife.

- High (although generally declining) *birth rates* also contribute to growing populations in Third World cities. This factor is heightened by the fact that large proportions of rural to urban migrants tend to be young adults who are most likely to produce children.

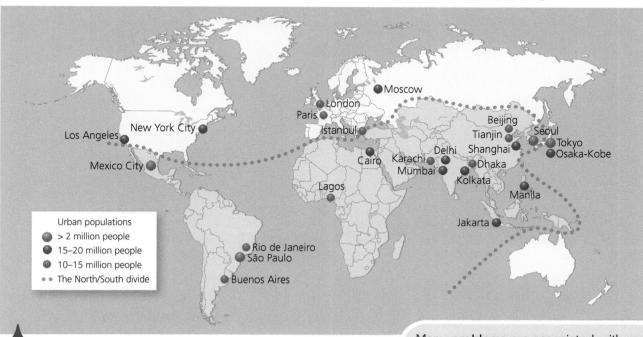

Urban populations
- \> 2 million people
- 15–20 million people
- 10–15 million people
- The North/South divide

1 Mega-cities of the world. Each of these mega-cities contains at least 10 million people.

(a) Which continent contains the greatest number of mega-cities?

(b) List the mega-cities of Latin America.

(c) Which cities in India have more than 15 million people?

(d) What is the largest city in the North?

(e) Account briefly for the large number of mega-cities in the South.

Many **problems** are associated with rapid urban growth in developing countries. This chapter will examine three of those problems.
1. The growth of unplanned shantytowns.
2. Inadequate services.
3. Widespread unemployment and underemployment.

Revise pages
31 and 69.

Urban problems in the developing world

1 The growth of unplanned shantytowns

Up to one-third of all Third World city dwellers (and most new migrants from rural areas) cannot afford to purchase or rent even the most basic accommodation in established urban areas. Some of these people become 'pavement dwellers' who are forced to live rough on the streets. Most, however, build shelters on land that they do not own. As these shelters multiply they form 'squatter camps', usually on the edges of cities. The squatter camps gradually develop into permanent shantytowns. Shantytowns are variously described as *favelas* in Brazil, *bidonvilles* in parts of Africa and *bustees* in Indian cities such as Kolkata.

Facts

Most large Third World cities contain several shantytowns. The Brazilian city of Rio de Janeiro, for example, contains more than 500 *favelas*. The largest of these – a shantytown called Rocinha – contains a quarter of a million people.

A large shantytown in Mumbai, India. *What does this photograph reveal about Third World shantytowns?*

2 Inadequate services

There are stark contrasts between wealthy and poor urban residential areas in Third World cities. These contrasts are reflected in the availability of services and amenities. Shantytowns usually suffer shortages of basic amenities such as electricity, sewerage systems and clean running water. They also lack adequately supplied schools, clinics, transport networks and policing services.

Revise
page 32

Inadequate services in the bustees of Kolkata are examined in detail on page 32.

3 Widespread unemployment and underemployment

Unemployment and underemployment (not having sufficient work to make a living wage) is rife in Third World cities such as Kolkata, Manila in the Philippines and Bangkok in Thailand. Relentless rural migration to these cities is driven more by the 'push' factor of rural poverty than by the 'pull' factor of actual urban employment opportunities. Such migration therefore contributes to ever-increasing urban unemployment and underemployment, especially in shantytowns.

Unemployment in Kolkata, for example, is compounded by the fact that manufacturing industry in that city has diminished in recent decades. Situated in an economically declining hinterland described as India's 'Rustbelt', the city relies too much on struggling traditional industries such as cotton weaving and carpet making. This reduces any remote chance that new migrants to Kolkata might find regular **mainstream employment** there.

With no unemployment benefits available to them, most jobless shantytown dwellers rely on the **'informal' sector** for work. Such people may work as casual builders' labourers, as shoe-shiners or as rickshaw pullers. They usually exist at *subsistence level* – earning just enough money for their families to barely survive.

A minority of unemployed poor people adopt **desperate measures** in order to survive. Some rummage among rubbish tips such as Manila's 'Smokey Mountain' in the hope of extracting items that might be saleable. Some try to eke out a living as professional beggars. Others, in cities such as Bangkok, resort to a notorious sex trade to make a hazardous living in prostitution. Some fall under the influence of criminal gangs and survive on the proceeds of theft, drug selling or other crimes.

A rickshaw puller in Kolkata, India.
Most rickshaws are now worked by pedal power rather than pulled by hand. But the life of a rickshaw puller continues to be underpaid, hard and hazardous. The working lives of many pullers are cut short by heart strain or by physical burnout.

Begging to live.
A lack of employment and unemployment benefits has forced this man to beg for survival on the streets in Kerala.

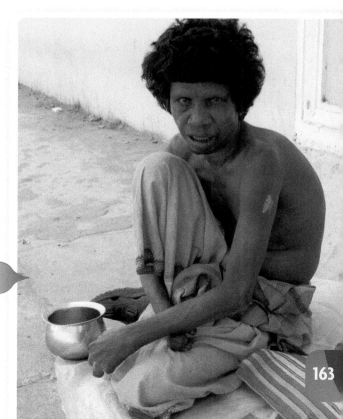

163

Attempts to solve poverty problems in Brazilian favelas

Successive Brazilian governments have made various attempts to solve the problems associated with favelas.

- In the 1970s, Brazil's military government tried to **eradicate favelas** by removing more than 100,000 residents from them. These people were to be placed in public housing projects or sent back to the rural areas from which they originally came. This 'eradication' scheme failed completely. No realistic housing projects were provided for evicted residents, while those sent to the countryside had very little work or services available to them and so drifted back to the cities. The 'eradication' policy failed because it did not recognise that favelas are the symptom rather than the cause of poverty. It failed to tackle the root cause of shantytown problems, which is poverty itself.

- A much more successful project is now in operation in the Diadema favela in São Paolo. This is a **self-help project** in which residents are encouraged to 'upgrade' their neighbourhoods by building better homes for themselves. Groups of local people are provided with building materials such as blocks and roof tiles on condition that they carry out the basic building work needed. The money saved is then used to provide clean water, tarred roads and community centres for the locals.

Self-help development in the Diadema favela. Local residents add colour to the facades of upgraded homes.

Test Yourself
eTest.ie

Sum Up

- **Urbanisation** is rampant in developing countries, mainly because of rural to urban *migration* and because of *high birth rates* among rural to urban migrants.
- **Problems** associated with Third World urbanisation include the growth of *shantytowns, inadequate services* and *widespread unemployment*.
- Poor people who cannot afford urban accommodation often live in 'squatter camps' on the edges of cities. These camps gradually develop into **shantytowns** or hastily built slums on the expanding edges of cities. More than 5 million people are crammed into tiny dwellings in the bustees of Kolkata. 'Pavement people' there have no homes at all.
- Shantytowns in cities such as Kolkata suffer from **inadequate basic amenities** such as electricity, sanitation systems and clean water supplies. They also suffer from shortages of educational and transport facilities.
- **Unemployment** and underemployment is rife in cities of the developing world. Many people work in the *informal sector* doing jobs such as shoe shining. Some rummage in waste tips, beg or even resort to prostitution or crime in order to survive.
- In the 1970s a Brazilian military government tried in vain to **eradicate** favelas and to relocate their inhabitants in housing projects or in rural areas. A current self-help project aimed at **'upgrading'** a favela in São Paolo appears to be achieving success.

1. The rapid growth of cities in the developing world has led to social and economic problems. Examine any two such problems, referring to examples that you have studied.

(LC Higher Level – 30 marks)

2. What do you think could be done to solve or alleviate some of the urban problems in developing countries? Make reference in your answer to an attempted solution that you have studied.

3. Using examples that you have studied, suggest how urban problems in the developing world differ from urban problems in the developed world.

(LC Ordinary Level – 40 marks)

Leaving Cert question with marking scheme and sample answer. Use the marking scheme to mark the sample answer.

The question

Explain two reasons why shantytowns develop near cities in the developing world.

(LC Ordinary Level – 30 marks)

The Marking Scheme

Two reasons explained at 15 marks each.
For each reason:

- Name the reason = 3 marks
- Explain the reason with at least 4 SRPs at 3 marks each = 12 marks

Total = **30 marks**

Note: one SRP will be allowed for naming a shantytown.

Sample answer

1 <u>Rural to urban migration</u> is the main cause of the growth of shantytowns in the developing world. Every year millions of people flock from poverty-stricken rural areas into cities such as Kolkata in India. Most of these migrants are 'pushed' out of the countryside by unemployment and by a severe lack of health, educational and other amenities. They are attracted or 'pulled' to the cities in the hope or alleviating these symptoms of poverty. Rural to urban migration causes cities such as Kolkata to grow at a rapid rate of more than 4 per cent a year. Most of this growth is concentrated in the shantytowns or bustees where most poor in-migrants live.

2 Up to one-third of all Third World urban dwellers (and almost all rural to urban migrants) cannot afford to purchase or rent even the most basic accommodation in Third World cities. Most of these people congregate in squatter camps at the edges of cities, where they live in tiny shacks made of wood, corrugated iron, or anything else they can access. In time, these <u>squatter camps develop into shantytowns</u> where people are usually recognised as the legal owners of the land on which their homes stand. Self-help projects have resulted in the further development of shantytowns in the form of improved housing and social facilities. This happened, for example, in the Diadema favela of São Paolo.

14 Future Urban Issues

As the world's population continues to grow, so do the number and size of its cities. Relentless urban growth has led to serious issues that must be addressed if cities are to remain socially and environmentally **sustainable** in the future.

Future urban issues include:
- continued urban sprawl
- social isolation and alienation
- energy sustainability.

Continued urban sprawl
The issue

Urban sprawl continues to grow steadily throughout the world. The metropolitan area of New York, for example, is now a **conurbation** that covers 8,700 square kilometres – more than ten times the size of Co. Louth. A conurbation is a continuous urban area that is formed when several cities and towns expand and merge together. Third World cities, though not as large as New York, tend to grow even more rapidly than do cities in the economically developed world.

Major problems will ensue if urban sprawl continues unabated in the future. Agricultural land and existing villages will continue to be swallowed up by advancing, monotonous suburbs in the developed world and by shantytowns in the Third World. As urban areas expand, commuting distances may also expand to the point of becoming unsustainable.

Resolving the issue

If migration into large urban areas can be controlled, excessive urban sprawl might be stemmed. One way of achieving this in is to encourage the growth of smaller, **alternative urban areas** to counter the attraction that dominant cities have for migrants. Ireland's National Spatial Strategy tries to achieve this goal. Its aim is to stem the growth of Dublin by encouraging the development of 'gateway' and 'hub' urban areas throughout the country.

The building of **higher-rise** apartment blocks rather than low-density housing would help to stem future urban sprawl around Dublin. Higher-rise accommodation projects would, however, need to be well serviced with local parks and other **green areas**. Large cities such as London already maintain 'green belts' around them to prevent continuous sprawl. Other cities such as Copenhagen use 'green wedges' to achieve the same effect.

Part of the New York metropolitan area – a reminder that continued urban sprawl could be a serious urban issue in the future

Social isolation and alienation
The issue

There is a danger that cities of the future may develop into places of social and ethnic division in which many people feel isolated and alienated from fellow citizens and from decision-making processes. Extreme **social stratification** is already a divisive feature of many cities. Rich or relatively rich people almost exclusively inhabit urban areas such as Brooklyn Heights in New York. Many rich people seldom mix outside their own social class and some live in 'gated communities' for fear of being robbed. Poor people tend to inhabit other areas of New York, such as parts of South Bronx. There is a danger that such poor **ghettos** could degenerate into focal points of unemployment, hopelessness, anger and alienation from government and decision-making.

Resolving the issue

Strong social policies are needed to create vibrant urban communities and to prevent cities from becoming centres of isolation and alienation.

- National and local governments may need to pursue housing policies that foster the creation of **mixed neighbourhoods** in which people of different cultural and socio-economic backgrounds can mingle.

- The inhabitants of mixed neighbourhoods should be given '**ownership**' of their urban government. Decision-making should be decentralised where possible so that people do not feel that they are being governed 'from the top down' by people they do not know. The division of Co. Dublin into four smaller administrative units was a positive move in this direction. Neighbourhood communities should have real inputs into city government, the policies of which should normally put community interests before those of private individuals.

- The layout and amenities of each neighbourhood should be designed to foster **enjoyment, pride and a sense of belonging** among its inhabitants. Pedestrianised streets, street furniture, numerous green areas and cheap, well-organised public transport might all play an important part in such designs.

Pedestrian streets and green areas would help to create a sense of pride and belonging in culturally and socially diverse urban neighbourhoods

Energy sustainability
The issue

Urban areas now account for approximately four-fifths of the world's **fossil fuel usage** and **carbon dioxide** outputs. If this situation is not resolved, the world's growing cities are likely to become environmentally unsustainable in the future.

Resolving the issue

A raft of **environmental policies** will be needed to achieve future energy sustainability in urban areas.

- The use of fossil fuel for **transport** should be reduced greatly, especially as finite oil and gas supplies grow more scarce and expensive. Financial charges could be used to discourage the use of *cars* in city areas, as has been done in Central London. Cheap and efficient *public transport* would be required to substitute for reduced car use. Cheap *bicycle hire* schemes, such as that already operating in Central Dublin, would also be helpful.
- The use of fossil fuels for **heating** could be reduced by improving the *insulation* of buildings. It might also be replaced where possible by the use of *renewable energy* such as solar, wind and tidal power. Solar power would be especially suited to many Third World countries such as Sudan and Egypt. Wind or wave power might be feasible in countries such as Ireland that experience relatively windy maritime climates.

Initiatives such as these would require great **capital** expenditure that would be well beyond the reach of many economically developing countries. It would be prudent, however, for rich countries to assist poor countries to achieve these initiatives, because such reforms would help to safeguard our entire planet from the menace of future climate change.

Test Yourself eTest.ie

Sum Up

- Relentless urban growth will give rise to serious **future urban issues**.
- Continued **urban sprawl** will overwhelm more and more farmland and village communities. It will also result in unsustainable levels of commuting. The development of *alternative urban growth centres* might reduce the relentless growth of very large cities. *Higher-rise buildings* and preserved *green areas* might also stem continuous outward urban sprawl.
- Cities of the future could become places of **isolation** and **alienation** in which people are divided into socially and ethnically divided ghettos. The creation of well-designed socially and ethnically *mixed neighbourhoods* should be encouraged and the people of such neighbourhoods should have an input into urban government.
- The continued overuse of *fossil fuels* could make cities **environmentally unsustainable**. More *public transport, insulation* and *renewable energy* should be used in order to avoid ecological threats such as climate change.

Activity

1. *'A sustainable urban area is one that meets the needs of the present without compromising the needs of future generations.'*
   (a) Examine **two issues** that might threaten the future sustainability of large urban areas.
   (b) What has been done and what can be done to ensure the future sustainability of large urban areas?

Optional Unit:
Geoecology
(Higher Level only)

This book contains two Optional Units.
You must **study one Optional Unit** only.

The composition of soil

Parent material (mineral particles)

Mineral particles are the largest ingredient of soil and can make up about 45 per cent of its total volume. These particles were once weathered or eroded from the soil's **parent rock.*** The parent rock might be local or might have been broken down and transported from other regions by agents of erosion such as rivers or moving ice.

- Individual mineral particles are generally very tiny. But their **size** can vary according to the type of rock from which they were derived. Particles of sandstone, for example, tend to be relatively large and coarse. Particles derived from clay, on the other hand, tend to be extremely small. The size of mineral particles affects the *texture** of soils. (Textures are examined on page 172.)
- Mineral particles may contain **compounds*** that help to make the soil fertile. Limestone, for example, provides plenty of *calcium* that strengthens the bones of grazing animals.
- Some minerals are **soluble**, which means they can dissolve in water and take a liquid form. Soluble minerals are very important. They nourish plants very well because plant roots can absorb liquid.

Organic matter

Organic* matter consists of living creatures as well as the remains of plants and animals. Although it makes up only about 5 per cent of the soil, organic matter plays a vital role in soil fertility.

Terms to know

- **Parent rock:** the rock from which a soil type is derived.
- **Soil texture:** how soil feels to the touch. Soils, for example, may feel smooth or coarse.
- **Compound:** something that is made up of two or more ingredients.
- **Nutrient:** in this case, something that nourishes plants.
- **Organic:** of or formed from living things.
- **Plant litter:** dead plant material, such as leaves or twigs, that has fallen to the ground.

Soils have four principal components or ingredients:
- **parent material**
- **organic matter**
- **air**
- **water**.

The proportions of these ingredients are approximately as shown in Figure 1. Their proportions may, however, vary considerably from one soil type to another and even according to changes in the weather.

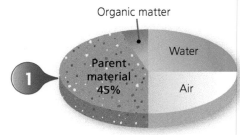

The composition of soil.

(a) Rank the components of soil according to their proportions shown in Figure 1.

(b) Calculate the proportion of soils that is made up of organic matter.

(c) Explain how each of the following processes might alter the proportions of the soil components shown:
- A period of drought.
- The laying of water-drainage pipes.
- The addition of animal manure to the soil.

- Multitudes of **living creatures** live in the soil. Some of these, such as earthworms, are visible to the eye. They help to keep the soil fertile while they live and their remains fertilise it when they die. But the vast majority of living creatures are microscopic. (They can be seen only with the help of a microscope.) Such *micro-organisms* include bacteria and fungi, millions of which could fit in a single teaspoon of soil.

- When **plant litter*** falls on the ground and when animals die, they are broken down by micro-organisms. This process causes the plant and animal remains to decay into a dark, jelly-like substance called **humus**. Humus increases soil fertility (see the box). It is found mainly near the surface of the soil, where it can give the soil a dark appearance.

Air

Air and water are located in the pores (spaces) between mineral particles. Air usually makes up about a quarter of the soil's volume, but it is more plentiful in loose-grained sandy soils than it is in tightly grained clay soils. Air is essential for soil **fertility**. It supplies the oxygen and nitrogen that plants need in order to live.

Water

Water can also make up about a quarter of the soil's volume, though this depends on **climatic conditions**. In desert areas, the amounts of water in soil can be so small that almost no vegetation can grow. In very wet areas, soils can become waterlogged or saturated with water.

A moderate amount of rainwater is usually good for soil **fertility**. As water seeps slowly through the soil, it dissolves soluble minerals. It then distributes these minerals to plants that can absorb them in liquid form through their roots. The water and the dissolved minerals nourish the plants.

How humus increases soil fertility:
- It nourishes plants with nutrients such as carbon and nitrogen.
- It absorbs minerals that might otherwise be washed down through the soil.
- It helps to hold soils particles together and so reduces the risk of soil erosion.
- It helps the soil to retain moisture.

Plant litter on a woodland floor in Co. Wicklow.
How does plant litter contribute to the formation of soil?

Wonderful worms. Earthworms play a huge role in the formation of fertile soils. As they burrow through soil:
- they help air and water to pass through;
- they loosen soil, which helps plant roots to penetrate it;
- they help to mix the soil together.

When earthworms die, their bodies decay into soil-nourishing humus.

Soil characteristics

The **four ingredients** of soil (examined on pages 170 and 171) are all **linked together**. This interlinking creates the following **soil characteristics** or properties:

Soil characteristics:
- texture
- structure
- pH value
- organic content
- colour
- water retention properties
- water content

Texture

Texture refers to the coarseness or smoothness of soil and it depends on the sizes of the particles that make up a soil type. Texture is important because it can control the ability of soil to retain nutrients or to retain or transmit water. It can also determine the ease with which plant roots can penetrate soil.

- **Sandy soils** have a loose, *coarse* texture because they contain **large particles** of up to 2mm in diameter. This loose texture allows water and air to pass easily through sandy soils and also makes the soils easy to cultivate. But water passing easily through the sandy soils can *leach** materials out of them. Such soils can also suffer from water shortage during long spells of dry weather. Farmers might therefore need to fertilise and irrigate sandy soils.

- **Clay soils** feel *smooth* because they contain very **tiny particles.** These tight-fitting particles tend to prevent air or water from passing through them. This causes clay soils to become *waterlogged** and sticky in times of rain. Such '*heavy*' soils* are difficult to plough and are more suited to the cultivation of grass. Farmers sometimes add lime or use land drainage schemes to make clay soils more fertile.

- **Loam soils** contain fairly even amounts of sand and clay particles. These soils are often ideal for farming and for gardening.

Terms to know

- **Leaching:** the washing of nutrients and minerals down through soil.
- **Waterlogged:** saturated with water.
- **Heavy soils:** soils that contain small clay particles and tend to retain water.

Cultivating loam in an Irish garden.
The texture of loamy soil allows it to be well drained, well aerated and very suited to agriculture and gardening.

Structure

The cementing action of water and humus causes individual soil particles to group together into small lumps of various shapes. These small lumps of soil are called **peds**. *The structure of a soil depends on the shape of its peds.* Two examples of this are given in Figure 2 below.

Soil structure	Ped type	Illustration	Effect on fertility
Crumb structure	Peds form rounded shapes, rather like breadcrumbs	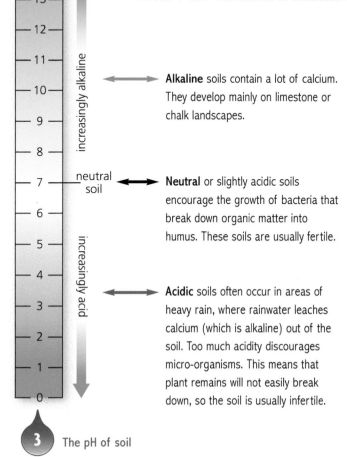	Water and air can move easily through the peds. This promotes soil fertility
Platy structure	Peds tend to be flat and overlapping, e.g. in soil that has been compacted.		Water cannot move easily down through the peds. The soil may therefore become waterlogged and infertile.

2

pH value

A soil's pH value indicates its level of acidity or alkalinity. Soils with low pH values are said to be **acidic** soils, while those with high pH values are **alkaline**. Soils with pH readings of about 7 are described as **neutral** (see Figure 3).

14
13
12
11
10
9
8
7 neutral soil
6
5
4
3
2
1
0

increasingly alkaline

increasingly acid

Alkaline soils contain a lot of calcium. They develop mainly on limestone or chalk landscapes.

Neutral or slightly acidic soils encourage the growth of bacteria that break down organic matter into humus. These soils are usually fertile.

Acidic soils often occur in areas of heavy rain, where rainwater leaches calcium (which is alkaline) out of the soil. Too much acidity discourages micro-organisms. This means that plant remains will not easily break down, so the soil is usually infertile.

3 The pH of soil

Do you think that the soil in this part of West Connemara is most likely to be alkaline, neutral or acidic? Explain your answer.

Organic content

The organic content of soil comes from the **remains of plants and animals** such as earthworms and insects. Plant litter and dead animals are broken down into *humus* by bacteria and other micro-organisms. Humus plays a vital role in making soil fertile.

Revise organic matter on pages 170–171.

It follows, therefore, that the more plant litter, animals and micro-organisms there are in soil, the more fertile that soil is likely to be. *Brown earth* soils, in Ireland, for example, are usually rich in humus. This is because they were formed where deciduous forests once provided the soil with abundant plant litter and animal remains.

Colour

Soil types vary in colour, which can be a sign of the soil's levels of fertility.

- **Black or brown soils** are usually very **fertile** for the following reasons:
  - They are dark because they contain lots of *humus,* which makes soil fertile.
  - Dark soils tend to be *warm* because they absorb more sunlight than light-coloured soils. Warm conditions help organic material to break down into humus and help seeds to germinate (develop) more quickly.

The *brown earth soils* of Ireland's midlands and eastern counties are examples of dark soils (see Figure 4).

Brown earth soil

- **Grey soils** are normally **infertile**. Their surface layers have a grey, 'washed-out' appearance because heavy rain has leached (washed) dark humus and other nutrients down through the soils and out of reach of many plant roots. **Podzols**, which are common on some Irish highlands, are examples of grey soils (see Figure 4).

Grey podzolic soil

4 Some Irish soils.

(a) Name two midland counties and two eastern counties with extensive areas of brown soils.

(b) Name two highland areas on which podzols are common.

brown soils
podzols
gleys
peaty soils

Red soils are common in tropical or equatorial areas close to the Equator. Their rusty red colour indicates high quantities of *iron oxide* (*rust*) in the soils. Hot, wet conditions create intense chemical weathering in these areas. This causes iron in parent rocks to break down into iron oxide, which is then passed on to the 'tropical red' soils.

Water retention properties

The degree to which soil can hold water or moisture depends largely on its structure and its texture.

- **Structure:** Soils with crumb structures (such as loam soils) allow water to move easily through them and so tend to be relatively dry. On the other hand, soils with platy structures do not easily let water through them and so tend to have a high water content.

- **Texture:** The photographs on the right show that soils of different textures have different water-retention properties.

Water content

The amount of water or moisture in soil is influenced by the following factors:

- The **water retention properties** of the soil (as described above).

- **Precipitation:** Soils in areas of high rainfall, such as the mountains of Kerry or Connemara, tend to contain more water than soils in the relatively dry southeast of Ireland.

- **The nature of the underlying rock:** Soils overlying permeable rock usually hold less moisture than soils overlying impermeable rocks. Permeable rock such as limestone allows water to pass through it and so to escape more easily from the soil above. Impermeable rock such as slate hinders the downward movement of water and so tends to increase the water content of the overlying soil.

- **The presence of a hard pan:** Soils that are heavily leached sometimes contain a thin horizontal layer called a hard pan. Hard pans are impermeable. They may block the downward movement of water and so cause the soil surface to become waterlogged.

Soil texture, water retention properties and agriculture

Coarse **sandy soils** can retain little water because they have large spaces between their big soil particles. While these soils sometimes favour the growing of vegetables, they may suffer from water shortages during times or in places of little rainfall.

Smooth and finely textured **clay soils** hold so much water that they may be poorly drained and even waterlogged. They often provide good grasslands for cattle, but are usually too 'heavy' for tillage.

Loam soils have a texture that is somewhere between sand and clay. Loam soils tend to be well drained, while retaining enough moisture to maintain high levels of fertility. They are therefore ideal for many forms of agriculture.

Natural processes that influence soil formation

We have already examined the general characteristics of soil. But no two soils are exactly the same. This is partly because a variety of physical processes may influence the formation of any particular soil. A list of these processes is given in the box.

Physical processes that influence soil formation:
- weathering
- erosion
- leaching:
  - podzolisation
  - laterisation
- calcification
- humification

Weathering

Elements of the weather, such as frost, temperature changes and rain, help to break down parent rock into smaller and smaller pieces. These pieces become the mineral particles or the 'parent materials' that make up about 45 per cent of most soil types.

Physical or mechanical weathering causes rock to shatter without altering its chemical characteristics. The main agents of physical weathering are freeze-thaw action and exfoliation.

- **Freeze-thaw action** happens where temperatures frequently move above and below freezing point. It is common on Irish mountains in winter, when the freezing and thawing of water within rock crevasses puts rock under extreme stress. This stress causes rock to break down into angular rock debris called *scree*. The scree is then further broken down over time until it forms mineral particle ingredients for soils.

- **Exfoliation or 'onion weathering'** happens when outside layers of exposed rock are shattered and broken down. This happens where extreme changes between day and night temperatures put stress on rocks by causing them to expand and contract repeatedly. Exfoliation is very common in hot deserts such as the Sahara, where day and night temperatures can vary by as much as 30°C.

Chemical weathering breaks down rocks by causing minerals within the rocks to dissolve or to otherwise decompose.

- Rainwater, for example, causes limestone to dissolve through a process called **carbonation**. This happens when carbonic acid in the rainwater reacts with calcium carbonate in limestone. Carbonation is very common in Irish midland counties such as Westmeath, where limestone is the dominant rock type.

- Rainwater also breaks down granite through a process called **hydrolysis.** This process turns feldspar in the rock into a clay called kaolin. Hydrolysis has been active in areas such as the Wicklow Mountains.

- **Oxidation** happens when iron in rock is exposed to oxygen in the air. The iron then oxidises or 'rusts' and this weakens the rock and causes it to crumble. When iron in soil is oxidised it gives the soil a rusty red colour. Such tropical red soils are common in hot wet lands near the Equator.

Oxidation gives these tropical red soils in Liberia their 'rusty' red colour

Erosion

Agents of erosion include rivers, moving ice and winds. They not only break down rock, they also carry away the resulting mineral particles and soils and deposit them in other regions.

- **Alluvial soils** are formed when *rivers* break down rock into fine particles and then transport and deposit these particles downstream. Alluvial soil or alluvium covers the flood plains of Irish rivers such as the Shannon. It usually consists of a mixture of fine silt and clay particles as well as coarser sand particles. It is normally very fertile.

- **Boulder clay** was formed when moving *ice sheets* ground down rock and transported a mixture of finely ground 'rock-flour', stones and boulders along their paths. This mixture – called boulder clay – is found in places such as Co. Monaghan and the Clew Bay area of Co. Mayo. Boulder clay tends to be 'heavy' and poorly drained and is better suited to rearing cattle than to tillage.

- **Wind** can erode rock that is not protected by surface vegetation. It can also transport eroded rock particles (as well as unprotected topsoil) over great distances before depositing them. **Loess** soil was deposited in the Paris Basin by wind. Loess is composed of fine dust that was blown southwards from the edges of great Scandinavian ice sheets at the end of the Pleistocene Ice Age. It is very fertile and is especially suited to growing tillage crops such as wheat and sugar beet.

A boulder clay area in Co. Galway. This drumlin-strewn area is covered in boulder clay. The fine clay in boulder clay tends to be impermeable, so that the soil is poorly drained and more suited to cattle pasture than to tillage.

Leaching

Leaching happens when rainwater soaks down through soil and carries soluble minerals and organic materials with it. It occurs where rainfall exceeds evaporation. It is therefore common throughout *Ireland* and especially in areas of high precipitation such the mountains of Donegal and Kerry.

Limited leaching can increase soil fertility when percolating water dissolves plant nutrients and delivers them downwards to plant roots. Severe leaching, however, can carry plant nutrients down through the A horizon and well beyond the reach of plant roots. This deprives plants of the nourishment they need and so damages soil fertility.

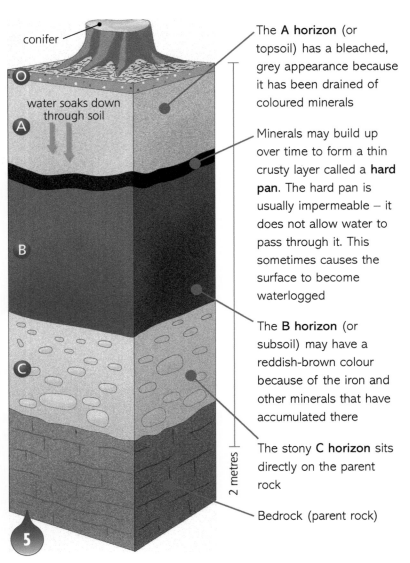

conifer

water soaks down through soil

O

A

B

C

2 metres

5

The **A horizon** (or topsoil) has a bleached, grey appearance because it has been drained of coloured minerals

Minerals may build up over time to form a thin crusty layer called a **hard pan**. The hard pan is usually impermeable – it does not allow water to pass through it. This sometimes causes the surface to become waterlogged

The **B horizon** (or subsoil) may have a reddish-brown colour because of the iron and other minerals that have accumulated there

The stony **C horizon** sits directly on the parent rock

Bedrock (parent rock)

A podzol soil profile.
A **soil profile** is a vertical section of the soil from surface to bedrock. It contains horizontal layers called **horizons**.
The layer closest to the surface is usually called the O horizon.
Below that are the **A, B** and **C** horizons.

- **Podzolisation** is an extreme form of leaching. It is common in areas of heavy rainfall, such as the Macgillycuddy's Reeks, where annual precipitation is more than 2000mm. It is also common in areas where the surface vegetation is *coniferous forest*, as for example in the great boreal forests of Russia and Canada. Water becomes very acidic (with pH values of 4.5 or less) as it percolates through the plant litter of coniferous forests. This acid water can dissolve and remove almost all minerals and plant nutrients in the soil, leaving the A horizon 'bleached' and infertile. *Podzols* are the types of soil that result from the process of podzolisation. They have very distinctive soil profiles, an example of which is shown in Figure 5.

- **Laterisation** is an extreme form of leaching that is common in equatorial and tropical regions. Hot, wet conditions and large amounts of forest plant litter give rise to a great deal of chemical weathering in these regions. This intense weathering breaks down rocks to great depths and so gives rise to deep soils. It also causes iron in soil to break down into a substance called iron oxide or rust. This process is called *oxidation*. It gives soils a rusty, reddish appearance that gives rise to their name of *tropical red soils*.

With the help of an atlas and the map on page 181, name three countries where the following soils are common:
- podzols
- tropical red soils.

A podzol soil horizon. *Identify the* **A horizon**, *the* **hard pan** *and the* **B horizon**.

Calcification

Calcification takes place in dry regions where evaporation exceeds precipitation. In such regions, ground water is drawn up through the soil by *capillary action*, a process that is the opposite of leaching.

Capillary action results in **calcification**, which is the build-up of calcium near the surface. Calcium helps to make soil very fertile, as in the *chernozem* or 'black earth' soils that cover the steppes (grasslands) of Russia and the Ukraine. Fertile chernozems are also found on the prairies of the United States.

How capillary action works
Following rain, gravity causes water to sink through the soil. But water is absorbed *upwards* through dry soil after long periods of dry weather. This is called capillary action. The water acts rather like water on a wet surface when a dry towel is placed over it to soak it up.

Humification

Humification is the process by which organic matter in the soil is decomposed into a black jelly-like substance called **humus**.

Organic matter consists of plant litter and the remains of dead animals. *Micro-organisms* such as bacteria and fungi attack the organic matter and cause it to decay. *Oxygen* is also needed to assist the breakdown of organic matter into humus. Air in the soil therefore plays an important role in the process of humification.

Humus makes the soil *fertile*. It converts nitrogen, calcium and other nutrients into soluble forms so that plant roots can absorb them easily.

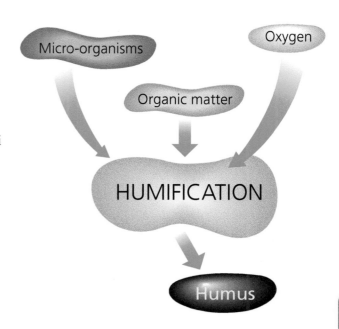

Micro-organisms

Oxygen

Organic matter

HUMIFICATION

Humus

Classification and global patterns of soils

How soils are classified

Zonal soils

Climate is the most important factor affecting soil formation. Soils are therefore usually classified according to the climate types that help to form them. They are called zonal soils because they occupy large **climatic zones** of the earth's surface. *Brown soils*, for example, are the zonal soils of Ireland and other areas with a cool temperate oceanic climate. *Tropical red soils*, on the other hand, are the zonal soils of equatorial regions.

Intrazonal soils

Within zonal soil belts, strong **local factors** can sometimes create different types of soils in certain areas. These local soil types are called **intrazonal** soils. Poor drainage, for example, creates *peaty soils* in Connemara and other areas of the west of Ireland.

Azonal soils

Azonal soils are soils that are recent in origin and **not yet fully developed**. These 'immature' soils do not have clear soil profiles. Recent deposits of *sand* – as in sand dunes – is an example of azonal soil. Azonal soils are also found in areas of newly deposited volcanic ash.

Brown earth is Ireland's zonal (and most common) soil type

Peaty, intrazonal soils are found in some poorly drained areas of Ireland

Sand dunes are an example of immature (not yet fully formed) azonal soil

Learn any **three** of the examples given below.

How zonal soils are related to climate and vegetation zones		
Zonal soil	**Climate zone**	**Vegetation zone**
Tundra soil	Tundra	Tundra
Podzols	Cold temperate continental	Coniferous forest (taiga)
Brown earths	Cool temperate oceanic	Deciduous forest
Chernozems/grassland soils	Warm temperate rainy and steppe	Grasslands
Aridisols (desert and semi-desert soils)	Desert/semi-desert	Desert/semi-desert
Terra rossa	Mainly warm temperate oceanic	Mainly Mediterranean
Latosols/tropical red soils	Equatorial/tropical	Rainforest
Mountain soils	Mountain climate	Mountain vegetation

Global patterns

The global pattern of soils is shown on the map in Figure 6. This map shows only the **general locations** of the world's most common *zonal soils*. It does not show the many intrazonal and azonal soils that exist within each zone.

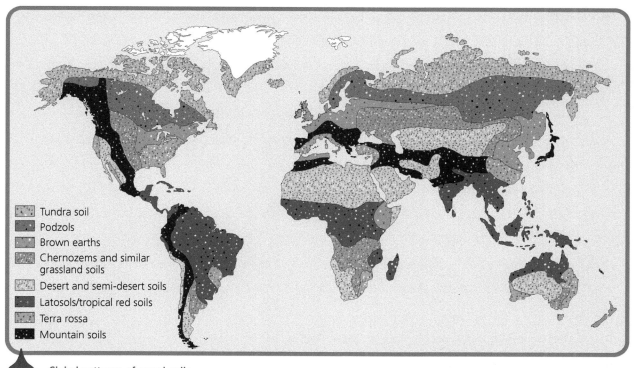

Tundra soil
Podzols
Brown earths
Chernozems and similar grassland soils
Desert and semi-desert soils
Latosols/tropical red soils
Terra rossa
Mountain soils

6 Global patterns of zonal soils.

(a) Name the zonal soil type in Ireland and the United Kingdom. What climatic zone exists there?

(b) Name the zonal soil type in each of the following places:
(i) Italy; (ii) Sweden; (iii) the Amazon Basin; (iv) the Sahara Desert; (v) the Rocky Mountains.

(c) Does this map show precisely the soil types in any part of the world? Explain.

Leaving Cert exam question, sample answer and marking scheme

The question

Examine the general composition and characteristics of one soil type that you have studied.

Mark the sample answer using the marking scheme on the facing page.

Sample answer

Brown earth soils or 'brown soils' are the most common soil type in Ireland. This answer will explore the composition and characteristics of brown soils, with reference to *parent material and bedrock, organic material and leaching.*

Parent material and bedrock

Mineral particles are the largest single ingredient of Ireland's brown earth soils and make up about 45 per cent of their total volume. These particles were weathered or eroded from the soils' parent rocks and so they contain many characteristics of these rocks.

Limestone is the parent rock for most of Ireland's brown soils. In parts of north Co. Dublin, for example, limestone provides local brown soils with an important mineral called **calcium**. Calcium is soluble. This means it can dissolve in water, take a liquid form and so be easily absorbed by grass. Calcium in grass strengthens the bones of grazing animals. Calcium-rich brown soils thus contribute greatly to the success of the blood stock (horse breeding) industry in counties such as Kildare. Limestone also affects the **drainage** capabilities of brown soils. Limestone is permeable, which means that water can easily pass through it. This facilitates good drainage on the soils that overlie limestone in places such as the valleys of the River Lee and the Munster Blackwater.

Organic material

Organic material consists of living creatures as well as the remains of plants and animals. It plays a vital role in soil fertility, although it usually makes up no more than 5 per cent of the volume of brown soils.

Brown soils were formed in areas of temperate climate and **deciduous forests**, which provided an abundance of both animal and vegetable organic material.

The forest environment supports a wide variety of **creatures** such as earthworms, which aerate soil by moving through it and which fertilise soil with their dead remains. It also contains a wide variety of micro-organisms, such as bacteria and fungi, many millions of which can live within a single spoonful of brown earth.

Deciduous woodlands also contain a wide variety of **plant life** that includes lush undergrowth as well as large tree species such as oak and beech. This plant life produces an abundance of *plant litter*, which consists of dead leaves, twigs, etc. that fall on the ground. This plant litter, together with the remains of dead animals, is broken down by the micro-organisms in the soil. This breaking-down process, which is called *humification*, takes place as animal and plant remains decay into a black jelly-like substance called humus. **Humus** is particularly abundant near the surface (in the O and A horizons) of the soil. It increases *soil fertility* in the following ways:

- It *absorbs minerals* that might otherwise be washed out of the soil.
- It *nourishes plants* with nutrients such as carbon and nitrogen.
- It helps to hold mineral particles together to create *crumb structured soils* that are well drained.
- It helps soil to *retain moisture*, which can be important in times of limited rainfall.

Limited leaching

Leaching is the process by which humus and other plant nutrients are washed by rainwater down through the soil. Slight leaching has the beneficial effect of dissolving humus and distributing it to plant roots that absorb soluble nutrients.

Brown earth soils are most common in the midlands and east of Ireland, where annual **rainfall levels** of approximately 800–1,000mm facilitate limited leaching. The crumb texture of brown soils, together with an abundance of burrowing animals such as earthworms, also assists the downward movement of plant nutrients.

Limited leaching tends to give most brown soils a **slightly acidic** pH value of 5 to 7. This is because rainwater absorbs carbon dioxide in the atmosphere and so is a weak carbonic acid as it seeps through the soil. The 'moderate' pH values quoted above favour the growth of most Irish agricultural crops, including grass and cereal crops such as barley.

It should be noted, however, that there are different varieties of brown earth soils throughout Ireland and that a minority of such soils experience relatively high levels of leaching. **Brown podzolic soils**, for example, can be found in parts of Donegal and Mayo, where rainfall levels are higher (and leaching is more severe) than in the midlands and east of Ireland. Severe leaching can also give the A horizons of these soils a pale 'washed-out' look, in contrast with the humus-rich brown colour of a 'typical' brown earth soil profile.

Marking scheme for 'Option' questions

Three or four aspects must be dealt with in answering an Option question. The marking schemes for these questions is as follows:

For an answer that deals with <u>three</u> aspects:
Three aspects at 27 marks + 27 marks + 26 marks

For each aspect:

Identifying (naming) the aspect	= 4 marks
Examination: at least 8 SRPs* at 2 marks each	= 16 marks
Overall coherence*	= 7/6 marks graded
Total	= **80 marks**

For an answer that deals with <u>four</u> aspects:
Four aspects at 20 marks each.

For each aspect:

Identifying (naming) the aspect	= 4 marks
Examination: at least 6 SRPs* at 2 marks each	= 12 marks
Overall coherence*	= 4 marks
Total	= **80 marks**

***SRP** stands for Significant Relevant Point. Each SRP must provide a clear piece of geographical information that is relevant to the question asked. Try to exceed the required number of SRPs in any aspect on which you write. You will get credit for the best SRPs that you present.

***'Overall coherence'** marks are awarded for qualities such as the fullness, accuracy, quality and 'flow' of the answer given. Make sure that your answers are relevant, clear and well laid out. Use well-structured sentences and paragraphs.

Leaving Cert exam question and sample answer

The question

With reference to one soil type, examine the factors that influence soil.

Sample answer

This answer will explore how *climate, parent material and bedrock, organic material and leaching* has influenced **brown earth soils**.

Climate

Climate is the most important factor that influences soil formation. The most common soil in any region is its **zonal soil**, which is associated with that region's climate. Brown soil (which develops in areas of cool temperate oceanic climate) is Ireland's zonal soil. Climate ultimately determines the **water content** of soil. Brown soil is most common in the midlands and east of Ireland, where well-distributed annual rainfall is generally a moderate 800–1,000mm. Moderate, well-distributed rainfall supports vegetation growth that helps to maintain a cycle of fertility in brown soils. It also gives rise to steady but *moderate leaching*, which will be examined later in more detail.

The climate of an area also determines **weathering**, which plays a vital role in soil formation.

- *Carbonation* is a form of chemical weathering that occurs when carbonic acid in rainwater reacts with and dissolves calcium carbonate in limestone. This provides soluble calcium that helps to enrich the brown soils of Ireland's limestone areas.

- *Freeze-thaw action* occurs whenever winter temperatures range frequently a\bove and below 0°C. This has helped to break down exposed rock and to provide the initial parent material (mineral particles) for brown and other soils.

Climate largely determines the type of **natural vegetation** in an area and this also affects the formation of soil. *Deciduous forests* once enriched Irish brown soils with abundant organic material. The role of organic material on soil will be examined later.

- **Parent material and bedrock**

  (Describe as in the sample answer on page 182).

- **Organic material**

  (Describe as on page 182).

- **Leaching**

  (Describe as on page 183).

The Leaving Cert marking scheme for 'Option' questions is given on page 183.

How did deciduous forests such as this one affect the development of brown soils?

Sum Up

- The main **components** of soil are:
  - *Parent material* or the mineral particles from which soil is derived. These tiny particles make up about 45 per cent of soil. They vary in size and may contain enriching compounds and soluble minerals.
  - *Organic matter*, which includes plant litter and animal remains. These decay to form fertilising humus.
  - *Air* and *water*, each of which make up about 25 per cent of soil and are essential for fertility.
- Soil components link together to provide the following **soil characteristics**:
  - *Texture* refers to how soil feels to the touch. Sandy soils have rough textures; clay soils have smooth textures.
  - Soil *structure* depends on the shape of groups of soil particles called *peds*. Round peds give (usually fertile) *crumb structures*. Flat peds give (often infertile) *platy structures*.
  - A soil's *pH value* indicates whether the soil is alkaline (high pH), neutral (around pH 7) or acidic (low pH). Neutral soils are usually the most fertile.
  - *Organic content* consists of plant litter and animal remains that are broken down by micro-organisms into humus.
  - *Colour* often indicates a soil's fertility. Brown soils are usually fertile and grey soils are normally infertile.
  - The *water retention* properties of soil depend largely on its structure and on its texture.
  - The *water content* of soil depends on its water retention properties, on precipitation levels, on the nature of underlying rock and on the presence of a hard pan.
- The following **natural processes** influence soil formation:
  - *Weathering*, such as freeze-thaw action, exfoliation, carbonation, hydrolysis and oxidation.
  - *Erosion* by rivers (which forms alluvial soil), by moving ice (which formed boulder clay) and by wind (which formed loess).
  - *Leaching*, which is the downward movement through the soil of soluble minerals and plant nutrients. *Podzolisation* and *laterisation* are extreme forms of leaching.
  - *Calcification*, which takes place when *capillary action* draws moisture up through the soil.
  - *Humification*, which is the decomposition of organic matter into fertile humus.
- Soils may be **classified** as follows:
  - *Zonal soils* occupy large climatic zones.
  - *Intrazonal soils* are influenced by local factors.
  - *Azonal soils* are recently formed soils that are not yet fully developed.

Test Yourself
eTest.ie

Activities

Leaving Cert questions:

1. With reference to one soil that you have studied, examine how parent material, climate and organic matter influence soil.

2. Describe and explain the characteristics of any one soil type studied by you.

3. Examine two of the natural processes that influence soil.

4. Examine the factors that influence soil characteristics.

Marking schemes
The marking schemes for all these questions are similar to the marking scheme described on page 183.

Soil is a *renewable resource* that can be used again and again provided it is managed properly. But soil usually depends on vegetation cover for its fertility and its survival. People sometimes destroy vegetation cover by deforestation,* by overgrazing* or by overcultivation.* The soil then loses its fertility and may become exposed to and destroyed by agents of erosion such as running water and wind.

Case Study 1:
Deforestation in the Amazonian rainforests

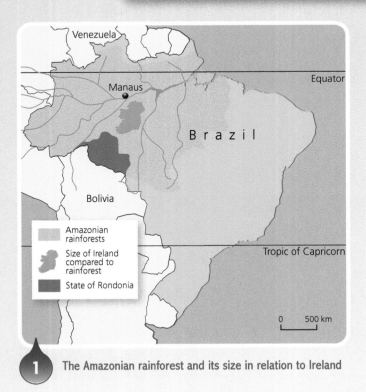

1 The Amazonian rainforest and its size in relation to Ireland

The Amazonian rainforest is a vast region of hot, wet **equatorial climate** (see Figure 1). Daily temperatures there average a high 28°C throughout the year and afternoons are typically marked by heavy convectional rain.*

Selva is the name given to the vast, dense rainforest that forms the natural vegetation of the Amazon Basin. These equatorial rainforests are among the most luxuriant and biodiverse* in the world. They contain a vast array of plant and animal species.

Yet the **soils** of the equatorial rainforests – which are called *tropical red soils* or *latosols* – are not naturally fertile. They maintain their fertility only through a delicately balanced relationship between equatorial climate, forest and soil (see Figure 2). They depend largely on the forest for their fertility.

For many centuries, the only human inhabitants of the rainforests were small numbers of **Amerindian*** people. These people did little to upset the delicate balance of the selva's ecosystems* or the fertility of its soil. Since the 1960s, however, the region has endured an ever-growing influx of people from outside the rainforest who are determined to clear the forests for short-term profit.

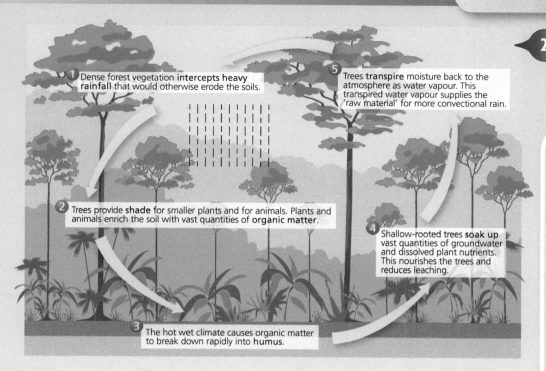

2 How Amazonian soils depend on the forest for their fertility

① Dense forest vegetation **intercepts heavy rainfall** that would otherwise erode the soils.

⑤ Trees **transpire** moisture back to the atmosphere as water vapour. This transpired water vapour supplies the 'raw material' for more convectional rain.

② Trees provide **shade** for smaller plants and for animals. Plants and animals enrich the soil with vast quantities of **organic matter**.

④ Shallow-rooted trees **soak up** vast quantities of groundwater and dissolved plant nutrients. This nourishes the trees and reduces leaching.

③ The hot wet climate causes organic matter to break down rapidly into **humus**.

Terms to know

- **Deforestation:** clearing forests without planting new replacement trees.
- **Overgrazing:** excessive grazing that causes land to become damaged.
- **Overcultivation (overcropping):** excessive cultivation that causes land to become damaged.
- **Convectional rain:** usually short periods of heavy rain; associated with hot air rising from the earth's surface.
- **Biodiversity:** the presence of a wide range of plants and animal species.
- **Transpiration:** the release of water vapour from the surfaces of plants into the atmosphere.
- **Amerindian:** American 'Indian'; people indigenous to the Americas.
- **Ecosystem:** an interlinked system of living things and their natural environment.
- **Desertification:** the spread of desert conditions into new areas, usually following the erosion of exposed topsoil.

Some of these '**outsiders**' are land-hungry *peasants* who, with the blessing of Brazilian governments, have tried to set up farms in the Amazon Basin. Some are commercial *loggers* who have torn through the forest in search of teak, mahogany or other hardwood trees for export. Others were businessmen who received *World Bank* aid to take part in massive settlement and farming projects such as the Polonoroeste Project in the state of Rondonia (see Figure 1). Many were wealthy *cattle ranchers* who cleared vast areas of forest in order to supply American fast-food outlets with cut-price beef burgers. Some are *miners* in search of the high-grade iron ore, copper and gold that lie beneath parts of the Amazon Basin.

The activities of all these 'developers' have contributed to the clearance of an astonishing 40 hectares of forest per minute. This massive **deforestation** causes soils to become more eroded and less fertile:

- When trees are cut, soils become exposed to the full force of equatorial rain. The rain sometimes erodes soil by **sheet erosion**, which is the even washing away of the soil's fertile upper layer.
- **Gully erosion** is even more common. This happens when rivulets of surface water cut deep grooves into the land.
- Without trees to soak up groundwater, **leaching** increases rapidly. More and more soil nutrients are then washed down below the reach of plant roots.
- The absence of trees deprives the soil of the **plant litter** that it needs to remain fertile.
- The 'development' of the selva has also resulted in the severe **pollution** of soil and groundwater. Pollutants range from household rubbish to deadly mercury that is used in gold mining.

Many scientists fear that relentless soil degradation is creating **a cycle of infertility**, **climate change** and **plant failure** that is already transforming segments of former lush forests into desertified* wastelands. This cycle is illustrated in Figure 3.

Cycle of infertility, climate change and plant failure in parts of the Amazon basin

3

- **Infertile and eroded soils** cannot support the **trees** that are needed to transpire water vapour back into the atmosphere.
- Reduced **water vapour** results in dramatically reduced rainfall.
- **Reduced rainfall** results in less vegetation growth.
- **Reduced vegetation** cover exposes soil to more erosion.

Part of the Amazonian rainforest in its natural state.
How does this area maintain its natural fertility?

The results of deforestation in another part of the Amazon Basin.
How has human interference damaged soil fertility in this area?

Case Study 2:
Desertification in the Sahel

Overpopulation in the *Sahel* was examined on pages 34–37.

Desertification is the spread of desert conditions into new areas, usually following the erosion of exposed topsoil. The world's worst instance of desertification is happening in the Sahel region of Africa. The **Sahel** is a narrow zone that runs east–west across Africa at the southern edge of the Sahara Desert (see Figure 4). It occupies large parts of Mali, Chad, Sudan and other countries. Desertification in the Sahel is so bad that desert conditions there are spreading southwards at a rate of 5 to 10 kilometres each year. Human activities have played a major role in this ecological disaster.

Rapid population growth is a major root cause of the problem. Sahelian countries all have high birth rates and declining death rates, which gives rise to rapid population growth in excess of two per cent a year. This has caused many parts of the Sahel to become **overpopulated** – they contain too many people for the resources available.

The increasing population has created a growing need for resources such as food and fuel. This need has in turn given rise to *overgrazing, overcultivation and vegetation clearance*.

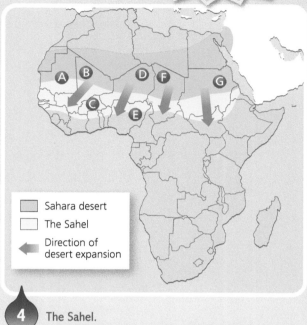

Sahara desert
The Sahel
Direction of desert expansion

4 The Sahel.

*Name each of the countries labelled **A** to **G**.*
Consult your atlas or the map on page 34 if necessary.

A large extended family in northern Nigeria.
Discuss some causes and effects of high fertility rates in the Sahel.

189

Overgrazing

Cattle rearing has always been a major feature of rural life in the Sahel, where ownership of cattle or goats often determines wealth and status. As the human population has increased, so has the number of cattle and goats. **Increasing animal numbers** degrade (damage) the soil in the following ways:

- Animals **overgraze** the land by grazing it beyond its ability to renew itself. They remove grass cover and even crop young trees and shrubs. This leaves the soil bare and vulnerable to wind erosion.

- Large herds of cattle trample and **compact** the soil with their hooves. This makes the soil less porous and results in more surface run-off and erosion in times of infrequent but heavy rainfall.

- Numerous **wells** have been dug to provide watering places for animals. Too many cattle tend to congregate around these wells, causing the land there to become very overgrazed and trampled. The overuse of wells has also used up groundwater that has taken hundreds of years to build up. The water table then falls and many wells dry up.

- In former times, almost all cattle farmers in the Sahel moved seasonally with their cattle in search of fresh pastures. This system of *nomadic herding* allowed soils to rest fallow (unused) for long periods and this allowed soils to renew their fertility. Increasing cattle numbers have now forced many farmers to **abandon nomadic herding** and instead to keep cattle permanently in fenced-off land. Such land is constantly in use and is often severely overgrazed and degraded.

A severely overgrazed area near a well in Agadez, Niger. *Suggest why areas near wells might become overgrazed.*

Overcropping

Rapid population growth has forced many farmers to **overcrop** land (cultivate land excessively) in an attempt to provide sufficient food for themselves and their families. In such cases the soil is not allowed to rest or is not fertilised sufficiently between crops. The soil then becomes progressively more bare and barren.

As overcropped areas become less productive, farmers are sometimes forced to cultivate **marginal land** in order to feed their families. Marginal land is land that that is not fully fertile enough for agriculture. When cultivated, such land quickly becomes barren and bare.

International debt has also contributed to overcropping in the Sahel. Countries such as Niger have gone into heavy debt to Western banks and governments. In order to raise foreign capital to repay such debt, the government of Niger has encouraged farmers to grow cash crops such as *groundnuts* (peanuts) for export. This has led to the following problems:

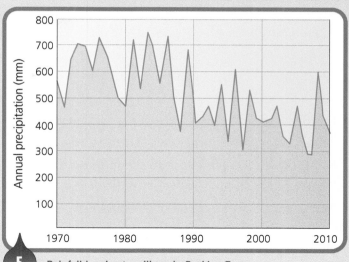

5 Rainfall levels at a village in Burkina Faso between 1970 and 2010.
Do you think the rainfall trends shown here are suited to crop growing? Explain.

- Groundnuts are usually not rotated with any other crop but are grown exclusively on the same ground year after year. This system is called **monoculture**. Groundnut monoculture exhausts the soil so much that after three years of cultivation the land needs to be left fallow for a six-year period. But most Niger farmers cannot afford to rest their land for such long periods. The land has therefore gradually become infertile.

- Many farmers were forced into personal debt in order to purchase the seeds and technology that they needed to grow groundnuts. To pay these debts, some farmers began to devote more and more land to groundnuts. This sometimes caused cattle herding and other land uses to be displaced and pushed into more '**marginal**' semi-desert areas. During particularly dry years, marginal lands produce very little vegetation. They then quickly became overgrazed and barren.

A groundnut crop in Niger.
What problems have been associated with the large-scale commercial growing of groundnuts in Niger?

191

Vegetation clearance

Rapid population growth has resulted in the widespread clearance of trees and shrubs throughout the Sahel. This vegetation clearance takes place partly to provide more land for agriculture. But it is also carried out to supply the **firewood** that most people need to prepare evening meals and to provide warmth. There is now a huge firewood and vegetation crisis throughout the Sahel. This is particularly severe near cities such as Ouagadougou, the capital of Burkina Faso. Almost all trees have been cleared within a **50**-kilometre radius of Ouagadougou.

The firewood collectors.
How might activities such as this contribute to desertification?

Large-scale vegetation clearance leaves much of the Sahel's surface bare and exposed to wind erosion. It also hastens the degradation of soil by depriving it of much-needed organic matter. Another problem is that, as firewood becomes scarce, many people are forced to use dried **animal dung** as fuel. This dung would normally fertilise the soil. Its use as fuel therefore contributes further to soil infertility.

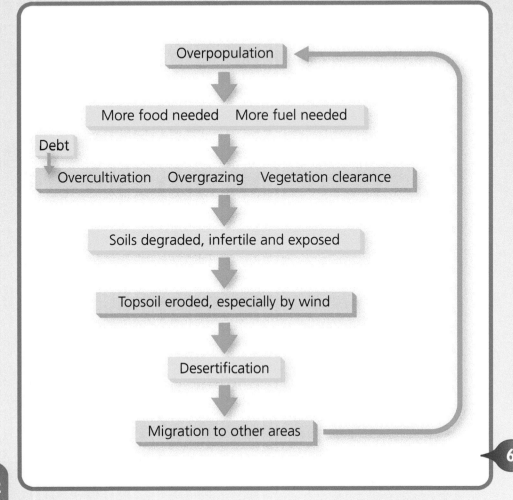

Overgrazing, overcropping and vegetation clearance have all contributed to soil degradation and **infertility** throughout much of the Sahel. With almost no surface vegetation to protect them, degraded soils become dry, dusty and exposed to large-scale **wind erosion.** Winds remove soil in dust storms, leaving large areas desertified and barren. As **desertification** spreads southward throughout the Sahel, millions of people are forced to migrate further southwards in search of food and fuel. These **migrations** serve only to overpopulate more land, creating a growing cycle of overpopulation, desertification and migration.

6 Human activities accelerate soil erosion and desertification in the Sahel

Conserving soil

People employ different methods of preventing or reducing soil erosion. Some of these methods of **soil conservation** are described here.

Contour ploughing

The traditional way to plough a hill is to plough up and down the slope. But this method allows water to flow freely down through the ploughed furrows. The flowing water can carry soil with it and result in destructive gully erosion.

> **Some soil conservation methods**
> - contour ploughing
> - terracing
> - stone lines
> - windbreaks

Contour ploughing is a technique that is used to prevent such gully erosion. In this type of ploughing the furrows and ridges go *across* a slope, following the contours of the hill. They therefore act like miniature dams or barriers that prevent water rushing down the slope. They hold back the water long enough for it to infiltrate (soak) into the ground. This improves soil fertility and leads to more vegetation growth, which further protects the soil from gully erosion.

Although troublesome to carry out, contour ploughing can reduce soil erosion by up to 50 per cent. It is practised widely in the Midwest of the United States where hydraulic equipment on tractors makes the technique less difficult or dangerous.

Terracing

Terracing can be used to prevent soil erosion on slopes that are too steep for contour ploughing. A series of walls are built one above another across a hillside. Behind each retaining wall a wide 'step' or terrace of land is flattened and farmed. The top of each retaining wall forms a little barrier called a 'bund' across the front of each terrace (see the photograph). The terraces and the bunds combine to trap water that would otherwise flow rapidly down-slope. They thus prevent gully erosion and allow water to enrich the soil by soaking slowly into it.

The building and maintenance of terraces is very labour intensive. Nevertheless, terracing is very common in China, Vietnam and other parts of East and Southeast Asia. Terraces there help to prevent heavy monsoon rains from severely eroding hill slopes. They retain enough water to support the intensive cultivation of rice, which is the staple diet of most people in East and Southeast Asia.

Terraced rice cultivation in China.
These terraces prevent serious gully erosion on steep slopes during periods of torrential monsoon rainfall. They retain sufficient water to allow the cultivation of rice.

Original slope

Terraces

Bunds

193

Stone lines

Burkina Faso is a country that lies within the Sahel. It experiences very infrequent but heavy bouts of rain that can result in sheet and gully erosion even on gently sloping land. Farmers in Burkina Faso place little walls or 'lines' of stones (or sometimes of hardened earth) across slopes. The stone lines trap rainwater behind them, so that the water gets time to soak into the ground rather than flow downslope. This prevents sheet and gully erosion and also helps to replenish local water tables.

Stone lines are most effective on very gentle slopes where they may take up less than two per cent of the land but can result in a 50 per cent increase in crop yields. They have the advantage of being cheap and easy to build. In Burkina Faso they are built and repaired during the dry season when other farming tasks require less labour.

Low stone walls are built across a gentle slope

Water trapped behind the stone lines can infiltrate into the ground

Building 'stone' lines in Burkina, Faso

Windbreaks

Windbreaks or **shelter belts** are an effective means of conservation in flat areas that are liable to suffer from wind erosion. They are barriers of trees and leafy shrubs that are planted along the edges of fields. They prevent the wind blowing the soil away or flattening or damaging cereal crops such as rice or wheat. Windbreaks can protect large areas of land. Studies in West Africa have shown that their presence can increase crop yields by up to 20 per cent. Many conservation projects in the Sahel include planting windbreaks of native varieties of trees and plants that are suited to local climatic conditions.

Windbreaks can also provide a variety of other benefits.

- The roots of windbreak vegetation help to bind soil together and so contribute to soil conservation.
- Fruit- or nut-bearing windbreak trees are sources of food.
- As windbreak trees multiply, they can be thinned occasionally and used to provide firewood or fencing posts.

Sum Up

- **Human activities** can destroy natural vegetation and damage soil fertility so that soils are exposed to and eroded by water or wind.
  - Tropical red soils in the **Amazonian rainforests** depend on selva vegetation for their fertility. Cattle ranchers and other people **deforest** vast areas of selva. Deforested soils soon lose their fertility and become exposed to sheet and gully erosion.
- Desert conditions are spreading rapidly in the **Sahel** region on the south of the Sahara Desert. **Overpopulation** has resulted in overgrazing, overcropping and vegetation clearance in the Sahel. These activities are major causes of desertification:
  - Increasing numbers of cattle **overgraze** land and trample soil. This happens especially where cattle numbers are concentrated near wells and on fenced-off land.
  - **Overcropping** is the excessive cultivation of land. It happens where people grow food crops in unsuitable marginal land. It happened in Niger where people grew groundnuts as a monoculture cash crop without resting or fertilising the soil sufficiently.
  - **Vegetation is cleared** to provide firewood and land for agriculture, especially in areas around large cities. The soil is deprived of the organic matter that vegetation would provide. This deprivation becomes worse if animal dung is also used as fuel.
  - All the above activities lead to soil degradation and infertility. Infertile soils become exposed to and are eroded by wind. This results in **desertification**. People are then forced to migrate into other areas, where the cycle of overpopulation, infertility and desertification continues.
- **Soil conservation** methods include *contour ploughing, terracing* and building *stone lines* on slopes. *Windbreaks* are used to protect land from wind erosion.

Activities

Leaving Cert Higher Level questions:

1. Discuss how human activities can accelerate soil erosion.
2. Examine how overcropping, overgrazing and desertification can affect soils.
3. Examine two ways in which human activities have impacted on **soils**.

See Leaving Cert marking schemes on page 183.

Suggested answering method and marking scheme for question 3:
Under two main headings, develop *three or four different topics or aspects*. These headings and topics might be as follows.

Overuse of land:

1. Overgrazing in the Sahel
2. Overcropping in the Sahel

Conservation of land:

1. Stone lines in the Sahel
2. Windbreaks in the Sahel

Each aspect/topic is allocated 20 marks:	
Identifying (naming) the aspect	= 4 marks
Examination: at least 6 SRPs at 2 marks each	= 12 marks
Overall coherence	= 4 marks

17 Biomes

Biomes are large natural regions in which *climate, soils, natural vegetation* and *animal life* are all interrelated. There are many different types of biome in the world. Ireland, for example, is located in a temperate deciduous forest biome.

This chapter will examine the **desert biome** in detail.

CLIMATE

Climate is the most important aspect of any biome because it determines the kinds of natural vegetation and animal life that will live in a region. Climate also influences soils.

1 How a biome works

SOILS

Soils are important because they influence the type of vegetation that will grow in a region.

VEGETATION

Natural vegetation is influenced by climate and soils. Vegetation influences animal life and soils.

ANIMALS

Animal life is influenced by climate and natural vegetation. The activities of people can seriously affect the soils, vegetation and even the climate of a biome.

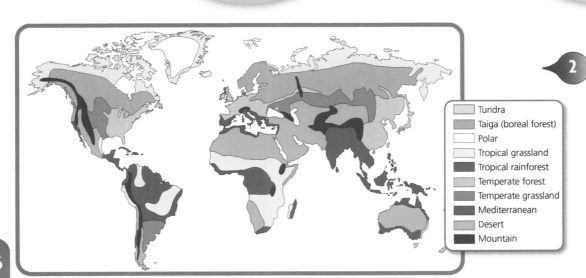

	Tundra
	Taiga (boreal forest)
	Polar
	Tropical grassland
	Tropical rainforest
	Temperate forest
	Temperate grassland
	Mediterranean
	Desert
	Mountain

2 The world's principal biomes.

Name the type of biome at each of the following locations:

(a) Ireland

(b) Greece

(c) The Amazon Basin

(d) Sweden

(e) Iceland

The desert biome

The term 'desert biome' refers generally to the world's hot low-latitude and cool mid-latitude deserts. This chapter will focus on **hot deserts**, which are the best known and most characteristic desert regions in the world.

A **desert** is a large arid (dry) area without sufficient rainfall to support much vegetation or human life.

Part of the Sahara Desert in Libya.
What impression of the Sahara Desert does this photograph give?

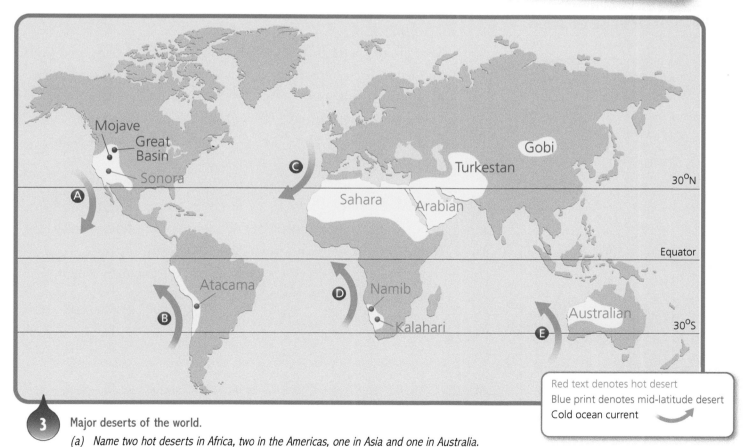

Red text denotes hot desert
Blue print denotes mid-latitude desert
Cold ocean current

3 Major deserts of the world.

  (a) *Name two hot deserts in Africa, two in the Americas, one in Asia and one in Australia.*

  (b) *Describe the general global location of hot deserts.*

  (c) *Identify by its letter label on the map each of the following cold currents:*
      West Australian Current, Benguela Current, Canaries Current, California Current, Peru Current.

Where are the hot deserts?

Figure 3 on the previous page shows that hot deserts are generally located in tropical and sub-tropical latitudes **between 15° and 30°** north and south of the Equator. Much of this zone is in the path of **the trade winds.*** Some of it lies in **high pressure*** **belts** that exist over landmasses about 30° from the Equator.

Most hot deserts are located **on the western sides of continents**, near **cold ocean currents**.

Terms to know

- **Trade winds:** prevailing winds that blow towards the Equator from latitudes of approximately 30° north and south.
- **High atmospheric pressure** occurs when dense air presses down on the earth's surface. It usually give rise to dry stable weather.
- **Dew:** precipitation in the form of moisture that collects on the ground. Dew forms when night temperatures fall and cause water vapour in the air to condense.
- **Fog:** cloud that collects on the earth's surface.

Hot desert climate

Hot desert climate is **very dry**, with a yearly rainfall of between 0mm and 250mm. Rainfall is as unpredictable as it is rare. When rain does occur, it usually comes in the form of short, *heavy downpours* that affect small, localised areas. These 'desert storms' are usually of limited use for plant growth for the following reasons:

- The heavy rains do not have much opportunity to infiltrate the soil. Rainwater runs rapidly on the desert surface, causing flash floods and eroding deep gullies.
- High temperatures cause rain to evaporate very quickly off the desert surface. Some rain evaporates even before it reaches the ground.

Very limited precipitation can occur in the form of **dew*** and **fog.*** Sudden drops in temperature can cause night dews in parts of the Sahara. Fog sometimes brings limited moisture to coastal areas where cool ocean currents flow offshore. Such fogs are common in the coastal sand dunes of the Namib Desert in southwest Africa.

The climate is **hot**, especially in summer, when daytime temperatures can exceed **45°C**. But temperatures can drop by up to 30°C within an hour of sunset and night temperatures can fall below freezing point in winter. This *diurnal* (day/night) *temperature range* is greater than the average summer/winter temperature range of between **20°C and 25°C**. That is why some geographers say the 'night is the winter of the desert'.

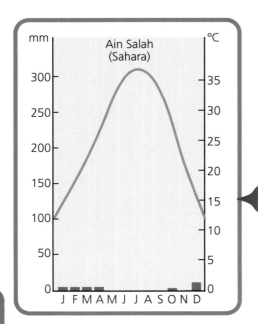

4 Climate graph for Ain Salah, Algeria, in the Sahara Desert.

(a) Calculate the annual temperature range at Ain Salah.

(b) Name and state the precipitation levels of the wettest month and the driest months at Ain Salah.

(c) Contrast summer and winter climatic conditions at Ain Salah.

(d) How do you think the climatic conditions shown might influence plant and animal life at Ain Salah?

Why deserts are dry

- Some hot desert areas lie in **high pressure** belts that run across much of the earth at about 30° north and south of the Equator (see Figure 5). Air descends towards the earth along these high pressure belts. As it does so, the air becomes warmer. Warm air holds more water vapour than cooler air, so the descending air absorbs moisture. That is why high pressure brings prolonged dry conditions.

- Most hot desert regions are in the path of the **trade winds** that blow over much of the earth from 30° latitude towards the Equator (Figure 5). As these winds blow towards the Equator, they become warmer. Warm air holds more water vapour than cold air. The trade winds therefore absorb rather than emit moisture, and they are therefore dry winds.

- Occasionally, moisture-laden winds can blow in from the western seas towards the deserts, but these winds must pass over cold **ocean currents**. As they do so, they are cooled and lose almost all of their moisture – usually in the form of fog – before they reach the land

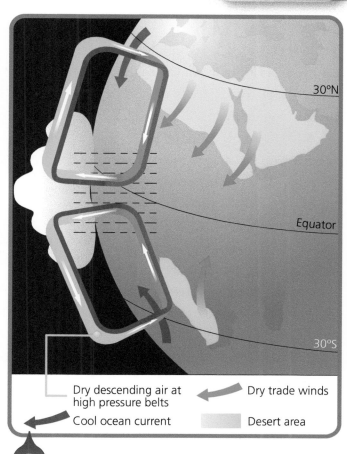

30°N

Equator

30°S

Dry descending air at high pressure belts

Dry trade winds

Cool ocean current

Desert area

5 Focus on desert locations in Africa

Why deserts are hot by day . . .

- Hot deserts are in the **tropics**, where the sun shines from almost vertically overhead in the summertime. These sunrays reach the earth's surface at almost right angles. They are therefore concentrated over small areas of ground and so give great heat.

- Another reason for high daytime temperatures is that the desert atmosphere contains little or **no cloud or humidity** that would help to block sunrays. This, together with a general absence of vegetation or water bodies, allows sunrays to be absorbed rapidly into the desert surface. The surface then returns great heat to the atmosphere, giving rise to high atmospheric temperatures.

. . . and cold by night

- **Cloudless skies** allow daytime temperatures to rise rapidly. But with no clouds and little humidity to blanket it, the heat escapes quickly after nightfall.

A night scene in the Sahara Desert.
What is meant by the term 'diurnal temperature range' and why is this range so large in hot deserts?

Soils

The dominant soil types in hot deserts are **aridisols** or dry (arid) desert soils. These soils are influenced greatly by hot, dry climatic conditions.

Some aridisols are potentially fertile and need only water to produce luxuriant plant life. This can be seen in *oases** within the Sahara Desert or where *irrigation** schemes have helped deserts bloom in parts of Libya and southern California.

Most desert soils, however, do not favour extensive plant growth. There are many reasons for this, most of them related to climatic conditions. Some of these reasons are outlined below.

Vegetation cannot easily survive in these stony, coarse-textured soils in the Namib Desert in Namibia

Little soil cover or coarse-textured soils

Many hot desert areas are rocky or stony and have little soil cover. Many other areas have coarse-textured gravelly soils. This is because dry climatic conditions have allowed winds to blow away finer dust and sand particles, leaving behind only coarser particles, stones or rock. Coarse-textured soils cannot retain what little moisture is available to them. They therefore tend to be infertile.

Lack of water and humus

Dry conditions and coarse-textured soils cause vegetation to be very sparse and, in some areas, non-existent. Sparse vegetation leads to a shortage of plant litter, which in turn leads to a scarcity of humus. A scarcity of humus contributes to soil infertility.

Poor development

Low precipitation leads to a lack of chemical weathering that would normally contribute to the formation of soil. This, together with a shortage of humus, means that aridisols are often poorly developed. They are without the clear horizons or the varied components (organic material, water, etc.) that exist in most Irish soils. Some aridisols consist of little more than a collection of broken-down mineral particles.

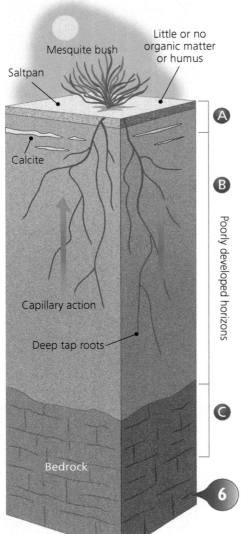

Little or no organic matter or humus

Mesquite bush

Saltpan

Calcite

Capillary action

Deep tap roots

Poorly developed horizons

Bedrock

A

B

C

6 Soil profile of a typical aridisol.
Why are there fewer clear horizons in this type of soil than there are in most Irish soils?

Capillary action and associated processes

Evaporation exceeds precipitation in hot, dry desert regions. In such regions, groundwater is drawn up through the soil by a process called **capillary action** (see page 179). Capillary action can lead in turn to salinisation and calcification.

- **Salinisation** is a process in which dissolved salts such as sodium and chloride move up to the surface. These salts are poisonous to most plants. Their presence on the surface may lead to the formation of barren *saltpans.**

- **Calcification** is the build-up of calcite or calcium close to the surface. Extreme calcification in hot desert areas can result in the formation of *hardpans* that plant roots cannot penetrate. Such hardpans further reduce soil fertility.

Terms to know

- **Oases** (plural of oasis): areas of desert that have been made fertile by the presence of water on or near the surface.
- **Irrigation**: the artificial watering of a dry area.
- **Saltpans**: areas in which evaporating water has deposited salt on the surface of the ground.

Saltpans and flamingos in the Kalahari Desert.

The northern part of the Kalahari Desert is famous for its saltpans and migrating flamingos.

Limited rainfall from January to March causes temporary shallow lakes to form on the impermeable hardpans of the desert surface. The northern Kalahari then becomes home to millions of pink flamingos that migrate into the region to breed.

Following the rainy season, the shallow lakes begin to evaporate quickly to leave blindingly white saltpans in their wake. As lake waters evaporate, crusts of salt can accumulate on flamingos' legs, making it impossible for some young birds to fly. These birds perish as the rest of their kind migrate out of the region in search of water and food.

Death Valley in California is one of the most barren desert areas on earth. But it contains more than 600 different plant species.

Vegetation (flora)

Vegetation is **scant** in hot deserts, mainly because of a **shortage of water** and **high rates of evaporation** owing to elevated daytime temperatures. Yet many plant species survive. They have different ways of adapting to desert conditions.

- Many desert plants use large **root systems** to find water.
  - Some plants have *taproots* that reach deep into the ground in search of water. The most famous of these is the *mesquite bush*. Its roots can penetrate the soil to a depth of 25m.
    - Some cacti and other plants have *shallow roots*, which spread outwards (rather than downwards) for great distances, so that they create a large moisture-collecting area in times of rainfall.
  - Some plants adapt to short and very infrequent desert downpours by growing very quickly. These plants are called **ephemerals**. The seeds of many ephemerals have waxy surfaces, which allow them to retain moisture for long periods of time. These seeds remain dormant, sometimes for years, awaiting desert rain. When rain does fall, the seeds develop into mature plants, burst into flower and produce a new generation of seeds, all within a few weeks. The old plants then die, while the new seeds become dormant and wait for the next period of rain. *Desert poppies* and the *creosote bush* of North America are examples of ephemerals.
  - Many plants are **succulents**. They store water for long periods in their impermeable, waxy stems, in their roots or even in underground bulbs. The *barrel cactus* and the *giant saguaro* (see opposite page) are examples of succulents.
  - Some plants produce **juicy fruits**, which are eagerly devoured and digested by birds. The digested fruit seeds are then spread over large areas in the birds' droppings.
  - The leaves and barks of some shrubs contain **poisonous or unpleasant substances**, which protect them from most hungry animals. The *Sodom apple*, for example, cannot be eaten by goats or camels.

The desert in bloom. These ephemerals bloomed suddenly following a rare desert downpour. Their life cycle will span only a few weeks.

(a) *What is meant by the term 'ephemerals'?*

(b) *How do the seeds of these plants survive long periods of drought?*

- Plants such as the *cereus or desert dandelion* **bloom only at night** when evaporation rates are lowest. The flowers of the cereus remain closed during the day to escape the drying effect of the scorching sun.
- Some plants use **several different strategies** to adapt to the hot desert environment. The *saguaro* or *giant cactus* of the Sonoran Desert in Arizona, USA is an example of such a plant (see below).

Oases

An **oasis** is an area of desert that has been made fertile by the presence of surface water. The water and the sun's heat usually contribute to the lush growth of vegetables, cereals, fig trees and other types of vegetation. The date palm is popular among oasis dwellers because it provides welcome shade as well as fruit.

People and hot desert vegetation

- Large herds of cattle or sheep have **overgrazed** semi-desert areas, such as parts of the Sahel in Africa. This destruction of natural vegetation has contributed to desertification (the spread of desert conditions).
- People in areas such as southern California have used **irrigation** to produce high crop yields in hot deserts. But the rapid evaporation of irrigation water can result in **salinisation**, or the build-up of salt, near the surface of the land. Too much salt makes the soil toxic to plants.

The elf owl – a little hider.

Despite its thorny skin, some animals manage to burrow holes in the saguaro. This hole was made by a woodpecker. It is now the home of the *elf owl*, which is the world's smallest owl. The elf owl is a nocturnal bird that hunts at night and rests in its little saguaro 'home' throughout the heat of the day.

The saguaro or giant cactus and how it adapts to hot, dry climatic conditions.
The saguaro can reach up to 15 metres in height, can weigh up to ten tonnes and can live for up to 200 years.

Pleats (grooves) in its stem and branches allow the saguaro to expand greatly. This allows the plant to store large quantities of water in its spongy inside during times of rainfall. The vertical grooves also help to direct **rainwater** to the base of the plant, where the plant's roots can absorb it.

Thorns (which are actually the plant's leaves) protect the saguaro from most species of hungry **animals**. The thorns also create areas of **still air** around the plant, protecting it from the drying effect of desert winds.

Waxy, impermeable skin acts like a plastic wrapper around the plant. It helps to prevent moisture in the plant escaping.

How plants adapt to desert soils

Desert soils usually suffer from *shortages of moisture and organic matter*. The process of *salinisation* may result in a build-up of harmful salts on upper soils, while the process of *calcification* can cause calcite hardpans to form close to the surface.

Desert flora adapt in different ways to these soil characteristics.

- The **roots** of many desert plants have evolved to survive in desert soils. The *mesquite* plant, for example, has developed deep *taproots* that can seek out moisture as far as 25 metres beneath the surface. Other plants, such as *cacti* and the *creosote* bush, have *shallow, wide-spreading roots* that draw water and organic matter from large areas of surface soil. These shallow roots may also avoid having to penetrate down through calcite hardpans.

- **Desert** plants such as the *creosote* bush tend to be **widely spaced**. This gives each plant a chance to draw moisture and nourishment from a wide area without competition from other plants.

- Desert flora have evolved various strategies of conserving the moisture that they draw from moisture-deficient soils. Cacti such as the *saguaro* and the *prickly pear* have thin **spines** or **thorns** instead of leaves. These spines transpire much less moisture than larger deciduous leaves. The **waxy, 'plastic-like' skins** of the saguaro and the prickly pear also help to prevent the loss of precious moisture.

- Some plants possess hardy and thick-skinned **seeds**. These seeds can hibernate for years in dry soils until a desert **rainstorm** provides enough moisture for them to take root and to grow.

- Plants such as the *Joshua tree* and the *mesquite* are **salt tolerant**. They can survive in the saline conditions that exist in some salinised desert areas.

The prickly pear.
How does this plant conserve the limited moisture that it draws from the soil?

Creosote bushes in the Sonoran desert of Arizona, USA. These strong-scented bushes are among the oldest living things on earth. Some creosote colonies are believed to be more than 11,000 years old. *Why are creosote bushes spaced widely apart from each other?*

Animals (fauna)

Hot deserts can support numerous animal species, but only if these animals are adapted to survive prolonged very hot, dry conditions. Desert animals have different ways of adapting to these conditions.

The rattlesnake

The rattlesnake is a native of the desert but is seldom seen there. Why?

The fennec fox

(a) How does the fennec fox obtain enough liquid to survive?

(b) Suggest two advantages of the fennec fox's very large ears.

The hiders

Many animals survive by avoiding the scorching heat of the sun.

- Some creatures are **nocturnal**. They hide away in cool places during the day and come out at night to hunt and to eat. Animals such as the *rattlesnake* and *kangaroo rat* (which live in underground holes and burrows) and the *elf owl* (which lives in holes burrowed out of cacti – see page 203) are examples of nocturnal animals.

- Some animals **hibernate** in order to survive long dry periods. They remain very still and underground for extended periods. Then, when rain finally arrives, they emerge to frantically eat, mate and breed. Examples of these are the *toads* of the Arizona Desert in the United States. They hibernate, often for more than a year, to await a desert rainstorm. They then emerge quickly to the surface and immediately enter flood pools to mate. Within 24 hours of mating, the females' eggs will be fertilised and hatched. Within two days, the pools will be full of tadpoles. Within two weeks (if the flood waters have not evaporated) a new generation of toads will emerge from the pools.

- Some animals avoid the heat by simply *staying in the shadow* of plants. The *jack rabbit* of North America uses cacti for shade, while many desert *insects* avoid the sun's rays by staying on the shaded sides of twigs or plant stems.

The non-drinkers

Some animals do not need to drink water: they get all the liquid they need from the food they eat.

- Carnivorous (meat-eating) animals, such as the *fennec fox,* get much of the liquid they need from the blood of their prey.

- The *desert gazelle* gets all the liquid it needs from the vegetation it eats. It conserves moisture by never urinating. Instead, it passes uric acid in the form of small, dry pellets.

Big-eared animals

Animals lose heat through their ears, which contain many blood vessels. The *fennec fox*, the *jack rabbit* and the *desert hedgehog* all have very large ears. This helps to keep them cool in heat of the day.

Birds

Most birds need regular water supplies, so few bird species live in deserts. Those that do have novel ways of adapting to their environment. The **roadrunner** of the North American deserts runs from place to place because it can use less energy by running than by flying. The roadrunner also has a very large tail, which it often spreads over itself like a parasol during the heat of the day.

The marvellous camel

Few large animals can withstand excessive heat or can retain moisture well enough to survive in the open in hot, dry desert conditions. The camel is a notable exception. Known for centuries as 'the ship of the desert', the camel is perfectly adapted to the desert environment.

The roadrunner
How does the roadrunner adapt to hot desert conditions?

During sandstorms, the camel can close its **nostrils** and can lower its inner **eyelids** to protect its eyes.

A tough-skinned **mouth** enables the camel to chew thorny desert plants.

The camel can drink more than 100 litres of water at a time. By not sweating, it conserves body fluids. It can thus survive for several months **without water**.

Fat in the **hump** acts as a food reserve. Because fat is concentrated in one area, the rest of the camel's body can cool more easily.

Coarse hair protects the camel's **back** from the sun.

Tough belly and kneepads enable the camel to lie on hot sand.

Wide, padded **feet** allow the camel to travel easily over soft sand.

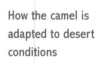

How the camel is adapted to desert conditions

- **Biomes** are large regions in which climate, soils, natural vegetation and animal life are all interrelated.
- One such biome is the **desert biome**. Hot deserts are generally situated between 15° and 30° of latitude and on the western sides of landmasses.
- Hot desert **climate** is **dry**, with annual precipitation of between 0mm and 250mm. Rain is very infrequent and tends to occur in short heavy downpours. The climate is dry because hot deserts lie on *high pressure belts* or in the path of the dry *trade winds*. Cool *ocean currents* rob any onshore winds of their moisture.
- Daytime **temperatures** can exceed 45°C in summer. Temperatures are very high because hot deserts lie within the *tropics* and usually have *no cloud* to block out direct sunshine. The *diurnal temperature range* can exceed 30°C. Cloudless skies allow temperatures to drop sharply after nightfall.
- Desert **soils** are mostly *aridisols*. Some aridisols need only water to make them very fertile. But many aridisols do not favour lush vegetation growth because they are very *coarse-textured*, lack *moisture* and *humus* and are *poorly developed*. They may also experience *salinisation* and *calcification*.
- **Plants** must adapt to hot, dry desert **climate**. Plants such as the mesquite bush have deep *taproots*. *Ephemerals* such as the creosote grow very quickly when rain occurs. *Succulents* such as cacti store water for long periods. The 'desert dandelion' *blooms only at night*. The *saguaro* adapts to desert conditions in a variety of ways. It uses its pleats, waxy skin and thorns to store water and to protect itself from drying wind and from hungry animals.
- Plants must also adapt to **soils** that are deficient in moisture and humus and that may possess calcite hardpans and harmful salts. The mesquite plant uses deep *taproots* to search for precious moisture. *Widely spaced* creosote bushes seek out moisture and humus with *wide-spreading roots*. The *spines and waxy skin* of the saguaro helps to conserve moisture, while the thick-skinned *seeds of* some plants can hibernate for years in dry soil. Plants such as the Joshua tree are *salt-tolerant*.
- **Animals** adapt to hot, dry conditions. Some animals *shelter* from the sun. These include nocturnal animals such as rattlesnakes, hibernating animals such as toads and animals such as jack rabbits that seek the shade of plants. The fennec fox needs to drink *very little water* and has *long ears* to help keep it cool.

Test Yourself
eTest.ie

Leaving Cert Higher Level questions:

1. Describe and explain the main characteristics of one biome that you have studied.
2. Illustrate the development of biomes, with reference to a specific example.

(Sample paper)

3. Examine the influence of climate on the characteristics of one biome that you have studied.
4. Describe how plant and animal life adapt to soil and climatic conditions in a biome that you have studied.

The official marking scheme and a sample answer to this question are provided on pages 208–209.

Leaving Cert exam question, marking scheme and sample answer

The question
Describe how plant and animal life adapt to soil and climate conditions in a biome that you have studied.

Marking scheme
- Use *three or four* aspects in your answer.
- At least one aspect must refer to *plant life* and at least one must refer to *animal life*.
- At least one aspect must refer to *soil* and at least one aspect must refer to *climate*.
- Allow 1 SRP for naming the chosen biome (once).

Number of aspects: 3 (27 + 27 + 26 marks) **or** 4 (20 + 20 + 20 + 20 marks)

For each aspect:
Identifying aspect of adaptation: 4 marks/4 marks
Examination: 8 SRPs at 2 marks each **or** 6 SRPs at 2 marks each
Overall coherence: 7/6 marks graded **or** 4 marks graded

The sample answer that follows examines four aspects. *Two* aspects will refer to plant life and *two* will refer to animal life. *One* aspect will refer to soil and *three* will refer to climate.

Use the marking scheme to mark the sample answer.

Sample answer

In a hot desert biome, <u>plant life has to adapt to aridisol soils</u> that commonly suffer from shortages of moisture and organic matter. Some desert soils also contain high levels of harmful salt and may contain impermeable calcite hardpans.

The <u>plant parts</u> of many species of desert flora have evolved to allow plants to survive in desert soils. The mesquite plant, for example, has developed deep taproots that can seek out moisture in the soil to a depth of 25 metres. Other plants, such as cacti and the creosote bush, posses shallow, widely spreading roots that absorb water and organic matter from a large area of the surface soil. Such shallow roots may also avoid having to penetrate down through calcite hardpans that are formed by a process called calcification. Cacti such as the saguaro and the prickly pear have thin spines (thorns) instead of leaves. These spines transpire much less moisture than deciduous leaves would. The 'waxy' skins of these plants also help to retain precious moisture that has been absorbed from arid soils. Some desert plant species possess hardy and thick-skinned seeds. These seeds can hibernate for years on dry soils until a rainstorm provides enough moisture to for them to take root and grow. Plants such as the Joshua tree are salt-tolerant, so they can survive the saline conditions that exist in salinised desert areas.

The <u>saguaro</u> or <u>giant cactus</u> of the Sonoran Desert in the USA is wonderfully adapted to very hot (45°C by day) and very dry (less than 250mm of rain per year) <u>climatic conditions</u>.

Grooves in its stem and branches allow the saguaro to expand greatly. This allows the plant to store large quantities of water in its spongy inside during infrequent but heavy rainstorms. The vertical grooves also help to direct rainwater to the base of the plant, where the plant's roots can absorb it. Thorns protect the saguaro from most species of hungry animals. The thorns also create areas of still air around the plant, protecting it from the withering effect of warm desert winds. Waxy, impermeable skin acts like a plastic wrapper around the saguaro. It helps to prevent moisture within the plant from escaping during the scorching days and long droughts of a hot desert climate. These assorted survival strategies allow the saguaro not only to survive but also to grow up to 15 metres tall and to live for up to 200 years.

Many animals hide away in order to survive in the hot, dry desert climate.

Some animals are nocturnal. They hide away in cool places during the day and come out at night to hunt and eat. Animals such as the rattlesnake and the kangaroo rat (which live in underground holes and burrows) and the elf owl (which lives in the saguaro plant) are examples of nocturnal animals. Some animals hibernate to survive long dry periods. They remain very still and stay underground for extended periods. Then, when rain finally arrives, they emerge to frantically eat, mate and breed. Examples of this are the toads of the Arizona Desert in the USA. They may hibernate for more than a year to await a desert rainstorm. They then emerge, mate and manage to create a new generation of toads within a two-week period – all before the waters resulting from the rainstorm evaporate. Some animals avoid the heat by simply staying in the shadow of plants. The jack rabbit of North America uses cacti for shade, while many desert insects avoid the sun's rays by staying on the shaded side of twigs or plant stems.

The camel – 'the ship of the desert' – is the animal that is most marvellously adapted to hot dry climatic conditions.

- During sandstorms, the camel can close its nostrils and lower its unique inner eyelids in order to protect its eyes.
- Its tough-skinned mouth enables the camel to chew the thorny plants that grow in hot, dry desert conditions.
- Its tough belly and thick kneepads enable it to lie on hot sand, while coarse hair helps to protect the camel's back from the sun.
- Its wide, padded feet allow it to travel easily over soft sand on which other large animals would struggle to walk.
- The camel can drink up to 100 litres of water at a time. By not sweating, it conserves body fluids. These two factors can allow camels to survive for several months without water.
- Fat in its hump acts as a food reserve that allows the camel to survive for long periods without eating.
- Because its fat is concentrated in one area (the hump), the rest of the camel's body can cool more easily. This is important for its wellbeing in hot desert conditions.

18 How Human Activities Alter Biomes

Human activities have severely altered biomes in many parts of the world. This chapter will examine how this has happened in the *rainforests of the Amazon* and in *Africa's Sahel region*.

📁 Case Study 1:
Some effects of human activities in the Amazon rainforests

Revise the Case Study on pages 186–188.

The Amazon Basin in South America provides one of the world's finest examples of a **tropical rainforest biome**. Its hot, wet equatorial climate supports a dense natural forest called *selva*. The selva is one the world's richest and most biodiverse regions. In its natural state, it contains an astonishing array of plant and animal species.

But Amazonia's* biome is very delicate and finely balanced. Since the middle of the twentieth century its survival has been threatened by the activities of people who began to clear the forests for a variety of purposes. Some of these 'outsiders' were road builders or miners. Others were land-hungry peasants who were encouraged by Brazilian governments to colonise the Amazon Basin. Some were loggers who tore down large areas of forest in search of teak, mahogany or other commercially valuable tree species. Wealthy cattle ranchers have been responsible for up to **60** per cent of **deforestation,** which in the mid-1990s took place at a staggering rate of up to **40** hectares per minute.

These human activities have altered or threatened the rainforest biome in several ways. Some of their **negative impacts** are described on the pages that follow.

Terms to know

- **Amazonia:** the Amazon Basin region.
- **Transpiration:** the process by which plants emit water vapour from their leaves.
- **Subsistence farming:** a system of agriculture that yields enough produce only to feed the farmer and his or her family.

Commercial loggers in action in the Amazonian forest

Impacts on water and soil
Water

Rainforest regions experience regular and large amounts of rainfall. The Amazonian city of Manaus, for example, receives more than 2,100mm precipitation annually. But **trees** help to control water systems in rainforests. In its natural state, the forest has an almost continuous *tree canopy* that protects the ground from the direct force of heavy equatorial rain. Much rainwater is *intercepted* by the tree canopy and evaporates from the trees before it can reach the ground. Some of the water that does soak into the forest floor is immediately soaked up by tree roots and is returned to the atmosphere through the process of *transpiration*.*

Deforestation disrupts this natural system of water control. It robs the rainforest of its intercepting canopy, so that *more rain* falls directly on to the ground. It also robs the ground of trees that would soak up groundwater and 'recycle' it back into the atmosphere. Deforestation also allows *heavy rain* to beat directly off the exposed soil. All this results in more groundwater flowing directly into rivers. Rivers then become larger and flood nearby plains. Heavy rain also transports *soil* into local river beds. This too causes river levels to rise and so contributes to **flooding**. Increased flooding has damaged many low-lying areas the Amazon Basin. It has also damaged some upper regions of the Basin in Peru and Ecuador. Flooding there has destroyed vegetation and animal habitats and has resulted in countless millions of animals drowning.

Water pollution has also impacted on Amazonia's biome. 'Developers' within the region have polluted rivers and groundwater with a variety of waste ranging from household sewage to deadly mercury used in the process of gold mining.

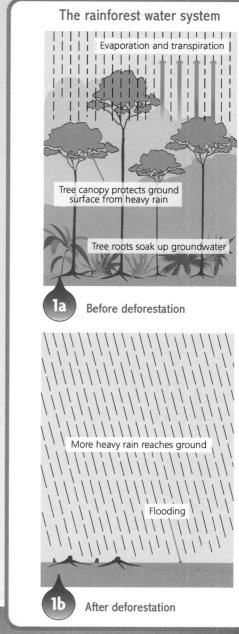

The rainforest water system

Evaporation and transpiration

Tree canopy protects ground surface from heavy rain

Tree roots soak up groundwater

1a Before deforestation

More heavy rain reaches ground

Flooding

1b After deforestation

Flooding in Amazonia.
Outline some causes and consequences of increased flooding in Amazonia in recent years.

Severe gully erosion in the Amazon Basin.

(a) *How can deforestation contribute to gully erosion in tropical rainforest biomes?*

(b) *How might severe gully erosion affect such a biome?*

Soil

Deforestation results in soil being exposed to the full force of heavy equatorial rain. The rain sometimes erodes soil by **sheet erosion**, which is the even washing away of the soil's upper layers. **Gully erosion** is even more common in deforested areas of Amazonia. It happens when rivulets of surface water cut deep grooves into the land. Without trees to soak up groundwater, **leaching** increases rapidly. More and more soil nutrients are then washed below the reach of plant roots, making the soil infertile. The absence of trees also deprives soil of the **plant litter** that it needs to maintain fertility. In these circumstances, infertility develops rapidly, especially where those who clear the land fail to fertilise it artificially.

Deforestation also has the effect of exposing soil to high temperatures (a daily average of 28°C at Manaus) and to direct, almost vertical sun rays. These cause the surface of the soil to be baked into a hard, almost brick-like substance on which plants cannot grow. This hard, baked infertile soil is known as **laterite**.

The use of bulldozers and other heavy **machinery** also has the effect of compacting and hardening soil surfaces. This has happened in deforested areas such as the west Brazilian state of Rondonia (see Figure 1, page 186).

Impacts on habitats

Human habitats

Forest peoples have inhabited Amazonia for many thousands of years. It is estimated that by the year 1500 about six million Amerindians (native Americans) lived in the Amazon rainforests. By the year 2000 this figure had dropped dramatically to below a quarter of a million and many forest tribes had disappeared completely. These figures reflect the grave problems that forest people face at the hands of those who deforest and 'develop' the rainforest.

The **Yanomami**, who live near the border between Brazil and Venezuela (see Figure 1, page 186) are an example of such a forest people. For many centuries the Yanomami lived off the forest in a sustainable manner. They hunted, fished and practised subsistence farming* in a way that did not damage or upset the delicate balance of the tropical rainforest biome. Since the 1970s, however, the Yanomami have seen their natural environment disappear as waves of cattle ranchers, miners and other 'developers' have invaded and deforested their territory. Some Yanomami may even have been *murdered* by the invading outsiders. Many others died of 'white men's' *diseases* such measles and the common cold, to which they had never before been exposed and against which they had no natural immunity. It is estimated that illnesses such as measles killed up to 90 per cent of the inhabitants of some Yanomami villages.

Those Yanomami who survived have been denied the right to live undisturbed in their own environment. Their *culture* has been diluted or disrupted by Western influences. Their traditional social structures and social life has been largely shattered by the introduction of outside influences such as money, roads, alcohol and sexual exploitation. Many members of this once-proud people have now been reduced to living a miserable roadside existence as beggars or prostitutes. The Brazilian government has in recent years given more recognition to the human rights of forest peoples such as the Yanomami. Laws have been passed that give Amerindian peoples ownership over limited but large tracts of rainforest. But such laws are often difficult to enforce in remote rainforest regions.

The Yanomami have lived for centuries in harmony with their tropical rainforest biome

Now the Yanomami face cultural ruin and possible extinction because of the 'development' of their home region by outsiders

213

Plant and animal habitats

It is believed that the Amazonian rainforest could contain up to two million species of plants and animals. Many of these species have so far proved **invaluable** to medical and other branches of science. Aspirin and quinine (used to treat malaria), for example, were first derived from rainforest trees. It is estimated that up to a quarter of all existing pharmaceutical drugs owe their origins to rainforest species. This is despite that fact that only about one-tenth of those species have yet been studied by people from outside the forests.

But rainforest plants and animals survive delicately in a very finely balanced biome. When the tropical rainforest biome is disrupted by deforestation, many plant and animal species may become **extinct**. It is calculated that deforestation in Amazonia alone may lead to the extinction of one or more species every day. The permanent loss of such species reduces the biodiversity of our planet. It may also deprive humankind of the future means to cure diseases such as cancer and AIDS.

Case Study 2:
The impacts of human activities in the Sahel

> Human activities and desertification in the Sahel were examined in the Case Study on pages 189–192.

Revise this Case Study.

The **Sahel** is a narrow zone that runs east–west across Africa at the southern edge of the Sahara Desert. It lies on a boundary between the Sahara's *hot desert biome* to the north and a *tropical grassland biome* to the south. But desert conditions are gradually spreading southwards over the Sahel. This process – called **desertification** – is partly the result of human activities.

The pages that follow contain a *Leaving Certificate question, marking scheme and sample answer* that relate to the impacts of human activities in the Sahel. Most material in the sample answer is derived from the Case Study on pages 189–192.

The Sahel

Leaving Cert exam question, marking scheme and sample answer

The question

Assess how biomes have been altered by human activities.

Marking scheme

- Use *three or four aspects* in your answer.
- Your answer can *refer to one or more biome*.
- A total of two SRPs can be awarded for naming two biomes.

Number of aspects: 3 (27 + 27 + 26 marks) **or** 4 (20 + 20 + 20 + 20 marks)

For each aspect:

Identifying aspect:	4 marks/4 marks
Examination:	8 SRPs at 2 marks each **or** 6 SRPs at 2 marks each
Overall coherence:	7/6 marks graded **or** 4 marks graded

Use the marking scheme to mark the sample essay.

Sample essay

The Sahel is a long, narrow region that runs east–west across the southern edge of the Sahara Desert in Africa. The Sahel lies on a transition zone between two biomes – a <u>hot desert biome</u> to the north and a <u>tropical grassland biome</u> to the south. Over the past half century, however, hot desert conditions have spread southwards over the Sahel. This biome-altering process – called <u>desertification</u> – is largely a result of human activities such as <u>gathering firewood</u>, <u>overgrazing</u> and <u>overcultivation</u>.

Gathering firewood

Much of the Sahel – especially the southern part – once contained a fairly extensive covering of trees and bushes. But this vegetation cover has largely disappeared rapidly, partly because of an ever-growing need for **firewood**. Firewood is an important <u>human need</u> in the Sahel. In the absence of expensive fossil fuels such as gas and oil, people depend on firewood to cook evening meals and to protect them from night temperatures that can drop suddenly to 20 °C below daytime temperatures. High <u>population growth</u> of more than two per cent per year means that more and more firewood is required. This is especially so in the case of <u>rapidly expanding cities</u> such Ouagadougou, the capital city of Burkina Faso, which has been consuming up to 95 per cent of the country's forest production.

The ever-growing demand for firewood has contributed to massive <u>deforestation</u> within the Sahel. This has been especially evident around large urban areas such as Khartoum in Sudan, where almost all trees within a 100-kilometre radius of the city have been felled.

The removal of trees and bushes is altering the Sahel's biome. It deprives the soil of <u>plant litter</u> that would supply it with humus and of <u>root systems</u> that would help to stabilise it. Without the nourishment of plant litter, the soil gradually loses its structure and its <u>fertility</u>. Infertile soil then produces little or no vegetation and so becomes bare, dry and exposed to the elements. Dry, exposed soil is then easily removed by <u>windstorms</u>. This completes the process of <u>desertification</u> that is making the Sahel part of a hot desert biome – a biome in which soils (and therefore vegetation and animal life) have become increasingly like those of the neighbouring Sahara Desert.

215

A large family in the Sahel region of Burkina Faso.
How has rapid population growth contributed to biome change in the Sahel?

The fencing off of cattle has increased in the Sahel in recent times.
State one cause and one consequence of this trend.

Overgrazing

Overpopulation has also led to overgrazing, which has been another major cause of soil degradation, desertification and biome change in the Sahel.

Cattle rearing has always been a major feature of rural life in the Sahel, where cattle ownership was traditionally a measure of wealth and status. As the region's human population increased rapidly, so did the number of cattle and goats. Too many grazing animals have degraded the soil (and so altered the Sahel's biome) in the following ways:

- Animals overgraze the land beyond its carrying capacity (its natural ability to renew itself). They remove grass cover and even crop young trees and scrubs. This leaves the soil bare and vulnerable to wind erosion.

- Large herds of cattle trample on and compact soils with their hooves. This makes the soil less porous and results in more surface run-off and erosion in times of infrequent but heavy rainfall.

- Thousands of wells have been built to cater for increased cattle numbers. Too many cattle tend to congregate around these wells, causing the land there to become trampled and very overgrazed. The overuse of wells has also used up groundwater that has taken centuries to build up. Water tables then fall and many wells dry up, making the land drier than ever.

- In former times, almost all cattle farmers in the Sahel moved seasonally with their herds in search of fresh pastures. This system of nomadic herding was a sustainable one. It allowed soils to renew their fertility by leaving them fallow (unused) for long periods. Increasing cattle numbers have now forced many farmers to abandon nomadic herding and instead to keep cattle in permanently fenced-off land. Such land is constantly in use and so is often severely overgrazed and degraded.

Overcultivation (overcropping)

Rapid <u>population growth</u> has forced many farmers in the Sahel to **overcultivate** (excessively cultivate) land in attempts to provide sufficient **food** for themselves and their families. In such cases, land was not allowed to rest or was not fertilised sufficiently between crops. The soil then became barren as its structure began to break down.

As overcultivated areas became less productive, farmers began to cultivate <u>marginal land</u> towards the north of the Sahel in places such as central Mali and central Sudan. This marginal land is dry, very close to the desert and not fertile enough for sustainable agriculture. When cultivated, it quickly became barren and bare.

Politics and international debt have also contributed to overcropping. From the 1960s onwards, countries such as Niger went heavily into debt to Western banks and governments. In order to raise foreign capital to pay such debts, the government of Niger encouraged farmers to grow cash crops of **groundnuts** (peanuts) for export. This has led to the following problems:

● Groundnuts are grown in <u>monoculture</u>, which means that they are not rotated with other crops but are grown exclusively on the same land year after year. Groundnut monoculture exhausts the soil so much that, following three years of cultivation, the land needs to be left fallow for six years. Most farmers ignored this requirement because they could not afford to rest their lands for such long periods. Land under groundnuts therefore became increasingly infertile.

● Many farmers went into <u>debt</u> to pay for the technology they needed in order to grow groundnuts. To pay these debts, some farmers began to devote more and more land to groundnuts. This sometimes caused cattle herding to be displaced and pushed into <u>marginal</u> semi-desert land. During particularly dry years, the marginal land produced very little vegetation. It then became easily overgrazed and consequently barren.

As in the case of deforestation and overcropping, land rendered infertile by overcultivation has become degraded, infertile and exposed to wind erosion. This has facilitated the widespread desertification that is now altering the biome of the Sahel.

The city of Timbuktu in Mali.
The rural area close to the city is almost devoid of trees or bushes. State one reason for and one consequence of this.

- The **tropical rainforest biome** of the *Amazon Basin* has been negatively impacted upon by human activities. These activities include **deforestation** for the purposes of cattle ranching, logging, road building, mining and other 'development' projects.
- Trees help to control **water** systems in the rainforests. But *deforestation* has allowed more rain to fall directly on the ground and has resulted in fewer tree roots being available to soak up groundwater. Heavy rain also transports exposed soil into riverbeds. All this leads to more *flooding*. People who deforest also tend to *pollute* groundwater with sewage, mercury, etc.
- Deforestation has led to increased sheet and gully **soil erosion**. It has also led to more leaching, less plant litter and more *laterisation* – all of which reduce soil fertility. Heavy *machinery* has also compressed and damaged forest soils.
- Native forest people such as the **Yanomami** are *endangered*. They have been murdered, killed by 'new' diseases, deprived of their lands and culturally ruined by the activities and influences of outside 'developers'.
- The Amazon Basin may contain up to two million species of **plants and animals**, many of which are invaluable to medical science. Deforestation may have resulted in the daily *extinction* of one or more of those species.

- Human activities have contributed to *desertification* that is altering the biomes of the **Sahel** region of Africa.
- Human population growth has increased the need for **firewood**. This has resulted in deforestation and bush clearance, especially in the vicinity of large cities. Soils are thus deprived of plant litter and root systems, so that they become infertile and exposed to wind erosion. Desertification takes place when soils are eroded.
- Population growth has also led increasing cattle numbers. This in turn has resulted in **overgrazing**, which has degraded soils. The concentration of cattle near wells has led to the trampling of soils there and to falls in water table levels. The enclosed fencing of cattle has also contributed to overgrazing.
- Farmers have **overcultivated** land for *food crops*. Overcultivation has damaged soils, especially in dry, marginal areas. The monoculture of groundnut *cash crops* has exhausted and degraded soils. Damaged soils become infertile and exposed to wind erosion. This facilitates biome change through desertification.

Test Yourself
eTest.ie

Activities

Leaving Cert Higher Level questions:
1. Examine two ways in which human activities have altered the natural characteristics of a biome that you have studied.
2. Assess the impact of human activity in a biome that you have studied.
3. Assess how biomes have been altered by human activities.

Marking scheme
The Leaving Cert marking scheme for each of these questions is similar to the marking scheme on page 183.

Optional Unit:
Culture and Identity
(Higher Level only)

This book contains two Optional Units.
You must **study one Optional Unit** only.

All human beings belong to a single biological species known as *Homo sapiens*. All members of this human species are basically similar. But different groupings within our human race differ somewhat from each other. These variations give rise to what we call different **ethnic groupings**. Ethnic groups may be broadly distinguished from each other by either or both of the following: *physique* *height* *head shape* *physical*

- Superficial **racial characteristics** such as *hair type* or approximate *skin colour*.
- **Cultural characteristics** such as *language, religion* and *nationality*. *music* *dress* *traditions*

Racial groupings and patterns

The idea of 'race' has been used to divide people into various groupings according to secondary **biological differences**. These generally superficial physical differences or 'racial traits' are gene-based and are passed on from parents to offspring. They typically refer broadly to:

- skin colour
- body build and stature (height)
- hair type (straight, wavy or curly) and colour (fair, brown or black)
- facial features (shape of head, eyes, lips, nose).

Contrasting racial traits developed slowly between peoples as they adapted to different geographical environments.

- **Skin colour**, for example, is determined by a human pigmentation called *melanin*. Melanin darkens human skin and protects it from sunburn and from skin cancers caused by very strong sun rays. People from hot, sunny climates are dark-skinned because they evolved over time to produce high levels of protective melanin. Pale-skinned people with little melanin usually evolved in cloudy or less sunny parts of the world. Low melanin levels allow pale-skinned people to absorb enough sunlight to provide them with sufficient levels of vitamin D3.

Colour and cancer.
Part of a light-coloured person's body showing a type of skin cancer called *melanoma*, which may have been caused by over-exposure to the sun's UV (ultraviolet) rays. Dark-skinned people have high levels of melanin that help to protect them from skin cancer.

Facts

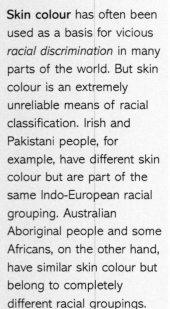

Skin colour has often been used as a basis for vicious *racial discrimination* in many parts of the world. But skin colour is an extremely unreliable means of racial classification. Irish and Pakistani people, for example, have different skin colour but are part of the same Indo-European racial grouping. Australian Aboriginal people and some Africans, on the other hand, have similar skin colour but belong to completely different racial groupings.

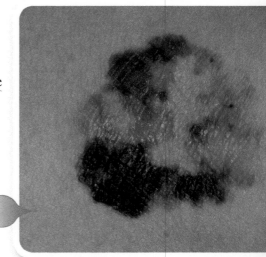

- **Body build and stature** also represent human adaptations to different environments. Tall, slender bodies help the Maasai and other peoples to remain cool in the tropical grasslands of East Africa. The Inuit people of the Arctic, on the other hand, benefit from shorter and plumper bodies that help to conserve heat. The Bambuti (pygmies) of the Democratic Republic of Congo are among the smallest peoples on earth. Their average adult height of less than 135cm (4ft 6in) helps them to move effortlessly through the equatorial forest that is their home.

Some racial misnomers

- **Pure race:** There is no such thing as a 'pure race'. Members of all ethnic groupings have at some time intermingled with people of other ethnic groups.

- **Black people:** In reality, there are no black people. So-called black people are brown in colour.

- **White people:** Neither are there any white people. If you are a 'white' person, look carefully at your skin and attempt to describe its real colour.

- **Coloured people:** Dark-skinned people are sometimes referred to as 'coloured'. This description foolishly assumes that 'white' people are without colour. In fact, all people are coloured.

People and their environments. From the top down, these three photographs show examples of the Inuit, the Maasai and the Bambuti peoples.

How are the physical characteristics of these peoples adapted to the environments in which they live?

Broad racial groupings and their locations

Some anthropologists (people who study the origins and other aspects of human beings) divide humankind into a small number of broad racial groupings, each of which tends to be concentrated in different parts of the world. The principal characteristics and locations of these groupings are described below. But these descriptions are very generalised. Large-scale **migrations** and intermingling between peoples have long since blurred the biological and locational differences between almost all racial groupings.

Irish
Ethiopian
Swedish
Pakistani

Some members of the Indo-European racial group

Mongolian
Chinese
Native American

Some members of the East Asian racial group

Indo-European

The Indo-European racial group is sometimes referred to as the **Caucasian** group. It is the largest and most widespread group in the world and is **located** mainly in Europe, North Africa, the Indian sub-continent and Western Asia. Colonial invasions and other migrations have caused this group to spread to the Americas, Australia, New Zealand and Southern Africa (see Figure 1).

Some very general **physical characteristics** of Indo-Europeans include the following:

- light-coloured to brown skin
- fair, brown or black hair that is usually straight to wavy
- light blue to brown eyes
- medium to tall stature.

East Asian

This very large group mainly occupies northern and eastern Russia, East Asian countries such as China and Japan and Southeast Asian countries such as Vietnam and the Philippines. East Asian people long ago crossed the Bering Strait into Alaska. Their descendants – Native Americans – then colonised many parts of North and South America.

General physical characteristics:

- light brown or sallow skin
- straight black hair
- narrow eyes and unpronounced noses
- short to medium height.

Sub-Saharan African

This racial group – sometimes referred to as the **black African** group – is much less numerous than either the Indo-European or the East Asian group. It is concentrated mainly in Africa south of the Equator. Large numbers of this group also live in parts of the eastern United States and South America and in Caribbean countries such as Cuba. They are mainly the descendants of millions of black Africans who were once kidnapped and brought to the Americas as slaves.

General physical characteristics:

- brown to dark brown skin
- dark brown to black hair that is typically curly and coarse textured
- dark eyes.

Nigerian

South African

African American

Some members of the sub-Saharan African racial group

Other groups

A number of much smaller and more isolated racial groups have been identified. They include the Aboriginal people of Australia and the Bushmen of the Kalahari Desert.   Pure race

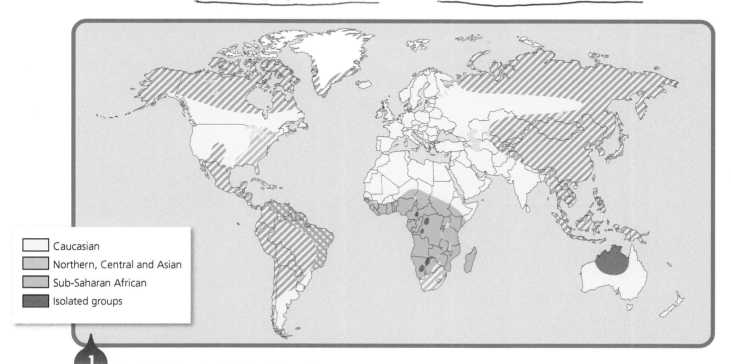

Caucasian
Northern, Central and Asian
Sub-Saharan African
Isolated groups

1 The distribution of principal racial groupings.

This is a very simplified map. In reality, members of all major racial groups inhabit most parts of the world.

Secondly the real 'borders' between racial groupings are gradual rather than precise borderlines as shown here.

Terms to know

- **Colonialism**: the military, political, economic and cultural domination of one country by another.
- **Colony**: a country that is dominated by another.
- **Colonial power** or **imperial power**: a country that dominates colonies.
- **Empire**: a colonial power together with its colonies.

Impacts of colonialism and migration on racial patterns and interactions

One of the key historical features of **colonialism** is that it was accompanied by large-scale migrations from colonial powers to their colonies. It has also led to later counter-migrations from former colonies to their former imperial powers. These **international migrations** have had enormous effects on racial patterns and interactions throughout the world.

This section will focus on **impacts of colonialism and migration** on racial patterns and interactions. In doing so it will consider the migratory effects of the world's greatest wave of colonialism. This colonial wave took place between the fifteenth and twentieth centuries when European powers conquered and colonised large parts of Africa, America and Asia.

The impacts of colonialism and migration relate to the following events or issues:
1. Out-migration from European colonial powers.
2. The oppression of colonised peoples. — *slave*
3. Counter-migrations from former colonies. — *people from colonies move back to origin country eg France*
4. Racial mixing. — *no mixing in South Africa (Apartheid)*

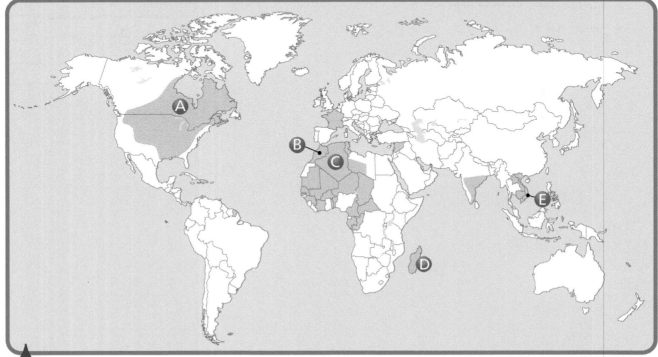

2 The French Empire at its height.
*Name each of the present-day countries labelled **A–E** that were once part of the French Empire.*

1 Out-migration from European colonial powers

From the fifteenth century onwards, European countries such as Spain, Portugal, Britain and France carved out huge colonial empires in the Americas, Africa, South and Southeast Asia and Australia.

European colonialism was accompanied by **massive out-migrations** from European countries to their various colonies. Most migrants were lured to the colonies by prospects of employment, cheap land and other means of material advancement.

Migration to the colonies reduced populations and eased population pressures in source countries such as France, Belgium and Britain. It also **transferred** hundreds of millions of white Caucasian (European) people to other parts of the world. Portuguese colonists, for example, migrated to Brazil, while Spaniards conquered other parts of South and Central America. British (and Irish) people poured into territories as diverse as Canada, South Africa, India and Australia. These migrants and their descendants changed the racial pattern of many colonies by adding a white Caucasian element to them.

Many Europeans harboured **racist** attitudes towards colonised peoples. They falsely believed that they themselves were naturally 'superior' to people of other racial backgrounds. Cecil Rhodes, a leading British colonist, believed '. . . that we are the first race in the world and that the more of the world that we inhabit the better it is for the human race'. Such racism was a barrier to racial mixing between colonists and colonised peoples. It contributed instead to the frequent **oppression** of colonised peoples.

A European example: focus on France

France acquired an empire between the seventeenth and the twentieth centuries. French **colonies** were mostly in North and West Africa, though they also stretched from the Americas to regions such as Vietnam in Southeast Asia (see Figure 2).

- Migration from France to the colonies **eased population pressures** in France itself. France's population had grown as a result of advances in food production and medical science in the eighteenth and nineteenth centuries.
- On the **negative** side, out-migration deprived France of many energetic, ambitious and adventurous young adults. They might have otherwise contributed to the social and economic development of the country.

Members of the French Foreign Legion. The Foreign Legion was once a symbol of France's overseas empire.

British settlers in the former African colony of Rhodesia (now Zimbabwe).
Colonialism introduced a small minority of white Europeans to the population of Rhodesia. Almost exclusive white control of government, land and other resources led to racial unrest. This in turn led to a successful independence struggle and later to the confiscation of some white-owned estates by the Zimbabwean government.
Rhodesia was named after Cecil Rhodes. What do you already know about him?

225

2 The oppression of colonised peoples

Mistreat peop. *— slau trade*

Colonial migrations affected racial patterns where they destroyed or displaced indigenous colonised peoples.

- Many native people died of **infections** such as measles and influenza that were carried by European colonists. Because these infections were new to many colonies, native peoples there had no natural immunity to them.

- Millions of indigenous people were **slaughtered** by European colonists. Such victims included Aborigines in Australia, Native American 'Indians' in the United States and Inca and Aztec people in South and Central America. It is estimated that the native population of Central and South America fell from nearly 25 million to 2.5 million within a century of the arrival of Spanish colonists.

- Shortages of local cheap local labour in the colonies caused Europeans to set up the **slave trade**. This resulted in millions of kidnapped black Africans being brought to work on the cotton, sugar and coffee plantations of Brazil, the United States and Caribbean islands such as Cuba. These slaves became the ancestors of most of today's black Americans.

- European colonists and their governments also **displaced** native peoples from their ancestral homes and territories. Native Americans, black Zimbabweans and black South Africans are examples of peoples who suffered such displacement.

The destruction and displacement of native peoples affected racial patterns in the colonies. It also led to **racial conflicts** and to several struggles for national independence, some of which (e.g. in India, Algeria and Angola) contributed greatly to the eventual collapse of European empires.

Focus on France

Like other European imperial powers, France profited from the exploitation of its colonies. **Cheap raw materials** such as rubber from Vietnam and sugar cane from the West Indies helped to keep French manufacturing profitable. France also benefited materially from the notorious **slave trade**.

The exploitation of colonised peoples by French settlers and their agents led to bitter **freedom struggles** that cost France dearly in money and lives. The Algerian War of Independence, for example, lasted for eight years and resulted in a total of up to one million deaths. The loss of colonies such as Vietnam in 1954 and Algeria in 1962 heralded the eventual collapse of the French Empire by the late 1960s.

Native Algerians being detained by French soldiers during the Algerian War of Independence.
The oppression of colonised peoples led to bitter wars of independence that eventually brought about the collapse of European empires.

3 Counter-migration from former colonies

From the middle of the twentieth century European empires began to crumble as more and more former colonies became independent. **Independence** was sometimes followed by migrations from former colonies to their former colonial powers.

- Some migrants fled from **racial** or **political unrest** within newly independent countries. People of Indian extraction, for example, used their status as British Commonwealth citizens to flee to Britain from persecution in Uganda in 1972.

- Most people migrated to their former colonial powers in search of **employment**. Because many migrants were willing to work for relatively low pay, they were often welcomed as 'guest workers' in countries such as Britain and France.

The Trellick Towers area of London.
Attempt to describe some causes and effects of the development of immigrant 'ghetto' areas.

Migrants from places such as Pakistan, the West Indies and Morocco added greatly to the multi-racial character of countries such as Britain and France. These migrants did not, however, always assimilate or mix easily into their destination countries. Many immigrants congregated together in **ghetto** areas such as Tower Hamlets and Hackney in London. Unemployment rates tend to be high and social problems acute in such 'ghettos' and it is often difficult for their residents to blend into 'mainstream' society.

Focus on France

The collapse of the French Empire was followed by extensive **counter-migration** from former French colonies to France. Some migrants, such as those of the old ruling colonial class in Algeria, were of French stock. Most, however, were of native North African or West African origin.

Throughout the economic boom of the 1960s, French employment agencies actively sought immigrant workers from countries such as Morocco, Algeria and Tunisia. Many such 'guest-workers' could speak French and were prepared to work for low pay doing menial work that most French people did not wish to do.

Many 'guest workers' were joined by their spouses and children, who made France their permanent home. They settled mainly in poorer suburbs of cities such as Marseilles, Lyon and Paris and added greatly to the multi-racial character of France's population. When France won the football World Cup in 1998, its national team was so multi-racial that it was described as *'Black, Blanc, Beur'* ('Black, White and Arab').

'Black, White and Arab' – French World Cup heroes of 1998

4 Racial mixing

Migrations associated with colonialism have helped to create **multi-racial** populations in many developed and developing countries. Black people, for example, make up 12.4 per cent of Britain's population, while white 'European' people make up a slightly larger segment of the population of South Africa. But multi-racial societies have not always led to **racial mixing** *in which people of different racial groups mingle, marry and have children together*.

Racial mixing has been very prominent in formerly colonised countries such as **Brazil**, where nearly 40 per cent of the population is of mixed race. The successful intermingling of white, black and Amerindian peoples in Brazil has been facilitated by a general absence of racism there and by the culturally unifying effects of a predominant language (Portuguese) and religion (Catholic).

Only 2.3 per cent of people in the **USA** are classified as being of multi-racial parentage. This may be partly because of a history of anti-black racial prejudice among some white people. Such prejudice led to the existence of racist organisations such as the Ku Klux Klan and to former racially discriminatory laws in southern states such as Alabama. **South Africa**'s former political system of *apartheid* led to even greater barriers to racial mixing. This will be examined further in the case study that follows.

Focus on France

Racial mixing has been hindered in France by the following factors:

- When immigrants from regions such as North Africa settled in France, many continued to cherish their Arabic language, Muslim faith and traditions relating to matters such as dress. They often lived together in so-called **ghetto** areas, where they were less likely to be overwhelmed by the French culture that surrounded them. The development of ghettos – many of which suffer from high levels of poverty and unemployment – hindered racial mixing in France.

- Racial mixing has also been hindered by **inter-racial distrust** and by racial riots such as those that occurred in several French cities in 2005. The emergence of political groupings and parties such as *Le Front National* (National Front) have sometimes provided platforms for prejudice and discrimination against black and Muslim immigrants.

Despite these obstacles, France has already experienced a considerable degree of **racial and cultural mixing**. This is shown by the fact that more than one in five French people has or had at least one immigrant parent or grandparent.

Images of racial disharmony and of racial mixing in France.
Racial rioting in Paris in 2005 and a racially mixed family in Paris in 2011.

Challenges created by international migration

Case Study 1:
Apartheid in South Africa

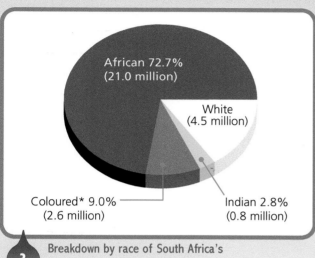

African 72.7%
(21.0 million)

White
(4.5 million)

Coloured* 9.0%
(2.6 million)

Indian 2.8%
(0.8 million)

3 Breakdown by race of South Africa's population in 1980. (*So-called 'coloured' people were mainly people of mixed race.)

(a) Calculate the total population of South Africa in 1980. 28.9 million

(b) What percentage of the country was classified as 'white'? 15.5%

Ever since the seventeenth century, South Africa has been subjected to major **migrations from Europe**, particularly from the Netherlands and Britain. European settlers gradually took over native black lands and became the rulers of South Africa. Many white settlers believed themselves to be naturally superior to black people.

In 1948, the white government of South Africa set up a system called **apartheid**. This was a racist system that was designed to separate people on racial grounds and to make 21 million black people completely subject to 4.5 million whites. Apartheid was enforced by a large number of penal laws that turned black people into second-class citizens or 'non-citizens'. These laws enforced what was broadly called 'petty apartheid' and 'grand apartheid'.

- **Petty apartheid** was designed to *separate* 'white' from 'non-white' South Africans in all aspects of everyday life. People were categorised at birth according to colour. Persons of different colour had to attend separate schools, hospitals, shops, post offices and churches. They had to use different beaches, playgrounds and sports fields. They had to play on separate sports teams, in separate sports grounds and in racially segregated competitions. The best facilities were reserved for whites. *Marriage* between black and white people was forbidden by an Act of Parliament called the Immorality Act. Black people could not move around freely. They had always to carry with them a special *pass* booklet that showed that they had 'permission' to be where they were. In urban areas, blacks were forced to live in specially built slums called *townships* that were well separated from white city areas.

A 'whites only' beach in apartheid South Africa. Petty apartheid ensured that South Africa's white minority had separate facilities that were better than those to which the black majority were restricted.

229

● **Grand apartheid** was designed to exclude black South Africans from *ownership* of their country. It worked as follows:

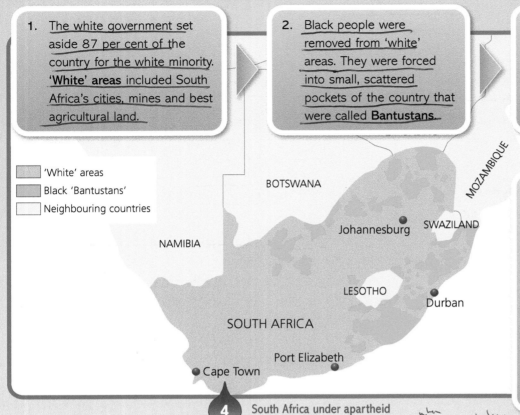

1. The white government set aside 87 per cent of the country for the white minority. **'White' areas** included South Africa's cities, mines and best agricultural land.

2. Black people were removed from 'white' areas. They were forced into small, scattered pockets of the country that were called **Bantustans.**

3. On being sent to Bantustans such as Transkei, blacks were given special passports that declared them to be Bantustan citizens. They were thus deprived of South African **citizenship**.

4. The barren Bantustans could not support their new populations. Their people therefore had to try to find work in 'white' South Africa. The South African government allowed physically fit young blacks to return to their old home areas. But they could do so only as **'foreign immigrants'** who could be sent back to the Bantustans once they ceased to be 'useful'.

Legend:
- 'White' areas
- Black 'Bantustans'
- Neighbouring countries

BOTSWANA
MOZAMBIQUE
NAMIBIA
Johannesburg
SWAZILAND
LESOTHO
Durban
SOUTH AFRICA
Port Elizabeth
Cape Town

4 South Africa under apartheid

Opponents of apartheid were silenced by fines, imprisonment, beatings and banning orders. Black people who opposed apartheid laws were treated particularly brutally. Many were tortured or killed. Even protesting children were shot dead on the streets of the black township of Soweto (see photograph).

But no amount of oppression could stifle opposition to apartheid both within and outside South Africa. Faced by a political and liberation movement called the **African National Congress** (ANC), apartheid was finally destroyed in 1994. In that year, the ANC, under Nelson Mandela, was swept to power in the country's first free general election. *Racial mixing* and equality was then at last made possible in South Africa.

Child victim of apartheid.
Young students were shot on the streets when they protested against apartheid in Soweto in 1976. The murdered boy shown here was 12-year-old Hector Pieterson.

Case Study 2:
Asylum seekers and refugees in Ireland

A common challenge of international migration has been the arrival of asylum seekers in countries such as Ireland. The challenge of asylum seeking relates to problems faced by the asylum seekers themselves and by the Irish authorities.

Problems faced by asylum seekers in Ireland – poverty, isolation and fear

- It sometimes takes years for an individual application for asylum to be judged. During that time, most asylum seekers are housed in hostels or in bed and breakfast accommodation. They are given three basic meals a day and adults receive €19.05 a week on which to live. They are not permitted to work and have no right to state-funded language classes, education or training. Most asylum seekers therefore experience considerable **poverty**. They find it difficult to purchase even basic necessities such as clothes, toiletries and bus tickets.

- Some asylum seekers have been dispersed in villages or towns throughout Ireland. Many such people feel socially and culturally **isolated**, especially if their knowledge of English is rudimentary. Their sense of isolation can increase if local people treat them with suspicion or distrust.

- Aggressive racist abuse has created **fear** among some asylum seekers. A survey by a Catholic organisation called Pilgrim House found that 95 per cent of black African asylum seekers in Ireland had suffered verbal racial abuse, often on a daily basis. More than one in five of these asylum seekers had also been physically assaulted.

Terms to know

- **Refugees:** people who get special permission to live in a country because of persecution or the fear of persecution in their native country.
- **Asylum seekers:** people who apply for permission to be accepted as refugees.

The Case of Mr Luyindula

Mr Luyindula is a journalist from the Congo who sought asylum in Ireland. Life in Ireland has not been a happy experience for Mr Luyindula. He was beaten up by a group of thugs in Temple Bar in Dublin. Nobody stopped to help him. An anonymous racist letter was then sent to 'The African' at his flat, and he has been told to 'go back to Africa' several times by people in the street.

'When I came here everyone seemed friendly,' said Mr Luyindula, 'but since the attack I have started to see some Irish people in a new light. Many of them think it's all right to have one or two black people living in Ireland. However, more than that irritates them. Older people are usually nice, but younger people are sometimes nasty and become particularly aggressive when they are drunk.'

(*Human Rights and Refugees*, Trócaire)

Discuss Mr Luyindula's views on Irish people.
Do you think they are well founded?

Problems faced by Irish authorities

- An independent body called the *Irish National Immigration Service* is given the task of judging whether or not asylum should be granted to asylum seekers. Those who judge individual applications need to be fair and just to the applicants. They may, on the other hand, grant refugee status only to people who have been persecuted or who reasonably fear persecution in their countries of origin. It is often very difficult to make such **judgements,** especially in relation to complex cases involving events and situations in far-off countries.

- Asylum seekers are frugally provided for in Ireland, but Ireland's international debts had reached a staggering €87 billion by 2011. This caused some Irish people to see any assistance to asylum seekers as an extra **burden** that our heavily indebted country can ill afford.

- The presence of asylum seekers has aroused **racism** among a minority of Irish people. False perceptions that asylum seekers are 'living well off the taxpayer' need to be refuted strongly in order to combat the spread of racism and xenophobia (the strong dislike of foreigners).

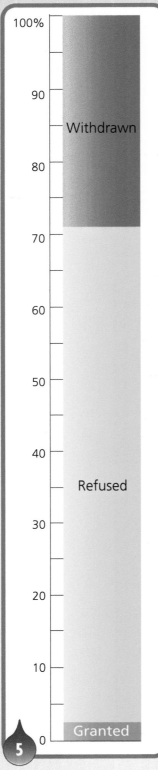

Year	Males	Females	Total	Male:female ratio (:1)
1992	31	8	39	3.9
1993	58	28	91	2.1
1994	264	97	362	2.7
1995	334	90	424	3.7
1996	875	299	1,179	2.9
1997	2,643	1,240	3,883	2.1
1998	2,869	1,757	4,626	1.6
1999	4,958	2,766	7,724	1.8
2000	6,602	4,336	10,938	1.5
2001	5,447	4,878	10,325	1.1
2002	5,773	5,861	11,634	1.0
2003	3,944	3,956	7,900	1.0
2004	2,521	2,245	4,766	1.1
2005	2,778	1,545	4,323	1.8
2006	2,875	1,439	4,314	2.0
2007	2,478	1,507	3,985	1.6
2008	2,469	1,397	3,866	1.8
2009	1,758	931	2,689	1.9
Total	**48,677**	**34,391**	**83,068**	**1.4**

5

The results of asylum application cases in 2009.

(a) What percentage of applications were (i) granted, (ii) refused, (iii) withdrawn?

(b) What do the above statistics suggest about Ireland's asylum procedures?

6

Yearly applications for asylum in Ireland from 1992 to 2009.

(a) What was the total number of applicants in 2009?

(b) In which year was the total number of applicants greatest?

(c) In which years did female applicants outnumber male applicants?

(d) What was the ratio of male to female applicants in 2005?

(e) Between which two years did the greatest decrease in applications occur?

(f) Calculate the total number of female applicants from 2006 to 2009 inclusive.

(g) Describe the trends in total applications between 2002 and 2009.

Sum Up

- People can be divided into **ethnic groupings** on the basis of *racial* or *cultural* characteristics.
- **Racial groupings** are based on variations in *biological traits* such as skin colour or hair type. These variations are usually determined by climatic conditions over very long periods of time.
- **Principal racial groups** include the *Indo-European* (Caucasian), the *East Asian* and the *Sub-Saharan African* groups.
- European **colonialism** and its related **migrations** have impacted on racial patterns and interactions.
- Colonialism resulted in massive **migrations from imperial powers** such as Britain and France to colonies such as India and Algeria. These migrations transferred Caucasian (European) people to the colonies. But *racism* among many Europeans hindered *racial mixing* between colonists and colonised peoples.
- Colonial migrations **destroyed or displaced many indigenous peoples**. Colonised people died from 'European' infections, were slaughtered, were transported as slaves or were removed from their lands. Colonial oppression eventually led to *independence struggles* that helped to bring about the collapse of European empires.
- Following colonial independence, **migrations occurred from former colonies** such as Algeria to former colonial powers such as France. Many poor economic migrants tended to live in *ghettos* and found it difficult to blend into local European cultures and lifestyles.
- Colonial or post-colonial migrations have created many *multi-racial* societies. But they have not always led to a large degree of **racial mixing** in which people of different races marry and have children. Racial mixing is more common in Brazil than it is in countries such as the USA and France.
- **Challenges** associated with international migrations included *apartheid* in South Africa and problems relating to *asylum seekers* in countries such as Ireland.
- South Africa was ruled by a **racist apartheid system** from 1948 to 1994. *Petty apartheid* discriminated against black people and separated whites from 'non-whites' in everyday life. *Grand apartheid* removed blacks from their homes, dumped them in barren 'Bantustans' and allowed them to return to their home areas only as temporary 'foreign' workers.
- **Asylum seekers** in Ireland usually live in *poverty*. Some feel *isolated* and *fearful* of racist attacks. It is often *difficult to adjudicate* on asylum applications. Some Irish people develop *xenophobia*, while others oppose any *financial support* of asylum seekers.

Activities

Leaving Cert questions:

1. Examine the principal characteristics and locational patterns of three major racial groupings.
2. Examine the impact of colonialism and migration on racial patterns.
3. Examine how migration can affect racial patterns.
4. Discuss the role of migration in any European region you have studied.
5. Examine two of the challenges created by international migration.

Exam training: Leaving Cert question, marking scheme and sample answer

The question
Discuss the role of migration in any global (non-European) region that you have studied.

Leaving Cert marking scheme for all 'Option' questions

Three or four aspects must be examined in answering an option question.
The marking scheme for these questions is as follows:

1   **For an answer that examines *three* aspects:**
    Three aspects at 27 marks + 27 marks + 26 marks

    For each aspect:
Identifying (naming) the aspect	= 4 marks
Examination: at least 8 SRPs* at 2 marks each	= 16 marks
Overall coherence*	= 7/6 marks graded
Total	**= 80 marks**

2   **For an answer that examines *four* aspects:**
    Four aspects at 20 marks each

    For each aspect:
Identifying (naming) the aspect	= 4 marks
Examination: at least 6 SRPs* at 2 marks each	= 12 marks
Overall coherence*	= 4 marks
Total	**= 80 marks**

> ***SRP** stands for Significant Relevant Point. Each SRP must provide a clear piece of geographical information that is relevant to the question asked. Try to exceed slightly the required number of SRPs in any aspect on which you write. You will get credit for the best SRPs that you present.
> ***Overall coherence** marks are awarded for qualities such as the fullness, accuracy, quality and 'flow' of the answer given. Make sure that your answers are relevant, clear and well laid out. Use clear sentences and paragraphs.

Sample answer

This answer will examine three aspects of the role of colonial and post-colonial migration in South Africa.

Mark this answer using the marking scheme provided.

1   The foundation of a racist society within a multi-racial population

White settlers from the Netherlands first arrived in South Africa in the mid-seventeenth century. These settlers were sometimes referred to as Boers ('farmers'). As more and more of them arrived they gradually overran the lands of black Africans in the Cape region in the west of the country. A wave of immigration from Britain followed. The British captured the cape from the Dutch in 1806, while the Boers moved eastwards to establish control over regions such as the Orange Free State. The Dutch had brought some slaves with them from West Africa and from the East Indies in Asia. The British brought with them forced labourers from their colony of India.

These colonial migrations introduced a diverse multi-racial element to South Africa's population. By 1980, approximately 73 per cent of the country's population was black, approximately 15 per cent was white and nearly 3 per cent was classified as 'Indian'.

Only 9 per cent of the population, however, was of mixed-race origins, showing that racial mixing was relatively uncommon in South Africa. This was largely because of racist attitudes among whites, who regarded themselves as being naturally superior to people of other colours. In 1948, the white minority government of South Africa introduced a racist political system of apartheid that forbade racial mixing under apartheid's 'Immorality Act'. Marriages or any sexual relations between people of different colours were strictly forbidden. Only since the ending of apartheid in 1994 has South Africa had the opportunity to develop as a racially mixed society.

2   The capture of the country's resources

European migration and colonialism resulted in the natural resources of South Africa being taken from the black majority and used for the benefit of white settlers and foreign investors from countries such as Britain, Germany and the USA. South Africa's vast gold and diamond resources in places such as Johannesburg and Kimberly all came under white control. The same is true of most of South Africa's land resources. A cornerstone of apartheid was a plan to set aside 87 per cent of South Africa (including all major mines and cities) as 'white' areas. Millions of black people were removed from these areas and exiled to remote and barren areas called 'Bantustans', such as Transkei. Some blacks were allowed to return to 'white' South Africa to seek work. But they now had Bantustan 'passports' and could enter 'white' South Africa only as temporary 'foreign' labourers. Black people were thus deprived of citizenship and land-ownership rights in their own land.

The above misuse of natural resources contributed to massive inequality among South Africans and to dire poverty among South Africa's black majority. In the 1980s, for example, the child mortality rate among blacks was thirteen times higher than it was among whites.

3   Racial discrimination and a resulting liberation struggle

Many European migrants and their descendants carried out appalling racial discrimination against South Africa's black population. This abuse began with the coming of the Boer settlers, who gave black people no political rights at all in the territories that they controlled. The establishment of apartheid (under a government dominated by whites of Boer descent) meant that racial discrimination was entrenched by law throughout South Africa. Under 'petty' apartheid, blacks were subject to a plethora of humiliating penal regulations that reduced them to the status of second-class citizens. Black people, for example, were compelled to carry with them special 'pass' booklets that showed that they had permission to be in 'white' South Africa. In 1960, when black people demonstrated peacefully at Sharpeville against the 'pass laws', 69 protesters were massacred by police.

Events such as the Sharpeville Massacre led to growing resistance against apartheid. The leading liberation movement was a political non-racial body called the African National Congress (ANC). The apartheid regime finally collapsed in 1994. In that year the ANC, under Nelson Mandela, was swept to power in South Africa's first free and democratic general election.

Language and Religion as Cultural Indicators

The term **'culture'** refers to the way in which people express their collective identity. Things such as language, religion, music, food, dress, sport, festivals and national identity are all *indicators* or facets of people's cultures. This chapter will focus especially on language and religion as cultural indicators.

Language as a cultural indicator

Language is the medium through which we speak and write. It is the medium of poetry, song and story telling. It is the medium through which we share most of our thoughts, feelings and emotions, as well as our collective experiences, traditional values and beliefs. It creates bonds between people who share a language and barriers between people who do not. Language is therefore a powerful cultural indicator.

What indicator or indicators of Irish culture are illustrated in this photograph?
List some other Irish cultural indicators.

Language families, language sub-groups and languages

There are more than **3,000** different individual **languages** in the word. Many languages are spoken by relatively few people and some are in danger of extinction. A few, such as English and Spanish, are spoken by hundreds of millions of people in different parts of the world.

Most individual languages can be grouped into major **'language families'**. Languages within each of these major groups or 'families' are 'related' to each other because they are descended from a remote common language.

The largest language group is called the **Indo-European Family**. It consists of several **sub-groups**, such as the Germanic, Romance, Slavic and Indo-Aryan sub-groups. Each sub-group has in turn given rise to several **individual languages**. English, for example, is part of the Germanic sub-group, French and Spanish belong to the Romance sub-group and Irish (Gaelic) is part of the Celtic sub-group. Languages derived from the Indo-European family are now spoken in many parts of the world (see Figures 1a and 1b).

Language families
(e.g. Indo-European)

▼

Language sub-groups
(e.g. Germanic)

▼

Individual languages
(e.g. English)

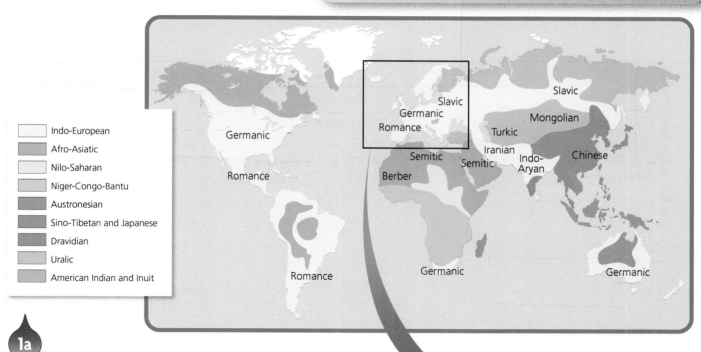

1a

The world's principal language families.

(a) Name four language families that are represented in Africa.

(b) Name four principal regions where Indo-European languages are spoken.

(c) How do you think languages of the Indo-European language family came to be spoken widely in Africa, the Americas and Australia?

Languages and language sub-groups in Europe.

(a) English is part of the Germanic sub-group of languages. Name three other languages of this sub-group.

(b) Which languages are most closely related to Irish? To which sub-group do they belong?

(c) Name five languages of the Romance sub-group.

(d) Identify which of the following languages is the 'odd one out' and explain why: Polish, Czech, Hungarian, Russian.

(e) Identify three languages in Europe that are not part of the Indo-European family of languages. To which language family or families do these languages belong?

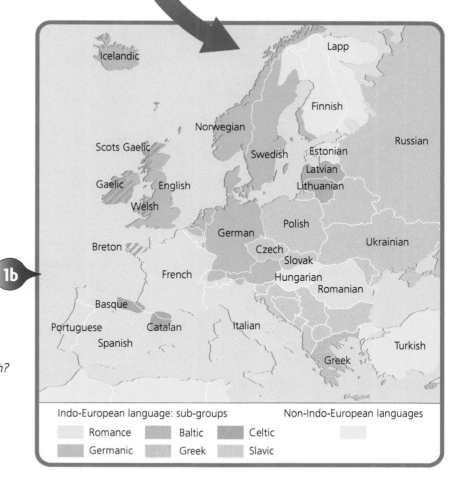

1b

The influence of English in Tanzania (above) and in Mumbai, India

Some facts about English

English is now the world's most influential 'international' language. It is the principal language of:

- the **internet**
- **multi-channel television**, where it is used in many music and sports channels
- international **aviation**
- international **science** publications.

The spread of international languages such as English

European languages such as English, Spanish and Portuguese are among the world's most spoken languages. These languages spread to many parts of the world as European imperial powers carved out empires in the Americas, Africa, Australia and parts of Asia.

English is the world's most influential 'international' language. Between the sixteenth and the twentieth centuries the **British Empire** grew to cover much of the world. As the empire grew, English became the official language and the language of political and economic elites in regions such as India, Australia, South Africa and North America. As the language spread, so did other aspects of English culture. British school programmes – featuring subjects such as Shakespeare and English history – came to be taught in parts of Africa. Colonial rulers and aspiring members of the 'upper classes' began to play cricket and 'take afternoon tea' in countries such as India. Other English pastimes, such as hockey and rugby, became popular in countries such as Pakistan and New Zealand.

As the British Empire began to decline, the **United States** began to dominate many parts of the world economically and militarily. As American influence spread, so did the influence of English as an indicator of American culture. Throughout the twentieth century, the USA became the centre of a developing **mass media** that included pop music, cinema, television and internet. English – and particularly 'American English' – became the leading language of this mass media. Through it, American phrases such as 'OK', products such as Coca-Cola, songs such as 'White Christmas' and Hollywood movies such as *Star Wars* have infiltrated much of the world.

The threat to other languages and cultures

The spread of the English language and of an Anglo-American culture can threaten the wellbeing of other languages and cultures. French authorities, for example, have become concerned at the increasing infiltration of English phrases such as 'le jogging' and 'le weekend' into the French language. To combat the spread of such '*Franglais*', an official body called the *Académie Française* now monitors the use of non-French phrases in the French language.

Small and minority languages and cultures have most to fear from the relentless spread of English and of an Anglo-American-style 'global culture'. Such minority languages and associated cultures include Irish, Welsh and Breton.

The spread of English language and rule has been associated with the gradual decline of **Irish language and culture** since the Norman invasion of Ireland in the twelfth century. Ireland's old Brehon Laws were replaced by English laws. The music and poetry of the Irish *fili* and bards disappeared in the seventeenth century. In more recent times, Irish customs such as 'wren boy' gatherings on St Stephen's Day have been replaced largely by American customs such as 'trick or treat' at Hallowe'en.

The Irish language also declined. By the mid-nineteenth century English was the language of government, commerce, wealth and formal education in Ireland. It was also the language of emigration to Britain and North America. By 1851, Irish was spoken widely only in the western half of the country. By 1926, Irish-speaking *Gaeltacht* areas had shrunk to about half of their size in 1851. The widespread use of Irish is now confined to small *Gaeltacht* areas in West Kerry, Galway, Mayo and Donegal. No more than **20,000** people live in these *Fíor Gaelteachtaí*.

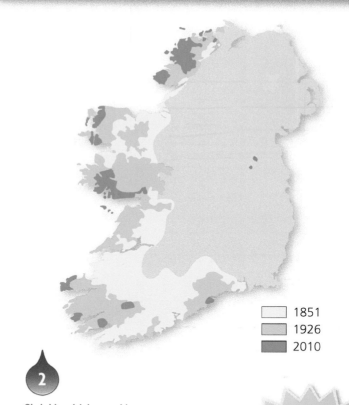

	1851
	1926
	2010

2

Shrinking Irish-speaking areas.
The map shows areas where more than 25 per cent of people spoke Irish on a daily basis in 1851, in 1926 and in 2010.
(a) Account for the decline over time of the Irish language.
(b) Why is the survival of Irish important?

Revise pages 339–340 in your Changing World core textbook.

Bhí fear ann fadó agus ....
Will you listen to me?

3 This old cartoon is from a humorous magazine called *The Dublin Opinion*.
What is the message or messages of the cartoon?

239

The Irish response

The Irish language and its related Gaelic culture might have disappeared completely but for the actions of Irish nationalists before and after national independence.

The late nineteenth century saw the rise of **Irish cultural movements** such as the *GAA* (which fostered a revival of Irish sports such as hurling and football) and the *Gaelic League* (which fostered the revival of Irish). Patriots such as Padraig Pearse strongly supported the Gaelic League because they realised that the Irish language was a vital indicator and medium of Irish identity and culture.

Successive **Irish governments** have tried to reverse the decline of Irish in Gaeltacht areas, to foster the wellbeing of Irish culture and to extend the use of Irish throughout the country. The following steps have been taken to promote this policy:

- A special *government department* called the Department of Arts, Heritage and the Gaeltacht is charged with promoting government policy on Irish culture and language.
- The *Official Languages Act 2003* requires that all public bodies provide services through the medium of Irish as well as English.
- The study of Irish is compulsory in *schools*.
- Irish-language primary schools called *Gaelscoileanna* and *Irish 'summer colleges'* receive government support.
- Irish *TV and radio stations* such as TG4 and Raidió na Gaeltachta have been set up and are subsidised.

These measures have so far had **mixed success**. A census in 2006 revealed that a healthy 1.66 million people in the Irish Republic claimed that they could speak Irish. However, only 53,000 people indicated that they used the language on a day-to-day basis outside school. This shows that ongoing and inventive efforts will be needed to preserve and revive Irish as a living indicator of our culture.

How has each of the features or activities shown in these photographs contributed to the survival and revival of Irish language and culture?

Case Study:
The Welsh language revival

Throughout most of the nineteenth and twentieth centuries more and more Welsh people began to speak only English. It looked then that the Welsh language would continue to decline and might eventually die.

Now, however, a **Welsh revival** is under way. A census in 2001 showed a two per cent increase in the number of people who spoke the language. It is now estimated that nearly half a million people speak Welsh and that this figure is up to 80 per cent in some northern and western parts of the country. The following **factors** are associated with the healthy and improving state of the Welsh language and culture.

- The *Welsh Language Acts* of 1967 and 1993 placed Welsh on an equal footing with English in all public services in Wales. Anyone in Wales may now carry out any public business through the medium of Welsh.

- Welsh is a *compulsory school subject* in Wales for children between the ages of 5 and 16 years. Many people who do not themselves speak Welsh now have their children taught through the Welsh language.

- Cultural festivals called *Eisteddfodau* are held each year to celebrate Welsh literature, music and dance. They are held through the medium of Welsh.

- Welsh is increasingly used in *media* such as some TV channels, local radio stations and newspapers.

- *Plaid Cymru*, the Welsh Nationalist Party, strongly supports the use of Welsh as a vital indicator of Welsh culture and independence.

Three signs of the Welsh language revival:
- the cover of Welsh language children's books
- a Welsh-language sign
- a Plaid Cymru rally in Cardiff.

Religion as a cultural indicator

Openly
– ?nfw ?
– " "os
– " "
– " "
Closing

Distribution of the world's major religions

The map in Figure 4 shows the spatial distribution of the world's major religions. It shows that different religions tend to be concentrated in different parts of the world. Each major religion began in one area and then spread outwards because of human migration and missionary activity.

migration, colonisation
European colonists brought christianity ...
the world

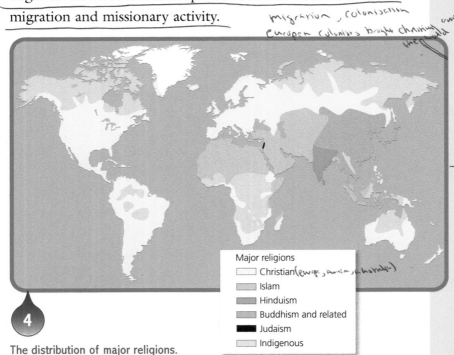

4

Major religions

☐ Christian *(europe, america, whandu-)*
☐ Islam
☐ Hinduism
☐ Buddhism and related
■ Judaism
☐ Indigenous

The distribution of major religions.

Note: this is a generalised map. It does not show minority religions or the extent of religious practice in any area. Western Europe, for example, is shown as 'Christian'. This does not allow for the fact that some Europeans belong to 'minority' religions such as Islam, while others profess to no religion at all.

(a) Christianity began in Palestine in the Middle East. Describe and account briefly for its spread to other parts of the world.

(b) What do you think is meant by the term 'indigenous religions'?

(c) Which major religion is associated with each of the symbols labelled **A–D** below?

The world's major religions
Christianity

Christianity is the world's largest and most widely dispersed religion. It is professed by almost one-third of the world's population.

Christianity was founded in Palestine by **Jesus Christ**, whom Christians believe to be the Son of God. It spread throughout the Roman Empire, of which Palestine was a part. It also spread along trade routes into parts of Asia. From the sixteenth century onwards, European conquerors, colonists and missionaries brought Christianity to many parts of the world, including the Americas, Australia and parts of sub-Saharan Africa.

Christianity split over time into different 'denominations'. The first great schism ('split') happened in 1054 when the *Orthodox Church* in Eastern Europe broke away from the *Roman Catholic Church* of Western Europe. A further split happened in the sixteenth century when the Reformation led to the emergence of several *Protestant* denominations. At the present time, South and Central America and most parts of southern Europe are strongly Catholic. Protestants outnumber Catholics in North America and in many parts of Northern Europe.

Islam

The Prophet **Mohammed** founded Islam in Arabia in the seventh century. Followers of Islam are called Muslims. They worship Allah (God) and believe that Mohammed was Allah's greatest messenger.

Soon after Mohammed's death, Arabic warriors began to build an empire that was later to stretch from southern Spain through North Africa to India. They introduced Islam into the lands they conquered. Muslim traders helped to introduce Islam to Indonesia in Southeast Asia. Economic migrants from countries such as Turkey and Pakistan introduced Islam to many parts of northern Europe in the twentieth century. Islam is now Europe's second largest religion.

Approximately one-fifth of the world's population now follows Islam. Most belong to the *Sunni* branch of Islam, while Iraq and Iran are predominantly of the *Shiite* (pronounced *'she-ite'*) branch.

Judaism

Judaism had its origins in the Middle East where it was the tribal religion of people who traced their origins back to **Abraham**. These Jews lived for a long period in *Palestine*, from which many were exiled at the time of the Roman Empire. The establishment and expansions of the Jewish State of *Israel* led to massive waves of Jewish migration back into Palestine from 1948 onwards.

Judaism has approximately 14 million followers, about five million of whom live in Israel and a further five million in the United States.

Hinduism

Hinduism dates back to about 1500 BC and is said to be the world's oldest religion. It is followed by more than 900 million people. Its followers are confined mainly to its source region of *India*, largely because Hinduism is not a missionary religion. Hindus give the name **Brahma** to their high god.

Buddhism

Siddhartha Guatama, also known as the **Buddha**, founded Buddhism in Northeast India in the sixth century BC. This religion was an offshoot of Hinduism. It spread to countries such as *Tibet*, *China*, *Korea* and *Japan*, where it sometimes merged with other local religions. Buddhism has more than 400 million followers, who believe that salvation can be achieved through self-knowledge and self-discipline.

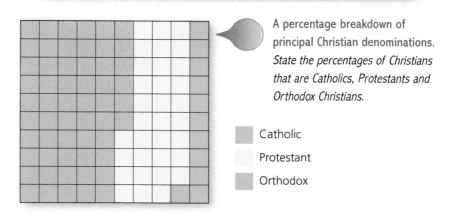

A percentage breakdown of principal Christian denominations. *State the percentages of Christians that are Catholics, Protestants and Orthodox Christians.*

- Catholic
- Protestant
- Orthodox

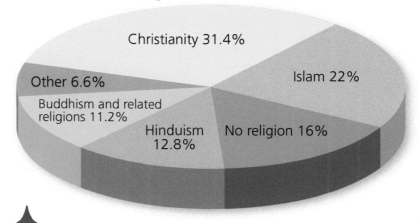

Christianity 31.4%

Islam 22%

Other 6.6%

Buddhism and related religions 11.2%

Hinduism 12.8%

No religion 16%

5 The world's principal religions in terms of followers.
(a) List in rank order the world's principal religions.
(b) By what percentage do the followers of Christianity exceed those of Hinduism and Buddhism combined?

A Buddhist temple in Kathmandu, Nepal.
The flags are called prayer flags because they have prayers or mantras written on them. Buddhists believe that as the wind blows the flags it carries the prayers around to the benefit of all.

Religion and culture

Religion can play a huge and varied role in people's culture and everyday lives. This section will consider the cultural role of religion with regard to:

- diet
- dress
- festivals and public events
- landscape features.

to harm or kill
a cow especially for
food is considered taboo
By most Hindus

Hindus believe cows are a
sacred symbol of life and
should be protected

20/29 India
Hindu prohibit
cow slaughter

7% of
Indians
eat
beef.

A sacred cow in India. Hindus consider cows to be sacred animals that may not be maltreated or killed.
How would such traditions impact on diet in countries such as India?

Women in the Islamic country of Pakistan.
Describe and account for the dress code of these women.

Diet

Religious beliefs and customs can impact greatly on people's diet.

Eating **meat** has been and is often regulated by religious belief and custom. Both Hindus and Buddhists, for example, share a belief that it is wrong to kill animals. This belief, which is called *ashima*, greatly affects their diet. The Hindu belief that *cows* are sacred animals also affects diets in countries such as India. Muslims are prohibited by their religious beliefs from eating pork or pork products.

Orthodox Jews observe complex rules regarding diet. They eat foods that their religion considers to be *kosher* or 'correct'. They eat only animals that have cloven hooves and chew the cud. They eat only fish that have fins or scales, so shellfish are excluded from their diet. They also observe strict rules for cooking and preparing foods. For example, they permanently set aside different pots for cooking dairy products and meat.

Religious **fasting** can also be a strong cultural indicator. Muslims fast between dawn and sunset for one month each year – a period called *Ramadan*. In the past, Catholics fasted and abstained from meat during the weekdays of *Lent* – a forty-day period that led up to Easter. In former times, Catholics also abstained from eating meat on *Fridays*.

Dress

Religion often influences human dress and body decoration. **Islam**, for example, insists that all its followers dress modestly. That is why women in countries such as Saudi Arabia are required to cover their legs and arms in public. Women in most Islamic countries are expected to cover their heads with scarves or veils. In Afghanistan, females were once required to wear burkas in public. These veils completely cover the face, which could not be exposed to men who were not members of a woman's family.

Some **Orthodox Jews** observe very distinctive dress codes. Men dress in black and wear beards and sideburns or side-curls. They wear a skullcap (*yarmulke*) or hat to cover their heads in respect for God's presence. Women wear long, 'modestly coloured' dresses and long sleeves.

Strict dress codes often govern **religious ceremonies**. In the past, Catholic women covered their heads and men exposed their heads in church. Both Jews and Muslims cover their heads in synagogues and mosques. Worshippers remove their shoes on entering mosques.

Festivals and public events

Many **festivals** or holidays throughout the world are based on religious traditions and beliefs. *Christmas* – the most celebrated holiday in the western world – celebrates the birth of Christ. *Easter* is another time of celebrations and school holidays in countries such as Ireland. It celebrates Christ's resurrection from the dead.

The old feast of *Hallowe'en* also has its roots in religious tradition. It is a relic of the ancient pre-Christian feast of *Samhain*, which marked the beginning of the Celtic year when animals were sacrificed to the god Dagda.

Each major religion contributes its own feasts and festivals to the cultural fabric of the world. Jews observe the feast of *Passover*, which commemorates the departure of Moses from Egypt more than 3,000 years ago. Muslims celebrate the feast of *Eid ul-Fitr*, which marks the end of the Ramadan fasting period. Hindus in countries such as India mark *Diwali* or the 'Festival of Light'. Buddhists celebrate feasts such as the *birth of Buddha*.

Describe the dress of these Orthodox Jews.

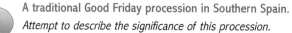

A traditional Good Friday procession in Southern Spain. *Attempt to describe the significance of this procession.*

245

Religious **pilgrimages** continue to be important cultural indicators in many parts of the world. *Croagh Patrick* in Co. Mayo is an Irish place of pilgrimage associated with St Patrick. Thousands of pilgrims climb that mountain, many of them in their bare feet, on the last Sunday of July each year. On an international scale, places such as *Bethlehem* (the birthplace of Christ) and *Rome* (the headquarters of the Roman Catholic Church) attract pilgrims and visitors from all parts of the world. One of the world's most important pilgrimages is the *hajj*. This is the journey that many millions of Muslims make to *Mecca* in Saudi Arabia. Islam encourages each Muslim who can do so to make at least one pilgrimage to Mecca.

Muslim pilgrims on hajj in Mecca.
Describe the dress of these pilgrims.

Pilgrims on Croagh Patrick. Tradition has it that St Patrick once fasted and did penance on Croagh Patrick in Co. Mayo. Thousands of people now make an annual pilgrimage to Croagh Patrick on the last Sunday of July each year. Some pilgrims climb the mountain barefoot.

Landscape features

Religious landscape features affect the everyday cultural lives of people throughout the world.

Churches are prominent landscape features in mainly **Christian** countries such as Ireland. Some churches, such as Cobh Cathedral in Co. Cork, are so large and prominently located that they dominate the local landscape. Church *towers and spires* are also significant landscape features. In Ireland these range from ancient round towers at places such as Glendalough, Co. Wicklow to more modern spires such as those on St Finbarre's Cathedral in Cork. Modern spires serve as belfries and provide religious imagery of buildings reaching up to heaven. Ancient round towers once also served as watch towers and places of refuge in times of attack. Christian landscape features also include *statues* that can range in size from the great statue of Christ that overlooks Rio de Janeiro in Brazil to life-size statues that decorate small religious grottoes in some Irish towns and villages.

Non-Christian religions have their own particular landscape features. Such features in **Muslim** countries include **mosques** with towers called *minarets* from which the faithful are called to prayer each day. Countries such as Nepal, which have large **Buddhist** populations, are studded with Buddhist *monasteries, temples, prayer flags* and *prayer wheels*.

Explain each of the following terms that have been used in this section:

- ashima
- kosher
- Ramadan
- Lent
- burka
- synagogue – Jewish place of w
- mosque – muslim pla el wofp
- Samhain
- Passover
- Eid ul-Fitr
- Diwali
- hajj

Landscape features associated with religion.

A The great statue of Christ overlooking Rio de Janeiro.

B A mosque in Malaysia.

C Buddhist prayer wheels in Nepal. Prayer wheels have sacred text or mantras inscribed on them. It is believed that spinning the wheels has the same beneficial effect as reciting the mantras.

247

Special study 1:
The varying influence of religion on politics

Religion normally impacts on the politics and civil governments of countries and regions. But the influence of religion on politics can *vary over time and from region to region*. This section will examine these variations.

Variations over time

Ireland and *Russia* provide good examples of how the influence of religion on politics has varied over time.

Ireland

Throughout most of the twentieth century, the Roman Catholic Church exerted **huge influence** over politics in **the Republic of Ireland**. In the decades that followed national independence in 1921, most Irish people were devoutly Catholic and would not tolerate any political programme that was not supported by the Church.

- When Taoiseach Éamon de Valera drew up a Constitution for Ireland in 1937, he did so in consultation with Dr John Charles McQuaid, the Catholic Archbishop of Dublin. The new Constitution recognised the 'special position' of the Catholic Church in Ireland.

- *Social policies and family law* at that time reflected Catholic teachings. Divorce and artificial contraception were banned and books and films were strictly censored.

Russia

At the beginning of the twentieth century, **Russia** was ruled by an emperor, or tsar, named Nicolas II. Like his father before him, Nicolas was an 'absolute ruler' or dictator. He was also a member of and greatly influenced by the *Russian Orthodox Church*, which was an integral part of the ruling establishment. This Church was therefore very politically influential in Russia.

In 1917, Communist revolutionaries under Vladimir Lenin overthrew the Tsarist regime. The Communist rulers were atheists who believed that religion was like an 'opium' (a drug) that helped to enslave people. Throughout the Communist era, therefore, the practice of religion was severely discouraged and many churches were closed throughout Russia. Religion then had no influence on politics.

Communist rule collapsed in Russia in 1991. Churches were reopened and religion was again encouraged and supported. As more people returned to the open practice of religion, the social and political influence of the Russian Orthodox Church increased. It is unlikely, however, ever to reach the levels of influence that it enjoyed during the time of the tsars.

A Russian Orthodox religious ceremony. *How did the influence of this Church vary over time in Russia?*

- The enormous influence of the Church over politics is well illustrated by the collapse of the *Mother and Child Scheme* in 1951. Dr Noel Browne was the Minister of Health at that time. He wanted to introduce free hospital and health care for all mothers and young children in the Republic. But the Catholic bishops opposed Dr Browne's scheme. They saw that it would increase State influence and so reduce Church influence over health matters in the Republic. When the bishops put pressure on the government, the scheme was dropped, Dr Browne resigned and the government collapsed.

Religious deference in Ireland.
Irish Taoiseach Éamon de Valera kisses the ring of the Archbishop of Dublin in 1933. The Catholic Church exerted great political influence in Ireland at that time.

Irish society has undergone radical changes in recent decades. Our society has grown less rural and less religiously devout and more urban, materialistic and politically 'liberal' in nature. The number of practising Catholics in Ireland has fallen considerably since 1990 and membership of the Catholic clergy has fallen dramatically in that time. These changes have resulted in a rapid **decline in Church influence** on Irish politics. This decline is illustrated by the 'liberalisation' of many of our social and family laws. Divorce, for example, has been legalised since 1997. The free sale of contraceptives has been permitted since 1992. The censorship of films and books has been greatly reduced.

Variations from region to region

The influence of religion on politics varies from region to region throughout the world.

- Religion impacts heavily on politics in many **Muslim regions.** The civil laws of countries such as *Saudi Arabia* are related closely to aspects of Sharia law, which reflects the religious laws and traditions of Islam. The consumption of alcohol is forbidden in Saudi Arabia, as is dressing immodestly. The laws also strictly forbid adultery, as well as false accusations of adultery. Even the national flag of Saudi Arabia illustrates the influence of religion on civil government: the flag includes a quote from the Holy Koran, which is the sacred book of Islam. Sharia laws and traditions are open to different interpretations and not all Muslim countries have laws as strict as those in Saudi Arabia. Some, however, have in the past imposed very strict versions of Sharia law. Throughout the 1990s, the Taliban government in Afghanistan compelled women to completely cover their faces in public with veils called burkas. The Taliban also forbade women to attend schools or to work outside the home, where they were likely to mix freely with men.

The national flag of Saudi Arabia.
This flag contains a quote from the Holy Koran.
It says 'There is no God but Allah and Muhammad is the messenger of Allah.'

- Communist countries such as Cuba, on the other hand, do not allow religious beliefs to directly influence their civil laws or government. Such countries are ruled according to strictly **secular** or *non-religious* principles. Many Western countries such as France are also ruled according to such principles. That is why religious symbols such as crosses or even Muslim headscarves or veils are forbidden in state-run schools in France.

But politics and civil government in many secular Western countries are influenced to some extent by particular religions. Britain, for example, is a multi-religious society that is credited with treating all religions equally before the law. But Britain's monarch continues to be the Head of the (Anglican) Church of England and so must herself or himself be an Anglican. This is a relic of former times when the Anglican Church was the 'established' Church in Britain. The United States is another country where a nominally secular civil authority is influenced considerably by religion. The influence of an extremely conservative 'Christian right' lobby can play a big role in the outcome of national elections. US dollar bills (rather like the Saudi Arabian national flag) even contain the religious declaration, 'In God we Trust'.

Extreme 'Conservative Christian' demonstrators in the US rally against gay and lesbian rights. The 'Conservative Christian' lobby exerts significant influence on politics and policies in parts of the United States.

Special Study 2:
Religious conflict

Religion has contributed over time to **conflict** and *cultural divisions* in many parts of the world. Such conflicts have occurred in many parts of *Europe*, in *Northern Ireland* and in the *sub-continent of India*.

Religious conflict in Europe

The **Protestant Reformation** of the early sixteenth century caused a major split in the Christian Church in Europe. Some princes and states remained loyal to the Catholic Church, while others followed new Protestant religions such as Lutheranism and Calvinism. By the middle of the century, open and bitter conflict erupted between Protestants and Catholics.

- Bitter wars broke out, for example between Catholic and Protestant princes in **Germany**. These wars ended with the Peace of Augsburg in 1555.
- An even more brutal religious conflict later broke out between Catholic and Protestant states in northern Europe. This was the **Thirty Years War**, which took place between 1618 and 1648. Both sides committed terrible atrocities before the war ended with the Treaty of Westphalia.
- **Religious persecution** was carried out by both Catholic and Protestant rulers and governments. Protestants in Spain were cruelly persecuted under the *Spanish Inquisition*. People who broke strict *Calvinist laws* in Geneva were beheaded or otherwise severely punished. *Penal laws* were introduced into eighteenth-century Ireland to 'suppress Popery'. Catholic priests were persecuted and people were forced to hear mass at 'mass rocks' or other secret locations.

Northern Ireland

There has been a long history of distrust between Catholics and Protestants in Northern Ireland. The **Catholics** tend mainly to be *nationalists*, who want to live in a united Ireland independent of Britain. The **Protestants,** some of whom are descended from settlers of the Ulster Plantation, are mainly *Unionists*. They want Northern Ireland to remain within the United Kingdom.

When Ireland was partitioned in 1921, Northern Ireland came under the almost exclusive control of its Unionist majority. Its parliament at Stormont was described by Prime Minister James Craig as 'a Protestant Parliament for a Protestant people'. Catholics were **discriminated** against in the provision of jobs and local authority housing. A system called 'gerrymandering' was used to rig constituency boundaries so as to prevent Catholics being elected to local government or to Parliament.

Such religious discrimination led to the formation of a *Civil Rights* Association that demanded equality for all. Violent attacks on civil rights marches by British soldiers and Unionists led to a complete breakdown of trust by the early 1970s. Northern Ireland then entered nearly three decades of **armed conflict** that involved the British army, the mainly Catholic *Provisional IRA* and mainly Protestant armed groups such as the *Ulster Freedom Fighters* (UFF).

Sectarian attack in Belfast.
Pupils of Holy Cross Catholic School in Belfast under attack from a Unionist mob in 2001.

The signing of the **Good Friday Agreement** in 1998 helped to bring an end to armed conflict in Northern Ireland. The Agreement recognised the 'diversity' of religious and other traditions in the North. It also guarantees equality and respect for the cultural rights of all.

Terror and conflict.
Both Unionist and Republican paramilitaries carried out shootings and bombings during the conflict in Northern Ireland. This photograph shows the aftermath of an IRA bomb in Enniskillen, Co. Fermanagh.

The Indian sub-continent

The Indian sub-continent was once a **colony of Britain**. Colonial India was much larger than India today: it included present-day Pakistan, Bangladesh and Sri Lanka, as well as present-day India. While most people in India were Hindus, a majority of people in the northwest (now Pakistan) and the east (now Bangladesh) were Muslims.

When Indians began to demand independence from Britain, **religious conflict** began to emerge within the colony. The independence movement was led by Mahatma Gandhi and his mainly *Hindu* National Congress Party. *Muslims*, fearing domination by Hindus in an independent India, set up a political party called the Muslim League to demand that Muslim areas should become a separate independent state. Rioting between Hindus and Muslims broke out in 1946 and resulted in the deaths of 7,000 people in Calcutta (Kolkata).

When India won independence from Britain in 1947 it was **partitioned** (divided) into two countries. Most of the colony – the country now called India – was mainly Hindu and under the Congress Party. The northwest and the east formed a separate, mainly Muslim country called Pakistan (see Figure 6).

The religious partition of colonial India did not take place peacefully. About 30 million people abandoned their homes as Muslims left India for Pakistan and Hindus fled from Pakistan to India. These *religious refugees* often attacked each other when they met and up to half a million people were killed. Even to this day, religious conflict simmers and erupts in *Kashmir* – a border area that is claimed by both India and Pakistan.

Colonial India

Kashmir

PAKISTAN

New Delhi

Arabian Sea

I N D I A   Kolkata

Mumbai

BANGLADESH (formally East Pakistan)

Indian Ocean

Bay of Bengal

Chennai

SRI LANKA

6 India in colonial times (circular map) and today

Religion as a unifying force

Religion can be a unifying force as well as a source of conflict. Countries such as the *Republic of Ireland* and post-independence *India* have experienced the culturally bonding effects of religion.

The Republic of Ireland

While religion has been a divisive force in Northern Ireland, it has tended in the past to be a **culturally unifying** force throughout the rest of the island. Since the *Penal Laws* persecuted Catholicism in the eighteenth century, the majority Catholic Church identified itself to some degree with Irish victims of British colonial rule. Some Irish popular movements, such as Daniel O'Connell's struggle for *Catholic Emancipation** were religious as well as national in flavour and were supported by many members of the Catholic clergy.

The *Irish cultural revival* of the late nineteenth and early twentieth centuries helped to mould the emerging Irish nation that was to form the Republic of Ireland. This cultural revival was supported and influenced by many members of the Catholic clergy. The hugely influential *GAA*, for example, was so strongly supported by Archbishop Croke that the Ireland's premier stadium – Croke Park – is named after him. The Church also controlled or played a major role in many popular social organisations. These ranged from youth movements such as the *Catholic Boy Scouts* to temperance movements such as the *Pioneer Total Abstinence Association*. Even local cultural events such as card drives, dances, feiseanna and variety concerts were often held in parish halls that were controlled by the Catholic clergy.

Pope John Paul II at the Phoenix Park.
The visit of Pope John Paul II to Ireland in 1979 showed the powerful influence of the Catholic Church here at that time. The country virtually came to a halt for several days as millions of people flocked to see the Pope. This event in Dublin's Phoenix Park drew one million people.

*Catholic Emancipation: a campaign aimed to give practising Catholics the right to sit in the British Parliament. It achieved this aim in 1829.

India

We have seen that divisions between Hindus and Muslims caused the break-up of the former British colony of India into the states of India and Pakistan. But religion has also been a **unifying force** in the region. The **Hindu religion**, for example, has helped to bind the present state of India into a stable unit.

India is a vast, sprawling country that is 47 times larger than the Republic of Ireland. It contains more than one billion people, 438 spoken languages and 645 distinct minority tribes. Were it not for the fact that 80 per cent of Indians are Hindu the country might not have survived as a political and cultural unit.

Hinduism is a *way of life* and a general philosophy as well as a religion. As such, it binds its followers together with a large degree of cultural unity. It does not limit itself to any particular scripture or narrow dogma and this makes it easier to maintain harmony among its many followers. It also preaches that spiritual happiness can be attained only through the absolute acceptance of God's will. This philosophy of '*acceptance*' has discouraged friction and dissent in India, even in situations where material poverty and social inequalities would seem to merit division and strife.

Sum Up

- The term '**culture**' refers to the way in which people express their collective identity. *Language* and *religion* are important indicators of culture.
- Most **languages** are members of major 'language *families*' such as the Indo-European language family. This family can be subdivided into language *sub-groups* such as the Germanic or the Celtic sub-groups. These sub-groups can in turn be subdivided into individual languages such as English and Irish.
- As the *British Empire* expanded, so did the use of **English** and other indicators of British culture. Growing *American influence* throughout the world added to the continued spread of English.
- The spread of English *threatened* the wellbeing of some other languages and cultural traits. It caused, for example, a gradual **decline in spoken Irish**, which is now confined largely to small Gaelteacht areas in the West of Ireland.
- *Cultural movements* such as the Gaelic League and *government initiatives* such as the Official Languages Act have fostered the **revival of Irish**. Continued initiatives will be needed to extend the everyday use of the language.
- Spoken **Welsh** is now in the increase. Factors such as *Welsh Language Acts, compulsory Welsh* in schools and the use of Welsh *media* have all contributed to this revival.
- The world's most practised **religion** is *Christianity*. It has split over time into Catholic, Protestant and Orthodox Churches. *Islam* is followed by 22 per cent of the world's population. It is particularly influential in North Africa and in the Middle East. About 14 million people follow *Judaism*. *Hinduism,* the world's oldest religion, is widely practised in India. *Buddhism*, an offshoot of Hinduism, is common in countries such as Tibet.
- **Religion is an important cultural indicator:**
  - Religion impacts greatly on human *diet*. The diet of Hindus and Buddhists are influenced by the belief that it is wrong to kill animals. Orthodox Jews eat only animals that have cloven hooves and chew the cud. Muslims fast during Ramadan and Catholics used to fast during Lent.

From cradle to grave.
With the help of the photographs above, discuss the influence of religion on the cultural lives of Irish people.

- Religion influences human *dress*. Muslim women wear headscarves or veils as marks of modesty. Some Orthodox Jewish men wear beards, side-curls and hats or skullcaps. Muslims and Jews cover their heads in mosques and synagogues.
- Events such as Christmas and Easter are religious *festivals*. So are the Muslim celebration of Eid ul-Fitr and the Jewish feast of Passover. Popular pilgrimages such as that to Croagh Patrick are also religious events.
- Many *cultural landscape* features have religious functions. These include Christian churches, spires and statues, Muslim mosques and Buddhist temples.
- **The political influence of religion has varied over time:**
  - The *Catholic Church* exerted great influence in *Ireland* in the decades following national independence. Ireland's Constitution and family laws reflected this influence, as did the collapse of the Mother and Child Scheme. Since the 1990s, the decline in Church influence was accompanied by more 'liberal' civil laws.
  - The *Russian Orthodox Church* had considerable influence in Tsarist *Russia*. This influence disappeared completely with the Communist Revolution of 1917. It has revived somewhat since the end of Communist rule in 1991.
- **The political influence of religion varies from region to region:**
  - The civil laws of *Islamic countries* such as Saudi Arabia have been greatly influenced by Muslim Sharia laws and traditions.
  - Religion has much less influence on the civil laws or government of 'secular' countries such as France.
- **Religious conflicts have occurred throughout history:**
  - *Religious wars* broke out in Germany and throughout northern Europe in the sixteenth and seventeenth centuries. Religious *persecution* took place in many countries, including Spain and Ireland.
  - Sectarian distrust and discrimination contributed to decades of armed conflict in *Northern Ireland* prior to the Good Friday Agreement of 1998.
  - Religious conflict between Hindus and Muslims led to the partition of colonial *India* into present-day India, Pakistan and Bangladesh.
- **Religion can also be a unifying force:**
  - Some *Catholic* clergymen played an important role in the cultural revival that accompanied Irish political independence.
  - The *Hindu* religion has helped to bind modern India into a cultural and political unit.

Test Yourself
eTest.ie

Activities

See Leaving Cert Marking Scheme on page 234.

Leaving Cert Higher Level questions:
1. Examine the significance of either language or religion as a cultural indicator.　　　　　　　　　　　(Frequently asked question)
2. Discuss how people express their culture and identity in everyday life.
3. *'The influence of religion on politics varies over time and from region to region.'* Discuss this statement with reference to examples that you have studied.
4. *'Religion can be a divisive as well as a unifying force.'* Discuss with reference to examples you have studied.
5. *'Multiculturalism is common in the modern world.'* Examine how multiculturalism may lead to conflict or may be a unifying force.

State boundaries and their effectiveness

Precise boundary lines separate states from each other. Some of these lines are **physical boundaries** that follow natural barriers such as coasts or mountain ranges. Others are **political boundaries** that were created by governments or treaties, often with little or no reference to physical geography. Different types of boundary vary greatly in their effectiveness.

1 Physical boundaries that follow natural barriers

The main function of boundaries is to separate peoples from each other. Many physical boundaries perform this function very well because they follow **natural barriers** such as sea coasts and mountain ranges. These barriers form natural zones of separation between peoples, so that distinct *nations** and *nation states** tend to evolve naturally on opposite sides of them.

Coasts

Island countries such as Ireland and Iceland are surrounded by coasts that form their natural boundaries. Some non-island countries also have coastal boundaries. The *Adriatic Sea*, for example, separates Italy from neighbouring Croatia and Albania.

Coasts probably form the best physical boundaries. Even in times of war, the sea has provided reliable defensive frontiers for nation states such as Britain.

Terms to know

- **Nation**
A nation is a large community of **people** who share a common identity. A shared race, language, religion and music can all help to create common identity. So can a shared history or the real or imagined presence of a 'common enemy'.

- **State**
The term 'state' usually refers to **territory** that is recognised as being independent or sovereign. There are more than 200 sovereign states in the world.

- **Nation state**
A nation state exists **when a people** (a nation) **controls a territory** (a state) of its own. Many states are not true nation states because they contain more than one people within their territories.

- **State boundary or 'border'**
A specific dividing line between states.

A mountain border.
The Andes mountains in South America form an effective natural boundary between Chile and Argentina. The border, shown by a broken line in this picture, generally follows the crest or chief watershed of the mountains.

Lakes

Very large lakes, like seas, form natural barriers between countries. Parts of Canada and the United States are separated from each other by the *Great Lakes* of North America. *Lake Victoria* in Africa forms a natural boundary between Uganda and Tanzania.

Mountain ranges

Because of their low temperatures, scarce oxygen, rugged terrain and light populations, high mountain ranges form effective zones of separation between nation states. Mountain ranges can also separate major nationalities and human cultures from each other. The *Pyrenees*, for example, form a natural boundary between French people to the north and Spanish people to the south. These considerations make mountain ranges excellent natural frontiers between nation states. National boundaries normally follow the highest crests or the chief watersheds of mountain ranges.

Deserts

Dry, lightly populated deserts form natural frontiers between countries, nations and races. The *Sahara*, for example, is the natural divide between the Arabic-speaking Caucasoid peoples of North Africa and the black peoples of sub-Saharan Africa. The civilisation of Ancient Egypt flourished for more than 2,000 years partly because it was 'protected' to the east and west by the inhospitable Sahara.

2 Rivers as physical boundaries

Rivers form **easily recognisable** physical boundaries between many countries. The River *Rhine*, for example, forms part of the borders between Germany and Switzerland and between Germany and France. Most of the border between Romania and Bulgaria follows the River *Danube*.

But rivers can **sometimes** prove **ineffective** as natural boundaries between countries.

● Fertile river valleys tend to attract rather than repel human settlement. Because of this, many river basins are populated by peoples of common races or cultures. They are *not*, therefore, *natural dividing lines* between different peoples. When used as such they may artificially separate people of common cultures and allegiances.

A hot desert area (above) and a river valley (below).
Compare the suitability of the desert area and the river as locations for international boundaries.

- Meandering rivers can sometimes *change course*, resulting in border disputes between neighbouring countries. Meander changes in the Rio Grande River resulted in several such disputes between the United States and Mexico. An artificial channel was eventually created in 1936 to regulate the river flow permanently (see Figure 1).

Changes over time in the course of the Rio Grande River that borders the USA and Mexico.

(a) What does this map suggest about the usefulness of rivers as international boundaries?

(b) Which country benefited more from the river course changes shown?

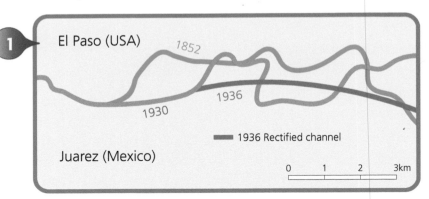

1

El Paso (USA)

1852

1930

1936

━━ 1936 Rectified channel

Juarez (Mexico)

0   1   2   3km

- A shared river boundary between countries can lead to international disputes relating to *navigation rights* or to the control of *water supplies* for irrigation or other purposes. The Central American countries of Costa Rica and Nicaragua quarrelled for more than a century over water rights on the San Juan River that separates them.

3 Political boundaries

Political boundaries are boundaries that have been created by government or treaty decisions with little reference to physical geography. Some political boundaries simply follow *lines of latitude or longitude*. Part of the border between the USA and Canada, for example, follows the 49°N line of latitude. Others are geometric straight lines that are drawn *obliquely* across territory, for example between the African states of Mali and Algeria. Some boundaries follow old *pre-existing political divisions*. The border between the Republic of Ireland and Northern Ireland, for example, follows ancient county boundaries. Some political boundaries even take the form of *walls* that are built to separate people. Such artificial boundaries once included the international wall/boundary that sliced through the city of Berlin. A present-day example is the Israeli government's 'separation wall' that cuts off Palestinians from Israeli-occupied land.

The Israeli 'separation wall' — a present-day example of an artificial political boundary between peoples

Political boundaries do **not always** make good or **effective** borders.

- They sometimes do not follow mountain ranges or other *natural barriers* between peoples.
- They may *cut through drainage areas*, mineral-bearing areas or grazing lands that tend to draw together peoples of common cultures.
- They sometimes *separate peoples of common cultures*, while trying to *amalgamate peoples of contrasting cultures* or clashing beliefs within single states.
- They are often drawn up with no reference to or consultation with *local populations*. This happened particularly in nineteenth-century Africa when imperial powers such as Britain, France and Germany 'carved up' Africa between them.

Weaknesses such as these often result in **international disputes** between countries and in **civil strife** within countries. The political border that partitions Ireland cut through and separated many local border communities. It also resulted in the creation of Northern Ireland – a political entity that has been plagued by tensions and violent strife between people of Unionist and nationalist traditions. Colonial political boundaries in Africa created many countries within which opposing peoples waged civil wars on each other. Sudan, Nigeria and Rwanda all suffered from such tragic and destructive civil wars.

Some international boundaries in northeast Africa in 2011, together with languages spoken by different peoples.

(a) *Identify political international boundaries that follow* **meridians** *(lines of longitude),* **parallels** *(lines of latitude) and* **other geometric lines**.

(b) *Following long periods of civil strife Sudan was partitioned in July 2011 when South Sudan became a newly independent state. How does this map suggest that poorly planned political boundaries may have contributed to civil strife in the original Sudan?*

(c) *Do you think the River Nile would make a suitable international boundary? Explain.*

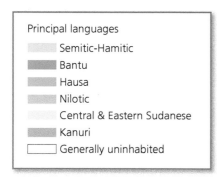

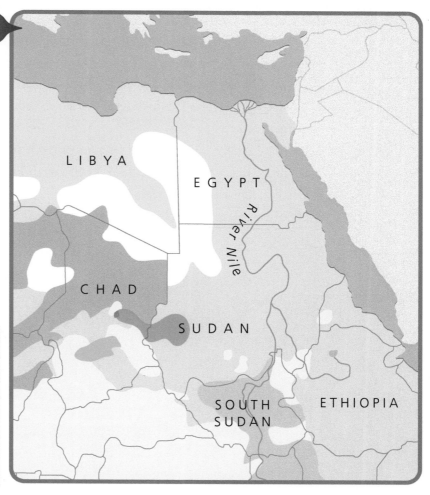

Principal languages
- Semitic-Hamitic
- Bantu
- Hausa
- Nilotic
- Central & Eastern Sudanese
- Kanuri
- Generally uninhabited

Cultural groups within states

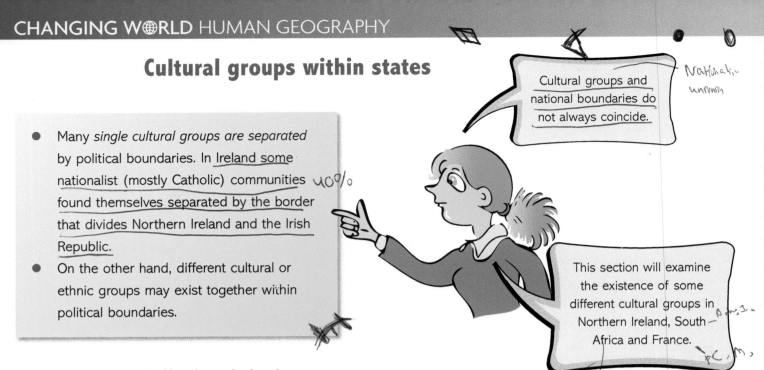

Cultural groups and national boundaries do not always coincide.

Nationalistic unimony

- Many *single cultural groups are separated* by political boundaries. In Ireland some nationalist (mostly Catholic) communities *40%* found themselves separated by the border that divides Northern Ireland and the Irish Republic.
- On the other hand, different cultural or ethnic groups may exist together within political boundaries.

This section will examine the existence of some different cultural groups in Northern Ireland, South Africa and France.

1 Northern Ireland

Northern Ireland contains two principal cultural groups – an approximately **60 per cent Unionist** majority and a large **nationalist** minority. These cultural groups tend to differ in politics, religion and the cultural activities they pursue.

- Unionists or 'loyalists' wish to maintain the **political** union between Northern Ireland and Britain. Nationalists or 'republicans' want to break the political link with Britain and would like the island of Ireland to be united as an independent republic.
- Most Unionists are **Protestants** (many are Presbyterians), while most nationalists are **Catholics**.
- Nationalists are more likely than Unionists to follows Gaelic **cultural pursuits**. They are more likely to learn the Irish language and take part in traditional Irish music and dance. They are also more likely to play or support Gaelic football and hurling, while Unionists are more likely to follow traditional 'British' sports such as hockey, rugby and cricket.

Revise Northern Ireland *on pages 251–252.*

Cultural contrasts in Northern Ireland. Loyalist murals decorate a wall in Belfast, while members of the nationalist community enjoy a St Patrick's Day concert in another part of the city.

Troubled relations between Northern Ireland's two main cultural groups go back to the **Ulster Plantation** of 1609, when Irish Catholic inhabitants were driven from their land to make way for Protestant planters from Britain. Tensions and animosity between the descendants of the planters and the dispossessed continued through the centuries.

When Ireland was **partitioned** (divided) in 1921, Northern Ireland came under the almost exclusive control of Unionists. Catholics were **discriminated** against politically, economically and socially, for example regarding the allocation of jobs and housing. By the early 1970s, this situation contributed to an outbreak of nearly three decades of armed **violence** involving republican and loyalist organisations. (This conflict will be examined in more detail on page 268).

Violence came to an end following the 'Good Friday Agreement' of 1998. This led to a **power-sharing government** in which Unionists and nationalists have shared power since 2007. These changes have helped to bring about increased harmony and co-operation between Northern Ireland's two principal cultural groups.

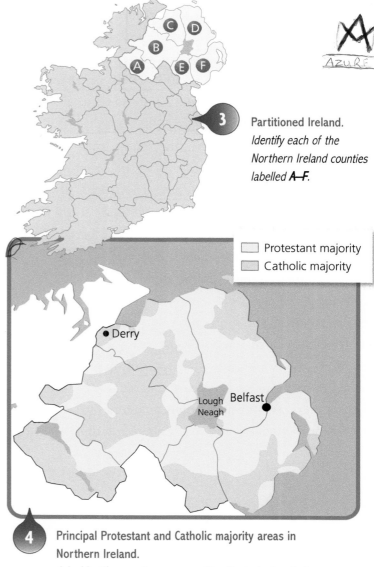

3 Partitioned Ireland.
Identify each of the Northern Ireland counties labelled **A–F**.

Protestant majority
Catholic majority

4 Principal Protestant and Catholic majority areas in Northern Ireland.
(a) Identify some large areas with a Protestant majority and some large areas with a Catholic majority.
(b) How was partition likely to have culturally affected people in South Fermanagh and South Tyrone?

Revise
Case Study 1
on pages
229–230.

2 South Africa

South Africa contains such as rich variety of cultural groups that it is sometimes referred to as a 'rainbow nation'.

- South Africa's **black majority** is descended from several different tribes, such as the Zulu and the Xhosa peoples. Many speak their own language and cherish their own traditional music, dance and customs.

- The **white minority** in South Africa is itself divided into two main cultural groups. Some are descended from English colonists. Others – the Afrikaners – are descended from Dutch settlers and speak a type of Dutch called Afrikaans.

- A small percentage of South Africans are descended from **Indian** immigrants.

Relations between South Africa's various cultural groups have been very troubled, largely because of the past political, economic and cultural *oppression* of black people. A white minority government established a political system called **apartheid** in 1948. This racist system aimed to separate white from 'non-white' South Africans in all aspects of everyday life. It set aside all the best social facilities for whites and used a 'pass' system to prevent blacks from moving freely in the country. It forced urban blacks to live in poverty-stricken 'townships' far from city centres and 'white' suburbs. It also set aside 87 per cent of South Africa for whites and forced black people into remote areas called 'Bantustans'.

Resistance to this oppression led to the eventual collapse of the apartheid regime in 1994. In that year the **African National Congress** (ANC) was swept to power under Nelson Mandela in the country's first democratic election. The ANC's non-racial policies have helped to promote harmony and respect between South Africa's various cultures. But harmony is hindered by the sharp economic inequalities that still exist in South Africa.

This multi-lingual road sign in South Africa is a reminder that the country contains several different cultures and language

The legacy of cultural and economic apartheid.

A Wealthy suburbs in South Africa continue to be inhabited mostly by white people.

B Millions of black South Africans continue to live in poverty-stricken townships, although the black majority government has improved township services and infrastructure.

3 France

The existence of different cultural groups in France is largely the result of large-scale **immigration** from former French colonies. Immigration has been particularly strong from North African countries such as Morocco, Tunisia and Algeria. It was especially rapid during the economic boom of the 1960s, when French employers welcomed foreign French-speaking 'guest workers' who were prepared to do menial work for small wages. Many of these 'guest workers' settled permanently in France, where they formed the core of a significant minority cultural group.

Revise
'Focus on France' on
pages 227 and 228.

Minority cultural groups from Africa and elsewhere have added greatly to the **multi-cultural** character of French society. This was reflected in the 'Black, White and Arab' composition of France's winning World Cup soccer team of 1998.

But cultural and racial mixing within France has been hindered by the following factors:

- Many North Africans immigrants and their descendants continue to live in poor **'ghetto'** areas in the suburbs of cities such as Marseilles and Paris. Many continue to cherish the Muslim faith, the Arabic language and old cultural customs in matters such as dress. Some tend to remain isolated from 'mainstream' French culture.

- The emergence of extreme right-wing political groups such as the *National Front* provided a potential platform for prejudice and discrimination against African and Muslim immigrants. This contributed to inter-cultural distrust that sometimes boiled over into **unrest** and rioting, such as happened in several French cities in 2005.

Culture clash.

A **Women in traditional North African dress in Paris.**

The French government bans the wearing of full face-veils on public transport or in public service buildings. It also forbids the use of Muslim headscarves (or any other religious symbols) in French public schools. These laws have proved controversial among France's five million Muslims.

B **An anti-immigrant protest in France.**

263

Cultural groups without nationality

Some cultural groups live within states to which they feel no allegiance and in which they have little or no political influence. Such groups are effectively without nationality and may seek to amalgamate with a neighbouring state or to found a state of their own.

This section will discuss three cultural groups that are or have been without nationality.

> **Cultural groups without nations**
> - Nationalists in Northern Ireland
> - Southern Sudanese (up to 2011)
> - Palestinians

Nationalists in Northern Ireland

When Northern Ireland was founded in 1921 it came under the almost exclusive political control of its Protestant Unionist majority. They were loyal to Britain and were determined to keep Northern Ireland within the United Kingdom.

> *Revise pages 260–261.*

But more than one-third of Northern Ireland's people consisted of nationalists who felt alienated and politically powerless within the new state. Many nationalists felt themselves 'cut off' from the rest of Ireland to which they wished to belong. They wanted to be part of a 32-county Irish Republic for the following reasons.

Nationalists in Northern Ireland at a Republican rally to commemorate the 1916 Rising.
Why might such commemorations be important to Northern Ireland nationalists?

- **Old enmities** between Unionists and nationalists went back as far as the Ulster Plantation, when the lands of Gaelic landowners were 'planted' with English or Scots settlers.
- Most nationalists were **Catholics** who felt out of place in the predominantly Protestant North. They wanted to belong instead to a Catholic-dominated state such as existed in Southern Ireland.
- Nationalists wanted to live in a more **'Gaelic'** Ireland in which the Irish language, Irish music and Irish games such as hurling and Gaelic football played an important cultural role.
- Nationalists were **discriminated** against in the allocation of jobs and local authority housing. They were also politically discriminated against by a dishonest political system called 'gerrymandering'. This system rigged local political boundaries so that Unionists were elected in many mainly nationalist areas.

The cultural alienation felt by Northern nationalists was lessened by the setting up in 2007 of a **power-sharing government** in Northern Ireland. Nationalists now enjoy a greater role in the political and cultural development of the state in which they live. But many still wish to be part of a 32-county Irish Republic. This is reflected in the popular support in Northern Ireland for *Sinn Féin* – a political party that favours the setting up of such a republic.

Southern Sudanese (up to 2011)

When Sudan gained independence from Britain and Egypt in 1956 it became Africa's largest state. The new state had a **Muslim Arabic majority**, most of whom lived in the north and centre of the country. But is also had a very sizeable **black Christian minority**, who lived mainly in the south and in the western region of Darfur. Tensions and suspicions gradually increased between these two groups, so that many black Christians felt increasingly alienated from the Sudanese state. The following factors contributed to this alienation:

- The mainly Arab Sudanese government made **Arabic the official language** throughout all of Sudan. This offended non-Arabic southerners, who spoke their own languages and who preferred English as a 'neutral' official language.
- In 1982 the government transferred command of all **armed forces** in the south to the central government in Khartoum. This broke an earlier agreement of 1973.
- The government introduced strict **Sharia laws** in the south. These laws reflected Islamic but not Christian traditions.
- Severe drought forced Arab herders to migrate southwards in search of grazing for their cattle. **Competition for land and water** then caused tensions and conflict between these herders and southern farmers.
- Almost all of Sudan's **oil reserves** are in the south of the country. Some southerners wanted local control of these reserves.

The alienation of southern Sudanese led to civil conflict and finally to the **break-up of Sudan** in 2011. You will learn more about this conflict on page 270.

People from north and from south Sudan.
List some contrasts between the two cultural groups that are evident from the photographs.

5

Africa and Sudan

The Palestinians

Palestinians are an Arab people whose ancient homeland in the Middle East is now mainly occupied by Israel. As their lands were gradually taken from them, the Palestinians became a people without an independent homeland.

By the end of World War II, Jewish people from many parts of the world wanted to establish a homeland of their own in Palestine. The United States supported this proposal and helped to persuade the United Nations to recommend that more than half of Palestine be set aside for a Jewish state. This state was called **Israel** and it was set up in 1948.

The establishment of Israel was accompanied by the removal of more than three-quarters of a million Palestinians from their homes. Those removed became **refugees** in neighbouring countries such as Jordan, from which neither they or their descendants have yet returned.

As time passed, more and more Jews migrated into Israel from all over the world. The amount of land controlled by Palestinians grew smaller and smaller, as Israel's military forces defeated those of neighbouring Arab states, suppressed Palestinian resistance and assisted in the take-over of Palestinian lands. By 2010 only small pockets of land in **Gaza** and parts of the **West Bank** of the River Jordan remained in Palestinian hands (see Figure 6). These fragmented pockets of land are not sufficient to form a viable Palestinian state.

The desire of Palestinians to have a state of their own is further obstructed by the creation of **Jewish Israeli settlements** in Israeli-occupied Palestinian territory and by the **demolition** of Palestinian homes. It has also been hindered by the creation of a huge Israeli-built **wall** that Israel claims is to separate Israeli from Palestinian territory. This wall slices through Palestinian land in many places and denies freedom of movement to many Palestinians.

The prospect of Palestinians returning to their old homes in Israel or obtaining a viable, **independent state** of their own seems remote at the present time. Many experts believe, however, that a just solution to Palestinian problems is vital to the creation of lasting peace in the troubled region of the Middle East.

Israeli settlers in Palestine.
More than 200 Jewish settlements have been built within Israeli-occupied Palestinian territory. These settlements range from entire towns to small collections of mobile homes.

Palestinian refugees in Gaza.
The right of refugees to return to their home areas could be central to solving the problems of Palestinians.

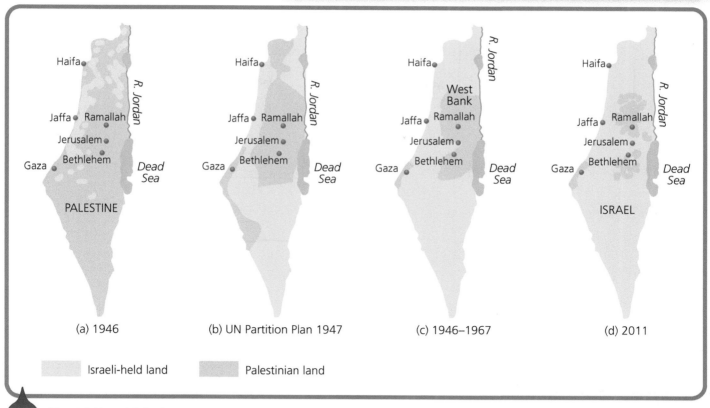

Haifa•

Jaffa• Ramallah•

R. Jordan

Jerusalem•

Gaza • Bethlehem• *Dead Sea*

PALESTINE

(a) 1946

Haifa•

Jaffa• Ramallah•

R. Jordan

Jerusalem•

Gaza • Bethlehem• *Dead Sea*

(b) UN Partition Plan 1947

Haifa•

West Bank

Jaffa• Ramallah•

R. Jordan

Jerusalem•

Gaza • Bethlehem• *Dead Sea*

(c) 1946–1967

Haifa•

Jaffa• Ramallah•

R. Jordan

Jerusalem•

Gaza • Bethlehem• *Dead Sea*

ISRAEL

(d) 2011

Israeli-held land   Palestinian land

6 The shrinking of Palestine, 1946–2010.
Describe and account for the changes over time illustrated by these maps.

Eviction.

Palestinian women watch an Israeli bulldozer demolish their family home in Israeli-occupied territory. Israelis sometimes claim that such homes are illegal or have harboured terrorists. Palestinians claim that such demolitions are part of an 'ethnic cleansing' policy to drive Palestinians from their land.

Conflicts between cultural groups and political structures

Minority or suppressed cultural groups sometimes feel alienated within a country. If these cultural groups are strong enough and if their sense of alienation is extreme enough, conflict may arise between the minority groups and ruling government establishments.

This section will examine conflicts that took place between cultural groups and political structures in Northern Ireland, South Africa and Sudan.

Conflict in the North.
Police violently attack a nationalist civil rights protestor in Derry.

Conflict in the North.
The aftermath of a Provisional IRA bombing in Belfast.

Conflict in Northern Ireland

We saw on page 264 that (mainly Catholic) nationalists in Northern Ireland felt politically and culturally alienated and discriminated against.

In the late 1960s, some people began to demonstrate peacefully for equal **civil rights** for all. When demonstrators were brutally and repeatedly attacked by Unionists and members of the RUC (police), Northern Ireland descended into civil conflict.

The **Troubles** (as the civil conflict was called) began with rioting and sectarian (inter-religious) strife in Derry and Belfast. Many nationalists joined the **Provisional IRA**, while some Unionists joined paramilitary (armed) groups such as the **Ulster Volunteer Force** (UVF). The **British army** was called in to prevent violence from spreading. But the army lost the trust of Nationalists when it killed thirteen unarmed people in the 'Bloody Sunday' massacre in Derry in January 1972. Nationalists were also infuriated when many of their members were **interned** (imprisoned without trial) in August 1971. The Troubles continued for nearly **three decades**. The IRA carried out devastating bombing campaigns throughout Northern Ireland and occasionally in England. The UVF and other loyalist paramilitary groups murdered many nationalists and Catholics throughout the North. Loyalist paramilitary groups are also thought to have been responsible for bombings in Dublin and Monaghan.

By the late 1990s, almost everybody in Northern Ireland was weary of the Troubles. Violence finally came to an end following the **Good Friday Agreement** of 1998. This led to the decommissioning (dismantling) of paramilitary arms. It also brought about a **power-sharing** government in which Unionists and **n**ationalists have shared power since 2007.

Conflict in South Africa

You have read (pages 261–262) that South Africa's black majority was severely oppressed by white governments and that the oppression of blacks became more intense under the apartheid system that began in 1948.

A body called the **African National Congress** (ANC) led the resistance against racial oppression in South Africa. Following its foundation in 1912, the ANC organised protests and strikes. It also published a *Freedom Charter* in which it outlined the equal rights of all citizens in a democratic, non-racist South Africa.

On 21 March 1960, armed South African police gunned down peaceful demonstrators in a town called **Sharpeville**. Sixty-nine men, women and children were killed that day. The government, fearing many more protests, then declared a 'state of emergency' and banned the ANC.

The ANC was then forced underground. It formed a **military wing** called the *Spear of the Nation* to fight South Africa's racist regime, and which attacked government installations ranging from police barracks to oil refineries.

In June 1976 the conflict in South Africa took a new turn when government forces massacred protesting schoolchildren in the township of Soweto. The **Soweto massacre** intensified the struggle against apartheid. Outside South Africa, **anti-apartheid movements** called for economic, cultural and sporting boycotts of apartheid South Africa. In Dublin, for example, a two and a half-year strike by eleven Dunne's Stores workers resulted in a ban on South African fruit and vegetable imports to Ireland.

By 1994, the apartheid regime finally **collapsed** under internal and external pressures. The ANC was swept to power in South Africa's first democratic election in which all adults could vote. The struggle against apartheid was over.

The struggle against apartheid:

A South African police and their victims at Sharpeville, 21 March 1960

B Striking workers and supporters picket Dunne's Stores in Henry Street, Dublin in protest against the sale of South African products

C Nelson Mandela, who was elected leader of South Africa after the defeat of apartheid

Conflict in Sudan

You read on page 265 of the tensions that exist between many Muslim Arab people and black Christian people in Sudan. Tensions have been particularly strong in the south of Sudan and in the western province of Darfur (see Figure 7).

These tensions led to two **civil wars**. A war between the (mainly Arab Muslim) government and (mainly Christian black) rebels began in southern Sudan in 1983 and raged for 20 years. No sooner had the first civil war ended than another broke out in Darfur.

The **results** of these largely cultural conflicts have been profound.

- Two and a quarter million people have been *killed*. Many more have been *injured* or driven from their homes.

- Massive *damage* has been done to buildings, crops and livestock. Hundreds of villages were destroyed in the Darfur region alone.

- By 2010, Sudan was spending 17 per cent of its income on its *armed forces*. This greatly reduced the amount of money that might have otherwise have been spent on development.

- In 2011 an internationally sponsored referendum was held to set up a *new state* of South Sudan. Most Sudanese voted for this proposal to divide Sudan in two. The new state of South Sudan consists mostly of desert; but it does contain 80 per cent of Sudan's oil reserves – something that could cause further conflict and self-interested foreign intervention in the region.

7 Sudan, showing the province of Darfur and South Sudan

A Janjaweed militiaman.
The Janjaweed or 'armed horsemen' supported government forces in the civil war in Darfur, where some were accused of committing atrocities against civilians. Many Janjaweed militiamen were from camel herding backgrounds and some fought on horseback or mounted on camels.

Sum Up

- Many states are separated from each other by **physical boundaries**.
  - Many physical boundaries follow *coasts, mountain ranges or deserts*. These boundaries are usually effective because they follow features that form natural barriers between peoples.
  - Some physical boundaries follow *rivers*. But rivers tend to draw people together rather than to separate them. Meandering rivers may also change course. Rivers may therefore make poor international boundaries.
- **Political boundaries** are usually created by treaties or by government decisions.
  - They may be inappropriate if they make no reference to natural boundaries or the wishes of local populations.
- **Some states contain different cultural groups** who may not easily mingle:
  - *Northern Ireland* includes a mainly Protestant Unionist majority and a mainly Catholic nationalist minority. Old rivalries between these groups and discrimination against nationalists led to violence and unrest.
  - In *South Africa*, a white minority oppressed a black majority under a racist apartheid system.
  - North African immigrants and their descendants form a distinctive cultural minority in *France*. Many live in urban ghetto areas, cherish their own culture and are distrusted by some right-wing French political groups.
- Some **cultural groups are without nationality** because they live in states or political situations from which they feel alienated.
  - Many *nationalists in Northern Ireland* felt alienated and discriminated against up to the formation of a power-sharing government in 2007.
  - *Black Sudanese Christians* felt aggrieved by issues such as the imposition of Arabic as their national language and of Sharia laws.
  - *Palestinians* feel aggrieved because more and more of their homeland has been occupied by Israel.
- **Conflicts** sometimes break out between alienated cultures and government establishments:
  - Nationalist grievances in *Northern Ireland* contributed to the outbreak of nearly three decades of violence.
  - The African National Congress spearheaded a long civil and armed struggle against apartheid in *South Africa*. This struggle ended with the collapse of the apartheid regime in 1994.
  - Black Christian unrest led to civil wars in southern and western *Sudan*. These wars resulted in more than two million deaths, widespread destruction and the eventual break-up of Sudan.

Test Yourself
eTest.ie

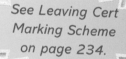

See Leaving Cert Marking Scheme on page 234.

Activities

Leaving Cert Higher Level questions:

1. Examine, with references to examples you have studied, the relative effectiveness of boundaries based on both features of the physical landscape and political decisions.
2. Cultural groups and national boundaries do not always coincide. Discuss.
3. Many states have different cultural/ethnic groups within their boundaries. Examine how these groups relate to one another, with reference to examples you have studied.
4. Conflicts exist between political structures and cultural groups. Discuss this statement with reference to examples you have studied.

Yugoslavia – the Life and Death of a Culturally Diverse European State

1 The formation of Yugoslavia in 1918

2 Yugoslavia and surrounding countries

3 New boundaries – the break-up of Yugoslavia

For most of the twentieth century a state called **Yugoslavia** was one of the largest countries in the *Balkans Peninsula* of southeast Europe. Yugoslavia stretched from Austria in the north to Greece in the south and from Romania and Bulgaria in the east to the Adriatic Sea in the west (see Figure 2).

A brief history of Yugoslavia

Yugoslavia has been described as a 'Versailles state' because it was set up by the **Treaty of Versailles** that followed World War I in 1919. Yugoslavia was an amalgamation of the pre-existing states of Serbia and Montenegro and part of the Austro-Hungarian Empire that had been defeated in the war (Figure 1). King Alexander and his family ruled Yugoslavia until World War II, when it was invaded, occupied and divided up by German forces in 1941.

Many Yugoslavians fought against **German occupation**. The most successful of these were Communist guerrilla fighters called 'Partisans' led by Marshal *Josip Broz Tito*. The Partisans succeeded in expelling the Germans in 1945. Tito – by then a national hero – was elected by referendum to lead Yugoslavia as an independent and **unified Communist state** (Figure 2).

Tito's Yugoslavia contained many different ethnic and cultural groups, some of which were hostile to each other. The country was managed as a federation of six separate republics, of which Serbia was the largest. Each republic had its own constitution, parliament and president, but was subject to the federal Yugoslavian government headed by Tito. Marshal Tito used a 'carrot and stick' approach to manage his culturally diverse and volatile country. On the one hand he offered equality to the country's different cultural groups. On the other hand, he banned extreme nationalism within any group and oversaw the arrest and execution of some nationalist leaders who disobeyed him. Despite underlying ethnic tensions and an economic crisis in the 1970s, Tito's personal authority and iron rule held Yugoslavia together.

After Tito's death in 1980, *ethnic tensions* grew in Yugoslavia as nationalism grew within each of its republics. Serbia tried to increase its influence over the federation, while non-Serbian majorities in other republics sought independence. *War* broke out in many parts of the federation and terrible atrocities were carried out. Between 1991 and 1992 the Federation of Yugoslavia *disintegrated* into seven different countries: *Slovenia, Croatia, Serbia, Macedonia, Kosovo, Montenegro* and *Bosnia-Herzegovina* (Figure 3).

Belgrade, now the capital city of Serbia and once the capital of Yugoslavia

Marshal Tito

Cultural contrasts in Yugoslavia

Yugoslavia was founded, not along rational ethnic or cultural lines, but by international treaty. A major reason for its eventual break-up was the cultural differences and historic suspicions that existed between its various ethnic groups. We will now examine some of these differences.

Some cultural differences:
- language
- religion
- ethnicity
- architecture

Language

There were three official languages in Yugoslavia: **Serbo-Croat**, **Slovenian** and **Macedonian**. The most spoken language – Serbo-Croat – is itself divided into Eastern and Western 'branches'. The Eastern branch is spoken mainly by Serbs. It uses the Cyrillic alphabet (similar to that used in Russian) which had been developed originally by members of the Orthodox Church. The Western branch, used mainly by Croats, uses the Latin alphabet (with letters similar to those used in English). There were also significant minority languages that included Albanian, Italian, Bulgarian, Romanian, Turkish and Romany.

The Yugoslav constitution guaranteed each ethnic group the right to use their own language and alphabet and the right to be educated in their own language through post-primary school. Nevertheless, the use of so many languages reflected the deep cultural diversity that existed within Yugoslavia's population. Such diversity contributed to eventual alienation between the ethnic groups and so to the break-up of Yugoslavia.

273

Religion

A diversity of religions existed in Yugoslavia, with **Eastern Orthodox**, **Roman Catholic** and **Islam** being the most widely followed religions. Different ethnic groups were often categorised by their religion and this added to the ethnic tensions that plagued Yugoslavia in its final years.

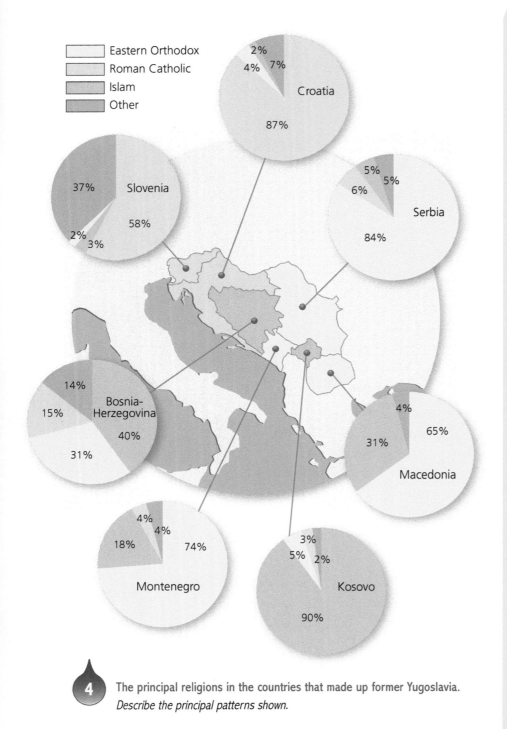

	Eastern Orthodox
	Roman Catholic
	Islam
	Other

Croatia 2% 4% 7% 87%

Slovenia 37% 2% 3% 58%

Serbia 5% 5% 6% 84%

Bosnia-Herzegovina 14% 15% 31% 40%

Macedonia 4% 65% 31%

Montenegro 4% 4% 18% 74%

Kosovo 3% 5% 2% 90%

4 The principal religions in the countries that made up former Yugoslavia. *Describe the principal patterns shown.*

- **Eastern Orthodox Christianity** is followed by **84** per cent of people in Serbia and by most people in Montenegro and in Macedonia. The Eastern Orthodox religion has priests (who are permitted to marry) and patriarchs who hold the highest positions of authority. Each family adopts a patron saint and honours that saint once a year with a celebration during which a candle is lit and special foods are consumed.

- **Roman Catholicism** is practised widely in the northwest of former Yugoslavia. Eighty-seven per cent of Croats and 58 per cent of Slovenians are Catholic. Catholicism permeates public life to some extent. Public holidays in Croatia, for example, include religious festivals such as the Epiphany (January 6) and Corpus Christi.

- Islam is widely followed in *Kosovo* (where **90** per cent of people are Muslim) as well as in *Bosnia-Herzegovina* and *Macedonia*. Many Muslims are descended from people who converted to Islam when Bosnia-Herzegovina was part of the Ottoman Turkish Empire. Like Muslims elsewhere, they read the Holy Koran, fast during the month of Ramadan and attend mosque on Fridays.

Ethnicity

Yugoslavia contained several ethnic groups such as **Serbs** (who were mainly Orthodox Christians), **Croats** and **Slovenians** (mainly Catholic) and ethnic **Albanians** (mainly Muslims). *Old hatreds* existed between some of those groups. Some Croats, for example, supported the Nazi occupation of the region during which many Serbs were massacred. Croats, on the other hand, resented Serbs who they thought received 'preferential' treatment during Communist rule.

Such ethnicity and hatreds were effectively suppressed during the rule of Marshal Tito (1945–1980). When Tito died, however, they emerged and contributed to the rise of 'ethnic nationalism' throughout much of Yugoslavia. This led to bitter ethnic conflicts and to the disintegration of the state by 1992.

Ethnic conflicts

Yugoslavia's ethnic conflicts have been described as **Europe's deadliest war since World War II**. Approximately 140,000 people were killed in a civil war that was infamous for its cruelty. Serb forces, for example, massacred more than 8,000 Bosnians in the town of Srebrenica and *'ethnically cleansed'* (expelled) more than 40,000 Muslims from the Bosnian town of Zvornik. Croatian forces, on the other hand, have been accused of taking over Muslim land and exiling more than 150,000 Serbs from Croatia.

Deadly conflict.
Ethnic tensions and war led to the break-up of Yugoslavia between 1991 and 1992. This photograph shows part of the town of Pec in Kosovo that had been destroyed by NATO bombing.

Contrasting architecture:

A The *Stari Most bridge* in Mostar, Herzegovina is a relic of old **Ottoman** architecture. When it was built in 1566 it was the world's widest single-arch stone bridge

B The **Eastern Orthodox** *Church of St Mark* in Belgrade, Serbia

C *Tomislav Square* in Zagreb, Croatia is an example of the well-laid-out architectural style favoured at the time of the **Austro-Hungarian** Empire.

Architecture

Buildings in the countries that made up Yugoslavia show a wide variety of architectural styles. This is partly because many of these countries have been influenced by *Eastern Orthodox* culture and have in the past come under the domination of the *Ottoman* and *Austro-Hungarian* empires.

- Countries such as *Bosnia-Herzegovina* and *Kosovo* have many buildings that typify the styles of the old **Ottoman Empire**. There are *mosques* that have domes and high towers and are decorated on the inside with rich wooden wall ornaments. There are public *fountains*, which were much beloved by the Ottomans. There are also ancient and spectacularly designed *arched bridges* that for Muslims once symbolised the meeting between heaven and earth.

- *Orthodox churches* in countries such as *Serbia and Macedonia* show **Greek and Russian** architectural influences. Many of these churches have domes and rounded arches. Their interiors are typically decorated inside with *frescoes* and *icons*. Frescoes are wall paintings that were painted on wet plaster. Icons are pictures of religious figures that are often painted on wood or carved in metal.

- *Croatia*, *Slovenia* and *Bosnia-Herzegovina* all came under the influence of the **Austro-Hungarian Empire**. It left a legacy of architectural '*discipline*' that included regulated building heights and wall thickness, together with straight, broad avenues that form right-angled grid patterns. It also left a rich legacy of *Catholic churches*. Some of these are in the Renaissance style with ornately decorated interiors.

Sum Up

- The Treaty of Versailles established the state of **Yugoslavia** in 1919. Yugoslavia was first ruled by a king, then occupied by Nazi forces during World War II and finally ruled by the Communist *Marshal Tito*. When Tito died, ethnic disagreements led gradually to civil war and to the break-up of Yugoslavia into seven different countries in 1992.
- **Extreme cultural diversity** played a part in the break-up of Yugoslavia. There were many facets to this diversity.
  - Yugoslavia had three official **languages** – *Serbo-Croat* (two distinct branches), *Slovenian* and *Macedonian.* It also had minor languages such as Albanian and Romany.
  - Different ethnic groups have often been categorised by their **various religions**. Most Serbs and Macedonians follow the *Eastern Orthodox* faith. Most Croats and Slovenians are *Catholic*. *Islam* is the leading religion in Kosovo and Bosnia-Herzegovina.
  - Old suspicions and hatreds existed between Yugoslavia's main **ethnic groups**. These hatreds contributed to '*ethnic nationalism*', to brutal *civil conflicts* and finally to the *disintegration* of the state.
  - **Architectural styles** illustrated the cultural and ethnic diversity of Yugoslavia. The architecture of the region was influenced by the *Eastern Orthodox* culture and by the old *Ottoman* and *Austro-Hungarian* empires.

Test Yourself **eTest.ie**

Activities

1. Describe how the three photographs on this page illustrate cultural differences in the former state of Yugoslavia.
2. The identity of any state or region draws on a variety of cultural factors such as ethnicity, language, religion, etc. Show how this has affected any named European state or region that you have studied. Refer in your answer to any three or four cultural factors of your choice.
3. Cultural identity is defined by many factors. Discuss this statement with reference to **one** case study of a European region that you have studied.

   (Leaving Cert question)

See Leaving Cert marking scheme on page 234.

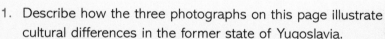

Acknowledgements

The authors wish to thank the many Geography teachers whose advice, encouragement and shared experiences have contributed greatly to this book. Special thanks to the teachers whose detailed, fruitful and encouraging reviews have contributed considerably to the script. We are also grateful to Ashling O'Neill and Claire Kelly for their valuable input.

We wish to thank all those whose expert endeavours played pivotal roles in the preparation, design and production of the work. Special thanks to the staff of Gill and Macmillan – to Anthony Murray, Hubert Mahony, Jen Patton, Denise Dwyer and Neil Ryan. We are extremely grateful also to Jane Rogers, Design Image and Brick.

The assistance of each of the following is appreciated and acknowledged: Aer Rianta; Joe Allen; Apple Computers; Peter Barrow; Belgian Embassy; An Bord Iascaigh Mhara; An Bord Gáis; Boston Scientific; James Bowen; Bray Urban District Council; Brick; Brendan Cannon; Siobhan Casey; Castlebar Chamber of Commerce; Sr Celestine; Central Bank of Ireland; Central Statistics Office; CHASE; Liam Coakley; Cork City Council; Sean Cotter; Chris Coughlan; Owen Deegan; Department of Arts, Heritage and the Gaeltacht; Department of Communications, Energy and Natural Resources; Department of Education and Skills; Department of the Environment, Community and Local Government; Department of Foreign Affairs and Trade; Department of Justice, Equality and Defence; Department of Transport, Tourism and Sport; Mary Doyle: Dublin City Council; Dublin Tourism; Emigrant Centre, UCC; Environmental Protection Agency; Fáilte Ireland; Fatima Mansions Project; Liam Fitzpatrick; Linda Fitzpatrick; French Embassy; Georgian House Museum; Aisling Gleeson; Mary Harrington; Maura Harrington; Ahmed Hassan; Tim Hayes; Darren Hetherington; Hewlett Packard; Michael Hussey; Cormac Hynes; Industrial Development Agency; Intel; Irish National Emigration Service; Irish Refugee Council; Islamic Cultural Centre of Ireland; John Joyce; Sheila Loughnane; Thomas McEvoy; John McGuinness; Joe Maher; Marine Institute; Mayo County Council; Mayo Enterprise Board; Medtronic; NASC; National Roads Authority; Guy Bertrand Nimpa; Northern Ireland Statistical Research; Lorcan O'Brien; David O'Connell; Finbarr O'Connell; Micheal O'Dwyer; Jill O'Neill; Ordnance Survey Office; Marie O'Rourke; Dolores Osborne; Seigfried Peinen; Pfizer Grange Castle; Roadstone Wood Group; Refugee and Migrant Project of the Irish Bishops' Conference; Sr Joan Ruddy; Ali Salim; Michael Sands; James Shannon; Elaine Sheridan; Sherry Fitzgerald (Estate Agents); Kevin Squires; Trócaire; Martyn Turner; Antoinette Tyrell; Údarás na Gaeltachta; University College Cork: Neil Warner; Waterford County Council; Welcome English: John Whelan; Wyeth BioPharma; Youghal Tourism; Youghal Urban District Council.

Charles Hayes, MEd, MA, HDE
School of Education, UCC

Una Nation, BA, MEd, HDE
St Mary's High School, Midleton, Co. Cork

Index